The Grass Catcher

The Grass Catcher

A digression about home

Ian Wedde

Victoria University Press

TE WHARE WĀNANGA O TE ŪPOKO O TE IKA A MĀUI
VICTORIA
UNIVERSITY OF WELLINGTON

VICTORIA UNIVERSITY PRESS
Victoria University of Wellington
PO Box 600 Wellington
vup.victoria.ac.nz

First published 2014

National Library of New Zealand Cataloguing-in-Publication Data

Wedde, Ian.
The grass catcher : a digression about home / Ian Wedde.
ISBN 978-0-86473-938-4
1. Wedde, Ian. 2. Poets, New Zealand—Biography. I. Title.
NZ824.2—dc 23

Printed in China by 1010 Printing international

For my brother Dave

Contents

The grass catcher

My first home, which I shared with my twin brother David, was our mother's womb. I seem to know in my cells that bargaining took place there and during the events that led to our moving in. Which of us would be left-handed? Which of us would have sons but not daughters (and vice versa)? Which of us would have a sanguine nature, and which that of a fantasist? In one way or another, this home and the trading that went on during our time there shaped our individual and collective identities. Our *fates*, the fantasist might have added, while his sanguine brother basked calmly in whatever present he was enjoying.

My brother left this home first, by twenty minutes – long enough for me to get the long-suffering expression that appears in most photographs of us as infants and little boys. Dave was strongly built, with a handsome, solid-boned frame, square head and a wide, delighted smile for the world. His twin, on the other hand, was slighter, with a notoriously rosebud mouth (my first affectionately disparaging nickname was Rosebud) and a forehead of foppish curls. An early memory: the smell of the spit with which my mother sculpted these ornaments. And my habitual expression, if the photos are to be believed, was querulous and introspective, as if an internal world or narrative kept distracting me from the obvious pleasures of the one out there.

I believe, without reason of course, that the companion of

my first exile didn't really notice what had happened. I'm sure I loved him then, in the weird, astigmatic way that twins do, but I may also have wished he had doubts about the situation we were in, as I did, instead of always beating me to the sunshine by at least twenty minutes. A family story, embedded deeply enough in my consciousness to have become something like a memory, concerns an event that was at once my revenge on my twin's diasporic equanimity and my acknowledgement that he felt pain differently from me. Our second home (after our mother's womb) was our maternal grandmother's house in Francis Street, Blenheim, where our mother and father also lived. Nana Horne (Agnes, or Aggie Horne née Tait) would take us for walks in our double wickerwork pram, and one day was alarmed by bellows of pain from the sunny-natured David: it was usually me who did the shrieking. After close inspection she discovered that the thumb his brother was gnashing with a sharp new tooth was not mine but his.

I wish I could recover the illicit pleasure of this displaced gratification, which involved my brother feeling my pain for me while I stole his comfort. At the same time, I know, guiltily, that something like this displacement would become my default imaginative condition: how I inhabited the first home-out-there-in-the-world about which, sixty-something years later, I can claim to remember anything.

Of course I can't really remember the notorious thumb-sucking incident, which the family enshrined as a tribal joke while simultaneously deploying it as a forensic lens on my developing character. Nor, of course, can my brother remember what happened. He, however, is certain that it was my thumb he was serenely sucking and biting as I shrieked. What Dave's 'memory' does to my version of the family's narrative is, of course, twist it away from the direction I want it to go in: away from the evolution of the duplicitous nature that serves my story best, that contrasts my perplexity about home with Dave's equanimity.

But I vividly remember another, later event. In 1954 we had gone to live in East Pakistan, now called Bangladesh. Dave and I, armed with air rifles, prowled the scrub that surrounded our house, hoping to shoot snakes or anything else that was alive and, in our view, deserving of death. We'd had an argument about something or other, and I ambushed Dave from behind the door to our bedroom. My memory of pulling the trigger of my air rifle has long been buried under self-protective tissue, but not my memory of the nauseating purple hole that appeared in my twin's thigh and the murky trickle of blood that ran from it. I went with my ashen-faced brother and grim mother to the hospital run by a Baptist missionary called Dr Bottoms. There was a veranda with lepers sitting in its shade, and a badly burned man in a kind of hammock filled with soothing oil. In a hot room smelling of dry wood-rot and strong disinfectant, the doctor probed the sickening hole below the leg of Dave's khaki shorts and, eventually, forceped out the slug I'd 'accidentally' shot into his thigh, while I drowned out my brother's stoic groans with my own theatrical shrieks of 'It hurts! It hurts!' – adding '*him*' after a grudging pause. But 'It hurts *me*' was certainly the subtext of the story that entered the family archive as additional hilarious evidence of my character's melodramatic inclinations. And, clearly, it wasn't my brother's pain I wanted, but our mother's sympathy. As with the pram incident, I wanted him to feel the pain so I could have the pleasure. Was there a pattern here? Did the family's wry anecdote contain an uneasy awareness of my duplicitous tendencies?

Another memory seems to belong somewhere along the arc from pram to gun. This memory is at once vivid and abstract, and I can't be sure whether the event I remember was single or typical. Our father was proud of his fine asparagus patch in the large back section of the home in Francis Street, and when Dave and I were about six we played in it after the plants had gone to seed and turned into a feathery, head-high jungle. This would have been about 1953. I don't remember the actual in-the-asparagus-bed story I'd become engrossed in acting out, but I do remember looking around at some point and noticing that Dave, Bobby Moss from next door, and whoever else had been involved, had gone.

This was probably because I was bossy – 'Now you be this, go here, do that' – and they just got sick of me. But *that* was because I was so absorbed in the game. There was an irresistible world I entered through my imagination – not so much an inner world as a physical one *out there*, but whose portal was inside me. Sooner or later it would dawn on those I was directing to play in this world that it was not one they cared much about, or even one they were *in*, and they would turn away from its obscurity – its essential privacy. They would leave me to it, as we say, and they would leave it to me, as we also say.

Both 'leaving' expressions point to another kind of leave-taking – that of the social diaspora, being-at-home in a place inaccessible to your brother. In my case, the inaccessible place in which I was at once displaced and at home was the world Dave and I shared – the house with our mother, father and grandmother in it, the asparagus patch, the nearby park, the public swimming baths, the town's aviary with its caged monkeys (one of which bit Dave), the turgid Taylor or was it the Opawa River with eels around the pongy sewage outlet, the lawnmower's green-stained canvas grass catcher hung up at the back of the garage. Does Dave also remember the funny smell of the pinkish Veet depilatory in the bathroom, the tastes-like-this smell of burned porridge in Nana Horne's black pot, the mothbally smell of the bedroom drawer where Nana kept her lolly bag?

But as well as – at the same time as – being the world we shared, it was another one whose familiar salients and objects were made strange to my companions, including my twin brother, by my different views of the shared familiar: the narrative warps and distortions that both estranged and absorbed me with their fabulously displaced gratifications, and that I became addicted to. Of course my companions, including my brother, had their own imaginative takes on the world – but my impression is that mine were more excessive. I base this impression on family anecdotes and my own accumulated fragments of memory, as well as on what I find when I try to look honestly into the person I have become. I hope I'm not giving my childhood self airs, or my adult self either.

A few years ago, I was writing about the road-trip photographs of Peter Black and recalling the dreamlike world that passed the car's windows when I was a child, and especially the indistinct, fragmentary world that appeared in the headlights as we drove home at night from a family outing; and in writing this memory down as a gloss on Peter's photographs I was suddenly returned to something far stronger than a vague image out of childhood. I encountered again, with a shock, as if through a portal to another dimension or reality, the image of the lawnmower's battered wire and canvas grass catcher hanging on the wall at the back of the garage and lit by the car's headlamps. As a child, the strangeness of this object verged on the terrifying – I looked at it with a shudder of fear and pleasure. Its fantastic weirdness had a lot to do with its ordinary familiarity. It looked like nothing on earth and like my father's grass catcher, the one attached to the chattering mower that he pushed up and down the front lawn, trying to make regular stripes of the mown nap – straightening out the warped world.

I saw that the thing he pushed through summer's pleasant aroma of mown grass and the thing on the back wall of the garage momentarily lit by the headlamps were the same, and were in the same world, but could be utterly different. The thing was not singular. And it was these differences – these uncanny lurches away from what was ordinary and familiar, these haunting, enchanting, mesmerising splits – that changed the world I played in with my twin brother. When the headlights lit up the grass catcher, this object at once known and unknowable, we had finally reached home. This was how I knew.

I arrived home then, and it was both a comforting place I lived in with my family and a place whose spookiness excited me into a kind of private trance; and again, many years later when I remembered the grass catcher, I arrived at a place that was at once homely and *unheimlich.* While Dave enjoyed tranquil sleep in the bed next to mine, I would pound on the wall to our parents' bedroom because *there really was* something in the big wardrobe and it was surely going to come out any minute now. Their weary, muffled reply was, 'Go back to sleep, it's only a dream.' *Go back to sleep*? That was where the dreams were, and what reason did I have not to believe them?

Fifty or so years later, I was in Blenheim for the opening of a Bill Culbert exhibition at the Millennium Art Gallery, the first time I'd been near my 'home town' for many years. I love Bill's work because it so often jauntily captures the paradoxical, uncanny natures of ordinary phenomena and objects, a view of reality endorsed equally by his mentor, the rigorous Marcel Duchamp, and by the congenial tip-faces and garage sales Bill likes to frequent. The day after the exhibition opening, somewhat hungover, I decided to find the house I'd spent my childhood in by retracing the once-familiar route from the town centre with its band rotunda or taxi stand, past where I remembered Paine's ice-cream parlour with its frosty milkshake containers used to be, and so on to Francis Street. This was a route Dave and I would have followed many times on our trikes, or walking with our mother or granny, and later on bikes. It was the way to and from Blenheim Primary School by the banks of the Taylor River across town. It was – it should have been – my first, indelible track, my migration route to and from home, locked in by narratives, games, encounters, landmarks and secret signs; the caravanserai track that could never be obliterated by drifting sand; a map on my brain; the spinal cord of my first epic; my *Odyssey*, my *Iliad*. It may have been the track Dave and I followed when we ran away, as we often did when we were little (once we were brought back in a fire engine) – not because there was anything to run away from, but (I suspect) because 'running away' was another worldly narrative that could be entered through the door inside my head, and which Dave mostly went along with, as a kind of amiable Sancho Panza.

But, that day in 2003, I couldn't find the track. I set off from the Presbyterian church on Alfred Street (a name I remembered because it had always seemed to condense my father's names, Frederic Albert), found the Memorial Fountain and Memorial Clock that had seemed so magnificent when I was a kid, thought I'd worked out where Paine's ice-cream parlour would have been (it had gone), followed my nose – and lost the way.

Then I thought, what might I have done on such an expedition back then? At what scale? The world I'd entered through the door in my head was, after all, no taller than an asparagus plant gone to seed. I might have scraped a stick along the corrugated-iron and paling fences of houses on the way, making that annoying rattle. I remember being told off for doing it, and then doing it anyway. I found a stick and, hoping no one was watching, set off again, crouched to something like my adult waist-height, rattling my way along the memory-track in my brain.

And then, as if in a dream, I arrived at a modest, sun-washed, single-storey California bungalow with a driveway down the side, a front lawn, a glimpse of a big back section, though no apricot tree at the corner on the driveway, no river-boulder balustrade with a front porch behind it, no . . . but it was the house. It was our childhood home. It was where the green dial of the radio glowed like a panther's eye in the front room, where Dave got carried inside by a distraught bloodstained motorist who'd bowled him when he biked out of the driveway without looking, where Nana Horne hummed the same brisk tune every morning along the corridor to the dunny and back again to her bedroom, where I once laid my father out cold in his workshop by hitting him on the back of his head with a hammer (I seem to remember a kind of scientific curiosity), where steam condensed down the cream enamel-painted walls of the kitchen near Nana's porridge pot. Now the house had been 'modernised', the big walnut tree at the back was gone – but this was still where we'd lived until Dave and I were seven. The garage that had housed the grass catcher was still there, in need of a paint job, its door by the footpath askew on rusty hinges.

This was an anticlimactic triumph, a compromised homecoming: the big signage of my memory had gone or been reduced in scale, and the lesson I learned was one I already knew in my heart. You can and you can't go back to the places you once called home, because the world you imagined then and the one you can recreate will never be the same; and I guessed, too, that the gap between 'can' and 'can't', where nostalgia may spread its melancholy spoor, may be the only true measure of what you've done with your life. And it may, too, be the measure of where you want to be going next, the place you have always and never been in, the place you are always running home to: *home*.

But I learned something else as well, or realised I knew it: that my best, even if compromised, chance of getting close to returning to those places I'd left whenever I'd left home would be by means of objects like the grass catcher. Because the grass catcher would help me to remember what everyone else had seen and what only I had seen. Its divided nature would guide me into the gap between can and can't go home again.

I don't remember when I first saw Don Driver's sculpture *Lawn Cuttings* (1976), but there was the battered canvas and wire grass catcher mounted at the end of a row of four coir mats, with a pair of old leather shoes and some other objects in attendance, in a stretcher frame of galvanised pipes – and I recognised it at once for what it was: the uncanny talisman that would get me as close as I was ever going to be to my first childhood home in the world. If I'm going to ask the question, Where are we when we're at home?, then I will have to find the objects or words or events that will get me close to the places I once called home, and where that question might disclose some answers.

I didn't have to bend double to find Horton Park at the end of the street I'd lived in as a kid – the open space with swings and slides where we'd played most days, and where I'd learned to ride a bike by taking off in a straight line towards an inevitable, distant tree. Where I'd leapt from the top of the swings with a bed-sheet parachute and been taken home screaming in the tray of Dave's trike after one of my big toenails was torn off during landing. But when I got to the park that day on my fifty-year-old nostalgia trip, I knew better than to go and have a swing with the kids there – me in my arty, city-slicker black with dark glasses and the faraway look of a lonely fantasist whose childhood friends had long since made themselves scarce. The other reason you can't go home again is because you are no longer who you were. Or rather, like the grass catcher that is both simply whatever it is in the world and something *other*, you are a kind of double: who you have become and the ghost fragment of the other you were when you were in this place you called home long ago.

I've been back a few times in the decade since that disenchanting return home in 2003, and something similar always happens. Most recently, in March 2013, I was in Blenheim with three other poets, Dinah Hawken, John Newton and Cliff Fell, to give readings in the same Millennium Gallery where Bill Culbert's work had been exhibited. Our theme was, as it happens, *home*. We arranged to meet for lunch and plan our evening. Cliff Fell came over from Nelson with his partner Pammy; they were in time for a long, talkative, preparatory lunch among the grapevines out at Rockferry, in a landscape that looked nothing like the nibbled pasture of my childhood. Dinah Hawken and her husband Bill also made it to lunch; they came over the hill from Waikawa Bay around from Picton, where I spent much of my childhood in a backwater that, then, had almost no houses, no marina, and a gravel road that petered out just past the boatshed where my grandfather's clinker dinghy waited to be pushed to the water along manuka rollers. Cressida Bishop, Director of the Millennium Gallery, also came to lunch; the gallery wasn't there when I was a kid, but the Memorial Clock Tower was, just over the road, along with the Floral Clock, both of them structures of awe-inspiring grandeur to my eyes in 1953, when the Queen visited and laid a wreath

(I couldn't see her). John Newton couldn't make it to lunch because he was moving house (home) on Waiheke Island, but he tore through the door of the gallery with minutes to spare before the evening reading, and would have been happy to see that copies of his new collection, *Family Songbook* (which is about home), were for sale.

In John's book, home territories radiate out from Robin Hood Bay at the entrance to Port Underwood: back inland to what used to be called Beavertown (or 'more/ fancifully still', Beaver Station) – now Blenheim; south from there to the Dashwood Pass and North Canterbury; or west through the Rai Valley to the Whangamoa Saddle, which my grandmother, Agnes Horne, was the first woman to drive a car over on the way to Nelson. We were all in our different ways trying to find that grid of locations, circumstances, memories and relationships that located us in some way somewhere.

Cliff, for one, was able to point out, from a perspective that had more to do with historical amusement than whakapapa or with what John characterises as 'homesickness', that his great-great-grandfather Alfred Fell was responsible for surveying the town that would become Blenheim, and named a disproportionate number of its streets after his children. Cliff came to New Zealand in 1997, and on visiting Blenheim for the first time may have found himself going along Francis Street, which his ancestor had originally called 'Frances'. Before coming to lunch, I'd gone on my usual pilgrimage to Francis Street. As usual, I tried but couldn't find it. Then I adjusted my scale, stopped walking nostalgically towards the yellow Wither Hills, and there it was, much closer to the centre of town than it seemed to be when I was a kid; and there was number 32, the slightly-the-worse-for-wear California bungalow, my childhood home, again.

Dinah Hawken said that, for her, being at home is both

utterly tangible: 'this room, this actual house – and garden, neighbourhood, coastline, town, country and world'; and intangible: 'the state of being at home with myself and with others'. I know what she means: after the reading, a woman my age came up and asked if I remembered her. Glenys. We used to play together. My answer had to be evasive to be truthful: no, I didn't remember her or the startling escapades she then reminded me of (we'd pinched someone's engagement ring); but yes, I did remember, because her name and the place we were in again after sixty years were drawn towards each other without quite making meaningful contact: somehow tangible and intangible, incongruous and even comic, as in Cliff's historical frame, and also melancholy, as in John's sense of 'homesickness'.

On my journey to rediscover these home places I will need the grass catcher to guide me to them, and my ghost fragments to guide me to the self I was when I was there – a self that may often have been a version of the counterfeiter who used his twin brother's pain to secure his own pleasure. Will I recognise these places called home and the dissembling play-actor who lived in them? Can my own experiences teach me anything about the experiences of others in the places I called home? How was it for them? This is what I need to find out.

The ivory bracelet

Under the paradoxical sign and faded colours of my dead father's weathered grass catcher, I begin the record of my journeys home.

I thought I'd begun this book long before I really started. In February 2004, I left the Museum of New Zealand after working there for ten years, and took out with me some incoherent questions about the country we live in, constructed as it is of almost indecipherable accumulations of memory, stories, objects, representations, and landscapes shaped by natural forces and human inhabitation. There were places I knew had been visited and represented obsessively by tourists, artists and writers: Mitre Peak, the Bay of Islands, the Otira Gorge, the Waipoua Forest. I wanted to go to these places and gawp; to drive in a dusty cavalcade of campervans towards Aoraki Mount Cook; to take a photograph of the railway station at Cass (through a viewfinder of the Rita Angus painting of it). I wanted to go to Ruapekapeka and see if I could imagine the British bombardment of Kawiti's fortified pa – I knew the 1846 John Williams painting of that event. I wanted to go to Maunganui and look at the places where Horatio Gordon Robley had painted the limb-shattering trench warfare of Gate Pa in 1864. I wanted to go to the Mackenzie Country and think about sheep dogs and Jock McKenzie, to eat whitebait in Westport, to walk up into freezing wind above the beeches in Arthur's Pass, to get to the top of the Panekiri Bluff on Lake Waikaremoana and imagine the lake before Tuhoe were cleared from its shores. I wanted to go to Ahipara on Ninety Mile Beach and look at the blunt hill through the eyes of McCahon's many paintings of it, and to walk along the foam-line at Muriwai, thinking about his beach walks, 'necessary protection', and an offshore island shaped like Moby Dick.

I wanted to stop and start among the unremarked or unremarkable places in the country whose stories I didn't know, the ones nobody had been interested in recording, or in erecting 'scenic' or 'historic site' signage next to – the mangrove-clogged creek behind the off-season camping ground; the pub with its row of diligent pokie players; the gravel back road with its sagging, mossy fence posts, busted, derelict farm machinery and dead, sodden lambs. I longed to go to all these places and look at them – half expecting to see or hear some answers to the questions I was still trying to work out how to ask.

I also just longed after ten years driving a desk nowhere to get out on the road and go around the country; to decide where to head for in the morning and change my mind before nightfall; to stop when I felt like it or when I was tired; to turn off the road on a whim or follow some vague memory spoor; to roll my sleeping bag out where I'd pulled the car over on a deserted coastline facing east into the sunrise I hoped to wake to; to rattle all the way down the gravel road to Tomarata just so I could hear the poet Ken Smithyman's laconic ghost-voice talking to me from rustling toetoe by the lake.

And so the following spring I threw a sleeping bag and some other gear in the car, and took off, all over the North Island, and subsequently on two separate occasions all over the South. Along the way, in a state between lonely, exhilarated and devastated, I babbled for hours into a tape recorder, took hundreds of photographs and wrote obsessively in notebooks. I talked to people in the dining rooms of backpackers and on mist-wreathed viewing platforms while waiting for their photo opportunity. I wrote a novel called *The Viewing Platform* and a long poem called *Letter to Peter McLeavey* based on these trips.

The Viewing Platform was written in France during the six months when I had the Katherine Mansfield residency in Menton in 2005. I went there intending to write the book about home, and thought *The Viewing Platform* was going to be it. It wasn't – or wasn't quite. On the way to France, I spent an emotional month in Bangladesh, looking for and finding the place where our family had lived in the 1950s. I thought that pilgrimage would be part of the *home* book project, and it was, but in the form of a Bangladeshi tourism operator I invented called Mohammed Baul Biswas, one of the six main characters in *The Viewing Platform*. Thus, the *home* book tore off on a tangent and became the one I wrote about leaving the Museum of New Zealand, not about leaving home.

On the way back to New Zealand from France, I stopped off in New York and went on another pilgrimage, this time through the flag-bedecked patriotic heartland up the Hudson Valley and the Catskills, to look at the places and landscapes that had informed the work of the Hudson River school of painters. Then I stopped in LA and drove up to Santa Cruz, following the nation-building visions of the Hudson River artists transposed through the redwoods of California and along the Pacific coast. It was research – it was also a continuation of the road trips I'd begun in 2004 in New Zealand. It was a project that was getting me closer to the *home* book by first taking me further from it.

In 2006 I went back to New York and attempted to recreate the experience I'd had of being there in September 2001 when the twin towers came down and the ash-clogged concept of homeland security rose up; I also went to look at dozens of the nineteenth-century Hudson, Pacific and Yellowstone paintings and photographs by nation-building artists in New York, Boston and San Francisco. This, too, was research, I told myself, and meant it, or meant it to be. I noticed then, and think about again now, the spatial performances of those artists, moving out to the wilderness to make pictures that would define home and nation for metropolitan sophisticates and captains of industry, and that would subsequently expand the popular imaginary of boundless frontiers, opportunities and entitlements – of a homeland that was always going to be greater than the sum of its parts: an *imperium*. All the time I was edging further away from writing about a home haunted by the mysterious double-life phantom of my father's grass catcher in Blenheim, New Zealand; and yet all the time I was also closing in on that haunting.

When I finally sat down to write *this* book, having summoned up the grass catcher to be my spirit-guide or lucky charm, two things happened. My youngest son Jack left home for the third or fourth time and got on a plane, intending to go first to Melbourne and then, a few months later, to his remotely ancestral home, Germany; and a second cousin, Paul Robinson, emailed me an item about a distant German ancestor:

> At the Alhambra Theatre, in Leicester Square, on July 8, 1882, appeared Marian the Giant Amazon Queen in an operetta called *Babil and Bijou*, billed as 'a grand fairy spectacular opera, with music by G. Jacobi'. According to the billing at this time she stood eight feet two inches high and was still growing.
>
> The theatre critic of the *Illustrated London News*, the famous journalist George Augustus Sala, wrote of the

> giantess: 'Notwithstanding her colossal height and build, she is very well proportioned, and she is decidedly handsome, possessing as she does the true pre-Raphaelite maxillary angle.' The *Daily News* remarked: 'She possesses a conspicuous advantage over most of her compeers, inasmuch as she has really considerable claims to good looks.'

My good-looking son Jack is taller than me, though not as tall as his distant relative, the giant Marian Wedde, born in Benkendorf in the Thuringian area of central Germany on 31 January 1865. Great-grand-aunt Marie, or Marian, or Marianne, reached eight foot three inches before she died. At twenty-five Jack was older than the poor giant was able to be – she died shortly before her nineteenth birthday in 1884. Some say she died in Berlin, where Jack was headed. Others say Paris.

Probably her wanderings were at the behest of theatre impresarios, but wandering also runs in the family. Wandering genes have flowed strongly into this home. Jack is a wanderer – no sooner back from a year in Japan than he was plotting this latest escape. His paternal great-great-grandfather, Heinrich August Wedde, became a sailor at a young age, apparently to the dismay of his family; he wandered as far as Wellington, New Zealand, where (in one version of the story) he jumped ship in pursuit of a woman from his home town of Kiel, Maria Reepen, with whom he raised a large family: Herman Conrad, Fritz (of whose wanderings more later), Herbert, Wilhelm Frederick, Bertha, Reinhold Heinrich, Freda, and my grandfather Albert Augustus. Jack's paternal grandfather, my father Frederick Albert, was an inveterate wanderer around New Zealand in his youth and around the world after we left Blenheim in 1954. So was my mother Linda – more so, if anything.

So was her paternal grandfather, Lewis Keele Horne, an English ship's doctor – or doctor who did his time on ships – born in 1832 or 1833. He married Ellen Clifford of Quebec in 1854, and finally settled in New Zealand, first in Collingwood in 1857, and subsequently in Marlborough, where he and Ellen raised a large family of eight sons and eight daughters. Perhaps the family was too much for him – Dr Horne seems to have been staying apart from it in the Criterion Hotel in Blenheim, and was presumed to have died when the hotel burned down in 1887. One account has him running back in to rescue his twelve-year-old son Leonard, and perishing in the attempt (Leonard had already been taken care of); but a descendant, Alexander Monro, was told by his father Herbert Monro on his deathbed that his grandfather the doctor had in fact left the burning hotel by a back door, taking his mistress with him; the following day they caught a river vessel down the Opawa and disappeared to Christchurch. This rumour continues to surface from time to time as an aside to semi-official accounts which treat Dr Horne as an exemplary pioneering figure in the province – which he was, in the public record. Horne Place in Springlands, Blenheim, is named after him; its serene, sunny house-fronts may conceal other discreet scandals.

The doctor's many children are said to have run wild at Dillon's Point and seldom went to school. The sons – George, Francis, Charles, Lewis, Ernest, Leonard, my grandfather Herbert, and Richard – were a wild bunch and ruined the family, my mother said. One contributed to the ruin by accepting a wager he could leap his new horse over the Blenheim town band – he killed the bass drummer in the process, or so we were told.

Linda's father Herbert's share of the Horne family fortune was said to have been a cast-iron kettle. Lillian, his sister, seems to have had better luck – she inherited a painting by Landseer, a friend of the doctor's, and left it to her son Gordon Gifford. Others of the 'wild bunch' became, variously, a gold miner at Kalgoorlie, a stewardess on the Opawa River ferry, a big-game hunter in South Africa and Rhodesia ('Had offspring to black ladies', according to my distantly removed cousin Pam Oliver's account), ran a boarding house, had a cattle run in Queensland . . .

The cast-iron kettle story is probably apocryphal; nonetheless, 'the colonial doctor of Dillon's Point', as the historical record is fond of calling him, despite his having also been an entrepreneurial landowner, drainer and flood protector on the Wairau flood-plain, seems to have left little for the son who became my grandmother's second husband. My brother tells me he once had, and may have stashed somewhere, receipts made out to Dr Horne from the New Zealand Government for payment of the salary he earned in his official position of 'Vaccinator of the Natives of the Wairau'. Our mother told us that Dr Horne was mostly paid in kind – vegetables and fish. When we were kids, Maori from Wairau used to come round with kerosene tins of whitebait, and Nana Horne would dip mugs of it into a big bowl. The memory of Dr Horne seems to have reached across to Waikawa Bay as well, where Aggie Horne's husband Bertie built a bach on 'Maori land' – though what that meant is unclear.

Apparently there was a long-running challenge to Dr Horne's will, of which his wife Ellen Horne was executrix. The dispute was referred to the Privy Council, but I don't know what became of it. Nana Aggie's and grandfather Bertie Horne's family was hard-up during the Depression and the war; our childhood was secure but very frugal, and when we left Blenheim in 1954 my parents had never owned their own house.

Also apocryphal may be the possibility that the Horne connection to Marlborough goes back further: the port of Picton is in Waitohi Bay, which Captain William Steine renamed Horne Bay in 1832 after the owner of his command, the *King William the Fourth*. In 1844, the New Zealand Company's Francis Dillon Bell (whence Dillon's Point) and Governor Sir George Grey bought Waitohi Bay off the local iwi, who then moved to Waikawa Bay. It would have been their descendants who later sponsored Bertie Horne on to a bit of land in Waikawa, where he built his bach. The Horne association with Maori probably owes much to Bertie's father and his work as Medical Officer of the district from 1870. If we have homes in history, mine seems at once irrelevant and inevitable.

My mother's Scots mother, Agnes Ogilvie Tait, was born in Dundee on the night of the great Tay Bridge disaster, 28 December 1879. In some illogical way, I associate the collapse of the bridge with the emigration of my Scottish ancestors – as if, at that moment, they said, 'Enow! We're oot o' here!'

They weren't the only Taits to move out from Scotland across the expanding global field of opportunity in the eighteenth and nineteenth centuries. And they may have had other reasons for being restless, or just for leaving. Sometime after starting this quest for what might be called the family home – that circumstance rather than place where my ancestors converged – I discovered that Aggie's grandparents can't have been the James and Martha Mein Tait whose headstones I found in the old Omaka graveyard in Blenheim, who died in 1897 and 1902 aged seventy-nine and eighty-one respectively. Martha would have been sixty-eight when the bridge went down and Aggie was born, which seems too old to become a grandmother. It's possible, though, that some members of Aggie's Tait family had already made their way to New Zealand, including perhaps a great-aunt and -uncle called James and Martha, and that her own father and mother, William and Susan (née Ogilvie) Tait, came to Marlborough to join family living at Tua Marina. I need to know more about Aggie's *faither* and her *màthair*, and why they chose to cross the world with a wee bairn, my grandmother.

Aggie stayed put in Marlborough, though. She married her first husband, Fred Cox, in 1904 – he died a few months later, and is buried in the graveyard at Tua Marina – and married my grandfather Bertie Horne in 1906; she lived most of her life in the house I was brought up in, at 32 Francis Street, Blenheim. As the first woman to drive a motor car over the Whangamoa, Aggie might have gone a lot further if she'd had the chance. She saved up and took my mother Linda for a cruise around the Pacific islands to make up for stopping her schooling and putting her to work in the hair salon she ran – I have a small Samoan tapa cloth Linda brought back.

Recently, when word got out that I'd been writing this book, I received a letter from a woman called Barbara Matthews. She remembered getting her hair done in 'that small town where nothing seemed to happen', where she lived from 1930 to 1948. She was taken by her mother to the hair salon 'in Girlings'. Reading Mrs Matthews' kind letter, and her reference to 'those old Wither Hills that seemed to enclose you', I felt the confinement of the place as well in her description of the small salon 'in one corner of the shop'. Mrs Matthews remembered my mother as being 'quite beautiful – tall and elegant, with lovely dark hair'.

Through the lens of Mrs Matthews' letter I locate that image of Linda in the small shop, the circumscribed history, the crowding hills, the bounded constituency of Wairau – and I think I understand her restlessness. I want to feel it. But then Mrs Matthews also remembered that 'there was a lot of music in that little town', and that there were productions at His Majesty's Theatre, in which my mother and father may well have been involved. In the end, though, Mrs Matthews 'became restless and just longed to leave that small town'. She became a librarian at the National Library in Wellington. My mother's own small-town blues drove her further away than that.

I too have the wandering gene – am restless, keen to go – when I can afford to travel, or when I can dress travel in the convenient camouflage of research – for example, into what it means to be at home, to leave it, to come back again. And so does my twin brother Dave, though in a different form. Dave and his wife Sue are often on the road, or on bikes, or tramping, or holidaying in various parts of the world – they send back snapshots of themselves on remote mountaintops, in deserts or floating down exotic rivers. They are usually grinning broadly, and in congenial company. Unlike me, they don't bother to camouflage the fact they're having fun by claiming to be doing anything more than travelling for the sake of it. In this they resemble our mother and father.

The day I finally stopped dithering and sat down to begin work on this restless project was the day Jack left and his giant ancestor arrived. I had to find a place where all the coming and going stopped for a moment. It was then that I knew, or decided, where that stopping-and-starting-place is – a place I didn't visit or revisit during the road trips of 2004, but a place I have kept revisiting one way or another all my life.

I also recognised something that should have been obvious long before this: I've seldom written about anything else but coming and going from home. My first novel, *Dick Seddon's Great Dive*, was about a character trying to retrace his steps towards belonging somewhere. The next, *Symmes Hole*, had three characters all trying to get, or find, home. In *Survival Arts*, Salvation is trying to find a home for his army-surplus M24 Chaffee tank (but really himself), and the book's other characters are all bewildered by the question of where they fit in. *The Viewing Platform* is a satire about the institutional culture of national home-building. In *Chinese Opera*, the gangster Little Frank is literally dying to recover the memory of when he was at home in love. The all-at-sea food and restaurant critic in *The Catastrophe* hopes, hopelessly, that he can at last make himself meaningfully at home in the homeless world of the Palestinian diaspora. I wrote about my wandering sons (and their ghostly, footloose ancestors) in *The Commonplace Odes.*

4.5 To my sons

Home's where you're always going, it's the place you've just
Left, where your father takes all the photographs
In the unfinished dwelling of the tribe. Tomorrow when it
rains
He'll fix the roof, dinner's over and music
Still follows you into the street as night falls

Across the face of the brooding, neighbourhood hillside.
Hair falls across the faces of young
Musicians. They're dancing, their paws are running and
running
In the dream chase, their hearts are broken and they cross
The world for love and then they come home

Again, these flâneurs – they have eaten the meats of strange
Lands and heard the call to prayer startle
Doves from the battlements of seaside resorts where the
gasoline
Was cheaper than at home. They've been where bear hunters
In the cold mountains make toys in the off-season.

They bring the toys back for us to look at.
There's a painted doll that fits inside another,
And so on, until the story disappears. The tall
Stories of the tall boys. They come back
Like their great-great-grandfathers before them, lacquer-

Ware in their sea chests, blue plates with unicorns
On the back, postcards of copulating gods,
T-shirts in languages not yet spoken,
An amulet, a faraway look. It's great to be home
Again, say our wandering sons, as they wave goodbye.

Thinking about all this, I feel myself being drawn as if by an undertow towards a specific time and location in my childhood. My second cousin Paul, who sent the item about the giant Maria Wedde, also sent a DVD copy of home movies shot in the late 1940s and early '50s by his Granny Vesey. Included is a tiny clip of Dave and I aged about four or five and dressed in white satin pageboy outfits at the wedding of Paul's mother, our beautiful grown-up cousin Norma. The little pageboys look tired and bewildered. The smaller one with the sculpted cowlick is screwing one fist into his eye and gazing with longing at an escape route. The other twin holds his ground – he seems anxious to make sense of where he is, rather than of where he might go.

The old movie clip immediately reminds me of a black-and-white photograph in which we hold up the train of Cousin Norma's sumptuous wedding dress. Here, our bewilderment is replaced by function, the distressing real-time of the movie by a split second of smiling certainty. Dave looks to be doing the heavy lifting; his cowlicked twin is rather more attentive to the photo opportunity.

And from this image – the two of us side by side, holding up the satiny shimmer of the train – I am towed away to shimmering sea. In another black-and-white photograph, taken about the same time, Dave and I are on the pebbly beach at Waikawa Bay in the Marlborough Sounds, probably at the bach my father and mother helped Bertie Horne build before we were born. I have no memory whatsoever of Norma's wedding, only the displaced, smell- and taste-free one of the photograph. I can't feel the weight of her sumptuous train – not because my brother's doing all the work, but because the moment of the image is without substance. But looking at the next snapshot I can feel the weight of the large, gutted fish, half our height, which Dave and I are holding up between us against a backdrop of ruffled, shining sea and bare, burned-off hills across the bay. I can smell the fish, which is also the smell of my father's forearms glittering with fish scales and of fish guts slithering from the bloodstained gutting board into the sea; and I can smell the popping Venus-necklace seaweed on the beach, the clay-stained water of the creek where it ran out into the bay, the bush-mould smell of the water where it was dammed further back, the smell of the long-drop dunny with its mason-fly nests of pale clay, the musty smell of the bunks we slept in on thin, lumpy squabs, the smoky wood-fire range burning manuka, fish frying on it in a heavy black pan, the fabulous aroma of the timber smokehouse up the back.

I can taste the fried fish, and especially the little garfish we had for breakfast after netting them at night with a Tilley lamp over the stern of the dinghy; and I can feel the weight of the big fish Dave and I are holding in the photograph – but the sensation of that weight has been displaced into the exciting, quivering weight of fish being pulled up on a hand-line. This would have happened later, when we were old enough to go out fishing in what had been Grandfather Horne's heavy clinker dinghy with its smoky outboard motor and its gunwales notched from years of cod lines being run across them. Those fishing trips, and others in larger launches, took us out to the kelpy reefs and deep sea-floor chasms where the tides run strongly in the narrows towards Tory Channel.

And it's out there, against a backdrop memory of shining, ruffled sea, and what I vividly recall of my earliest sensations, that I find the one place I can never leave and yet always return to – a kind of paradoxical eddy, at once turbulent and fixed, a whirlpool that my family ancestors seem to swirl around in, and a centre from which I go on measuring my distance from my first home-in-myself when I was separate from my mother and also from the brother who took the weight of our cousin's bridal train, and who held the other end of the manuka stick from which the big fish hung on its knotted length of flax, its weight pulling us towards each other even as we strained to stay apart by lifting the trophy we held up between us.

1.4 To My Twin Brother

There are some things I still need to know:
How can I talk to you when we have forgotten our language?
Where can we meet now that our mother is long dead?
How can I bring you gifts when you
Are bringing me gifts? How could our father

Be in the picture when he was always taking it? What
Is this we hold up between us – is it a trophy,
Did we compete for it, is it alive or dead? And how can
My sons speak to your daughters
When they have never learned our language? Where

Can they meet now that their fathers have no place
To meet? How can they share what they have when they have
Nothing in common? And what is this they hold

Up between them? Is it their grandmother's wedding band,
That gateway through which their fathers entered

Life, through which their grandfather left it?
Why are you left-handed while I am right-handed?
Why did you have daughters while I had sons?
Which of us could have been the other's sister?
And what is this we hold up between us?

Is it perhaps a mirror? Or a moon trail
On the placid ocean where the reflections of our mother and
  father
Are not disturbed, sitting under Royal palms
On the Picton foreshore, tinkle of jazz from the ferry,
Sons unborn, cheek by cheek under Gemini?

Once again, I surprise myself by remembering that I've thought about this before, but glancingly, so that the page of *The Commonplace Odes* on which that poem is written gives way quickly to the next one, on which 'To Donna's Young Dogs' ends with a plea:

                                        Seat me
Again at tables loaded with hope, in the baffling
Milieu of the tribe, in its dwelling that cannot be finished,
In a persistent shower of light like sawdust – your doggy
Boys running home through rain to be towelled.

There are two more photographs I've found while preparing to write this. Neither seemed until now to have any bearing on that diagram of counterweighted attraction and repulsion, the effort of self-identification captured by the images of heavy fish and bridal train. In one, I'm aged about eight and doing most of the holding up, this time of a dead snake hanging perpendicular between me and a boy called Billy McKenzie, a Scots kid who lived in the same place as us up the Karnaphuli River in East Pakistan in the early 1950s. Billy's grip of the snake is wincing at best – a forefinger and thumb touching it at waist height. I, on the other hand, although wearing an expression of disgust, have hoisted the thing aloft. At very least, the occasion seemed to demand triumph, an appropriate gesture for the camera.

In the other photograph I'm unaware of being looked at – or don't care. Skinny, bearded, smoking a cigarette and staring off into some distance or other, I seem uninterested in two of my kids, Carlos and Conrad, and their friend Brandon. There's no display of triumph, no mugging to the camera, and certainly no sign of the symbolic happy-family enactments that would later fill my photo albums. In the indifferent photograph, the kids and I are on the foredeck of the launch that had suddenly appeared one morning in the remote Queen Charlotte Sound bay where I'd been holed up alone for weeks, finishing off my novel *Symmes Hole.* My wife then, Rose, had had enough, or was worried, or both, and she came over with the kids to take me home.

As luck would have it, I'd just finished the book, much of which was set in the Sounds around the whaling station at Arapawa Island on Tory Channel. That might be one explanation for my haggard indifference. Another might be my marooned diet of whatever fish I'd been able to catch, and cress from the creek. But the most likely one has to do with that attraction and repulsion that seems to characterise the wanderer's feelings about home – the place you long for and long to leave; the place in which you long to immerse your identity in the tribe's, and from which you long to be free and alone with your freedom.

That day, returning to the ferry terminal from the western

side of the Sounds, we'd have passed under the steep, rocky flank of Allport Island. I have a vivid childhood summer memory of puttering in the clinker dinghy around the Snout that separates Waikawa Bay from the harbour at Picton, and of my father tying the boat to a tree root so he could clamber up and fetch my mother a branch of crimson pohutukawa flowers. Chick, as he was known to family and friends, adored Linda – he called her Lindy. As a young man he'd bashed his face on an underwater rock after accepting a dare to dive from the crosstree of a yacht sailing in the Sounds. The damage wasn't great but he concealed some twisting of his top lip under a jaunty moustache. The effect when he smiled was sometimes slightly unnerving – no more so than when he smiled admiringly at my mother. In many photographs of Chick gazing at Lindy across the wine glasses of dinner tables, his tipsy, adoring smile has a slightly lecherous lift to one side. She was strikingly beautiful – the family album contains many photographs of Linda as a young woman on boats in the Sounds, often surrounded by salty-looking men, the crookedly grinning Chick among them. All of them are smoking, and in some pictures my mother is wearing the heavy ivory bracelet that I would later become obsessed with.

My mother's vivacious beauty was clearly legendary in that region. After the publication of *Symmes Hole*, only days after Linda died in November 1986, I met an elderly Maori man known as Uncle Arthur, whose Waikawa Bay whanau was connected to the descendants of James 'Worser' Heberley, the hapless whaler hero of my novel. Uncle Arthur worked as a messenger at Parliament buildings, and after our first encounter on the occasion of the book launch we sometimes met for a beer at De Brett's on Lambton Quay near Parliament.

'Your mother was a very beautiful young woman,' he

informed me carefully. What was left politely unspoken was that he'd been besotted with her, though only a boy at the time.

A sad phantom comes part-way into view at this stage in my hesitant return to Dieffenbach Point – the place I know I have to get back to in order to leave again on this journey home. My maternal grandfather, Herbert Stacey Horne, known as Bertie, was born in Blenheim in 1877. Among the many memories Uncle Arthur had of my mother at Waikawa Bay, the most central was of helping to launch Bertie's heavy clinker dinghy down the beach on the mainland side of the bay – the same dinghy whose wet, cod-line-grooved gunwales were central to my childhood world. The help was needed not just because the boat was heavy but because what I came to know as our family bach was built on the Snout peninsula, across the bay from the road and the boatsheds, on land provided to Bertie Horne by Uncle Arthur's hapu. Uncle Arthur's help was also needed because Bertie had only one arm. According to my mother, he'd lost the other one as the result of an accident at a farm-equipment trade show where he'd volunteered to demonstrate a new harvesting machine. One coat sleeve got caught in the conveyor, and his left arm was dragged through the sprockets.

Why is my grandfather Bertie Horne a sad phantom? One reason is the ever-present moral of the harvester story as told by my mother. Bertie was an alcoholic, and she says he was drunk when he volunteered to demonstrate the harvester. Linda adored her father who, like his son, my Uncle Keele, was blessed with an anarchic sense of humour; as a child, however, she had also been terrified when he appeared covered in blood after yet again falling off his bicycle on his way home from the pub. She had a fear that one or another of her twins would inherit Bertie's alcoholic gene. It was certainly her heavy smoking that killed my mother, and from time to time when she worried that I might be showing signs of inheriting the alcoholic Bertie gene we'd make a pact – Linda would knock off smoking if I'd moderate my drinking. On a couple of occasions when I stayed at her house after Chick died, we surprised each other at dead of night, she having a furtive smoke and me getting an insomniac's shot from the liquor cabinet.

Bertie Horne's a sad phantom for another reason. On my mother's death certificate her father's Christian name is left blank. It was Dave who had to look after the official records in Auckland after our mother's funeral, and like me he had little or no knowledge or memory of our maternal grandfather. We were apparently presented to him as babies while he was an invalid in bed at the house in Francis Street, but of course I don't remember that. In one of only two pictures I've ever seen of him, he's sitting on the front step of the house, next to the river-boulder balustrade he built, his stump arm tucked inside a pinned-up shirtsleeve, a durrie stuck to his bottom lip. Linda told me he'd been in constant pain from the botched amputation of his mangled arm but that he'd managed it with medication, had stopped drinking and had spent much of his time out at Waikawa Bay. Though there's no evidence to support my hunch, a medical historian I talked to about Bertie agreed that he'd quite probably been put on a maintenance dosage of morphine by a friendly family doctor – not so uncommon in small-town New Zealand in the 1930s and '40s – which would explain why he was able to knock off the booze.

On Linda's death certificate Bertie is described as a 'shopkeeper'; and in a family tree, 'Descendants of Randolph Horne', assembled by Pam Oliver, it's recorded that he 'owned a Hairdressing Saloon in Blenheim' – the one remembered by Barbara Matthews, where Linda worked. Though he may have been the legal owner of the business, the reality, according to Linda, was different – it was his wife Agnes Horne who established the business and saw the family through the Depression and the war with it. Another male Horne, Lewis Clifford or Lew (1913–1974), is described in Pam's yellowed family tree as having 'worked in Bert Horne's saloon in Blenheim' – so perhaps Bertie also cut hair there before losing his arm.

Linda had to leave school young and work in the 'saloon', which was also a tea shop, to help support the family. This caused her great sadness and some bitterness, and by her own admission was one reason she wanted to get out of Blenheim when the time came. While she and Agnes (and perhaps Lew) worked the salon and tea shop, Bertie did nothing much – or couldn't do anything much – except go fishing from Waikawa Bay. I suspect he also did so to put some distance between himself and his formidable wife.

The impression I have of Agnes is a composite of childhood memories – brisk, no-nonsense, a piercing gaze, a judiciously eked-out bag of hard blackball lollies in the bloomers drawer of her Scotch chest; of my mother's chagrin at the control Agnes had over her; and of anecdotes like the one about her being the first woman to drive a car over the Whangamoa Pass.

Uncle Arthur remembered that one-armed Bertie sculled the dinghy expertly with a single oar over the stern once it was in the water. My father taught us how to do that, using kid-sized oars. I remember how the seawater ran along the oars and on to my hands when I rowed – me on one side, Dave on the other, an oar each, and also with two oars, 'putting our backs into it'. Chick knew a few stirring poems by heart, one of which he adapted as a rowing-chant – John Masefield's 'Cargoes'.

Dirty British coaster with a salt-caked smoke stack
Butting through the Channel in the mad March days,
With a cargo of Tyne coal,
Road-rail, pig-lead,
Fire-wood, iron-ware, and cheap tin trays.

He'd haul back on the stress syllables and reach forward in between: '*Dir*-ty British *coas*-ter with a *salt*-caked *smoke*-stack . . .' He didn't so much love poetry as respond fervently to hearts-of-oak jingoism amplified by meter. But I've remembered the Masefield poem; and I remember how to row.

Chick also showed us how to line up a marker astern and keep it in place as we rowed so as not to have to look over our shoulders at where we were going. Looking into those astern viewfinders, still sharp in my memory, it's the scrubby bush of the Snout that I can still see, a fold where the creek ran down, the yellow stain of clay in the sea by the creek mouth, a little pebbly beach. When I go back to Waikawa now I can still spot the place as if I'm rowing across the bay with my back to the little store by the road, the old boatsheds, the big Arthur house on the hill with the Royal palm in front. These days there's a marina, the town of Picton has extended its suburb all the way out past Waikawa, and there are expensive holiday homes overlooking the Sound. But from the foreshore on the mainland side, standing on familiar pebbles, sticky yellow clay and wave-smoothed broken glass, I can return without effort to the place across the murky bay from which we'd have set off early in the morning to Dieffenbach Point.

I don't know where my mother's heavy ivory bracelet came from – not from my father, though it appears on her wrist in a photograph of her as a young woman at the tiller of a boat in the Sounds. I think this image may predate their marriage, but I don't know for sure; it may have been taken on their honeymoon. They certainly honeymooned on a yacht in the Sounds, and the bracelet seems to belong there – I can hear it clacking against the hard kauri of the tiller. It may have come from her grandfather Horne, the former ship's doctor, who was said to have brought exotic objects back from his voyages in the China trade.

It also appears in photographs of a theatre production in which my mother took part. Both she and Chick were founding members of the Marlborough Repertory Society in 1948; Chick was a president from 1952 to 1953, and a vice-president in 1951–52. According to the theatre's records, the Society's farewell to them in 1953 included a production of *Tony Draws a Horse.* Until 1975, the Society staged productions in the classic Her Majesty's Theatre, which was a cinema most of the time – Dave and I saw our first movie there: almost certainly *Against All Flags*, with Errol Flynn as the pirate Brian Hawke; we both remember Flynn swinging from ropes. There was a props- and set-building space somewhere away from the theatre, where Chick used to take us while he painted flats; the water-based paint he sloshed on with big brushes had an unforgettable, chalky smell. I don't remember shows in which Linda took part, though Dave says one of them was *The Arcadians* – 'I remember the title, and the hero arriving by parachute, possibly into Arcadia where who knows what awaited?' Our cousin Norma, who went to drama school and was a regular and glamorous lead in the company's productions, says that Linda was mostly involved with costumes and make-up. The record shows that she did have a part in a 1951 production of *Fresh Fields* by Ivor Novello – but the commemorative theatre prints I have of her can't be tracked back to Repertory productions.

When we were clearing out their house in Auckland after Chick's death, I found a set of photographs from Gordon McCusker Studios, Blenheim, in which Linda appears to be barely out of her teens. When I asked her about the photographs, she said only that she'd enjoyed the performances and endured her stage-fright because she also loved the whole fantasy world of costumes, make-up and accessories.

The McCusker photographs document her romantic lead as Lady Mary Lasenby in a production of *The Admirable Crichton*, J.M. Barrie's gently comic 1902 satire of the English class system. According to my cousin Norma, this was a Blenheim Operatic Society production and took place before Linda and Chick were married. The ivory bracelet is conspicuous in all these photographs. In one, of a scene from Act Two in which the characters are marooned on a tropical island, Linda aka Lady Mary appears with the company, all of them clad in fanciful homemade deerskin costumes. Hers is the most elegant, as are the stylish sandals she's wearing, and she alone wears a neat chaplet of leaves. She's crouched on one knee next to a rugged-looking Crichton, with other castaways standing behind them. They look variously alarmed or expectant (one through a monocle) but my mother's expression is calm and focused – with a slight smile, she's bending a bow and aiming an arrow at some off-stage prey, presumably the dinner that only Crichton knows how to prepare and cook. The ivory bracelet has slid halfway up her slender left forearm, the one with which, as I now think, she was aiming at a future beyond the life she led in Blenheim – a life in which the fantasies of play-acting would become real, in the equivalents of tropical islands.

I see the same smile in a photograph taken when Linda would have been in her late fifties, in the Casino du Liban, north-west of Beirut, overlooking the Bay of Jounieh. This time, it's a cigarette she's pointing in her right hand. Her left, bracelet-bearing arm is concealed, but I know the ivory bracelet's no longer there, because by then she'd given it to me.

My father died of a heart attack on 6 September 1981 when Dave and I were thirty-four. He was only seventy-four years old. He was cremated at Purewa Cemetery in Auckland and his ashes were scattered there. Dave, who looked after the arrangements for him, as he did also for our mother, said that Linda refused to have a memorial marker for her Chick. When we visited the place a couple of years ago, he told me that, typically, she didn't want to be 'a bother'. More importantly, she couldn't bear the thought of a marker for Chick falling into disrepair, and couldn't imagine anyone sticking around long enough to look after it. Most importantly, she saw no reason to remember him in that place. It had nothing to do with him – it wasn't his home – and she wanted to remember him in all the different places where they'd lived together: in East Pakistan, England, Geneva, Korea, Cairo, Amman, Zambia, and in the many other places they'd passed through in their restless lives. As Dave told me this, I wanted to add 'and the Sounds' – but he would already have known where I was heading. So we talked a bit about how our mother and father came and went in our lives, and how their unmarked passing was somehow appropriate.

Linda died on 7 November 1986 when Dave and I had just turned forty. That means she was thirty-six when she had her twins. Her death certificate says she was twenty-eight when she married; Chick was thirty-three. They were married for eight years before they had children. I know there were miscarriages, and Chick was away at the war. She was seventy-six when she died, having been ill with emphysema and associated conditions for many years. That didn't stop her getting on a plane and going all over the world to see her old friends once affairs had been sorted out and their house in St Heliers, Auckland, sold after Chick's death.

She knew the trip away would kill her and said as much when we went out for lunch before she left. I asked her if she'd rather be making up drapes for her new flat. She laughed at the joke – she knew exactly what it meant. Some months later, she came back off the plane in a wheelchair, and died soon after. She, too, was cremated at Purewa. On the day we visited, Dave wasn't sure if there was a memorial anywhere. He confessed to feeling guilty about such apparent neglect. But really, what did it matter? That neither of us could feel any kind of connection between those two wanderers and the lawns and memorials of Purewa Cemetery seems natural enough.

That day, Dave lent me a hat to keep the sun off, and made his customary joke about me needing a bigger one because of the size of my brain. In fact, his head is bigger than mine, his mind is capacious and agile; he has an exceptional memory, and his ability at word-games and puzzles is phenomenal, like our mother's for cryptic crosswords. My thinking constantly veers off into digressions. It gets distracted and sidetracked – for example, by the Qing Dynasty jade bull I went to find in Auckland Museum after we'd visited the crematorium's memorial garden. I was still wearing the hat borrowed from my brother. The bull is called Yu-shek, and dates from some time before 1860. It's in the Sir George Grey Collection, and I used to visit it regularly when I was a student at Auckland University and living in a flat in Parnell. Back then, it seemed to have a zone of calmness around it. When I found it again, I remembered the uncertainty and unhappiness of that time, how I couldn't work out how to be peaceful. I also remembered my mother's ivory bracelet. Later, on the way down Parnell

Rise, I passed a shop called Home. Nothing in its window fitted the disordered cryptic crossword in my brain – but the ivory bracelet did. It made sense; it completed something.

I felt miserable about my mother and father for years after their deaths. Something remained unresolved. I kept a number of talismanic objects with me, vaguely intending to do something with them one day. They included our mother's ivory bracelet. In 2004, the year I left the museum, I was asked to write the concluding chapter in a book, *Figuring the Pacific*. I finished the chapter with an account of what I did with the bracelet.

> As a kid, I'd once told my mother that I was scared of her dying, and that her heavy ivory bracelet frightened me, because I thought of it going into the grave with her. In my memory, she took it off and gave it to me. As a kid, I was prone to histrionics – I may still be; my twin brother is sceptical this gifting happened (he may have his own reasons for this). After her death, though, I did have the bracelet, and it wasn't on her body when she died. I also had one of my father's old Omega Seamaster watches, and a scarf of my mother's with a pohutukawa motif on it. I kept these objects together in a box in my office, with a couple of photographs: they comforted and disturbed me. They haunted me.
>
> In the summer, I often used to sail with one of my cousins in his ferro-cement yacht across Cook Strait from Wellington, through Tory Channel past the flank of Arapawa, and past Dieffenbach Point with its light. Sometimes when it was rough I'd do the strait sailing while he wrapped up, morose and miserable. That was the part I liked; he didn't. Inside Tory Channel he'd brighten up, open a beer, and sail the rest of the way. One year not long ago, I took the ivory bracelet and my father's Omega Seamaster watch, and wrapped them in the scarf with the pohutukawa motif. I weighted them down with a piece of obsidian I'd found years ago by

> a spilling midden in Otanerau Bay on the southern side of Arapawa Island across from Ship Cove. As my cousin took the boat around the light on Dieffenbach Point, I dropped the wrapped-up objects over the stern. They sank quickly. Though the tides are ferocious there, I know pretty much where they ended up.
>
> I don't really understand how I came to this decision – I think it came to me. It felt right then, and it still does, especially when I think of my parents. I have a sense of well-being whenever I go past the Point. My cousin teased me all the way to Picton. Drolly, affectionately, he raised his beer-can in a salute as we passed the entrance to Waikawa Bay. I felt tremendously happy.

Is there any point trying to explain this happiness? It's possible that I succeeded in appeasing some guilt at leaving my brother to deal with the miserable bureaucratic mopping-up after our parents' funerals. The happiness may be entirely selfish, more sign than substance. Perhaps the bundle with the ivory bracelet and the watch was what the English psychoanalyst Donald Winnicott called a 'transitional object'. I was certainly no longer a child when I dropped the bundle over the side of John's yacht, and had long ago ceased to expect my mother to 'bring the world to me'; yet I needed an object, an 'act' that would bridge the abyss between me and a world without my mother and father.

But I think the best answer is simpler. There's a black-and-white snapshot of my mother and Nana Horne on the mainland beach at Waikawa. My guess is that it was taken while Chick was away during the war. Nana's wearing a warm, sensible coat and the thin-framed glasses that gave her a piercing expression. She has one hand on the familiar clinker dinghy. My mother has her thick, dark, wavy hair pinned back above her ears – the cloudy background and ruffled bay behind them suggest it's one of those cold, windy Sounds days when gusts rip down between the steep hills and drive whitecaps up against the tide that pours strongly through Tory Channel and past Dieffenbach Point. She's wearing a stylish wind-cheater and trousers. Nana, bending to steady the prow of Bertie's dinghy, is looking at her daughter sideways, with a conspiratorial grin. Linda's looking at the camera: her rather aquiline nose directs her characteristic chevron-shaped smile straight at me.

They look at home together, mother and daughter, probably making fun of the photographer. Though Linda was frankly resentful of her mother's restriction of her schooling, and made no secret of the fact that Nana Aggie had been one reason she'd wanted to get out of Blenheim, still, they'd lived in the same house in Francis Street until my mother was forty-three, had got the family through the Depression together, run a business, got through the war, managed alcoholic and then one-armed Bertie, and raised twin boys to the age of seven. In the photograph on the beach, they seem to fit in to the place – Linda especially, with her wind-cheater; and Bertie seems almost present too, because his dinghy's there. The one thing I want to see, but can't, is the ivory bracelet, because my mother has her hands behind her back. But of course I imagine it's there.

At the simplest level, I think my Dieffenbach Point happiness came from the sense, present in the snapshot, that my mother too was happy there – away from the domestic, which she didn't like much ('Would you rather be making up drapes?'), and blowing away her irritation at the narrow circumstances of her life in Blenheim in the breezy, unpredictable environment of the Sounds, with its boat trips, fishing expeditions, beach picnics, make-do bach life and fun in general.

There's also an incongruous snapshot of a smiling Linda with her lanky, scowling, one-armed father, both of them standing in a neatly excavated trench with steps at what I think is the bach section at Waikawa, though it could have been the air-raid shelter trench they were required to dig back at Blenheim. Bertie is leaning back, holding his pipe; he's covered in mud. My mother, dressed in a chic costume with smart shoes, is striking a modelling kind of pose, with her hands on her hips and one knee forward. The caption on the back of the snapshot, in Linda's neat handwriting, concludes, 'N.B. House coat cut down & navy & white wedgie shoes of which I've told you. Do you like them dear?'

Her wicked smile on the windy beach or in 'the trench' is one I see over and over in the hundreds of photographs my father took of her during their wandering years; and so I resist the impulse to suggest that my mother's happiness at Waikawa Bay is a sign that she was 'at home' there. But, as a final resting place, a last home, haunted by the clatter of the ivory bracelet on a boat's tiller, and raked by tides that resist any attempt to stay in one place, Dieffenbach Point still feels right.

The asynchrony of my twin brother's and my left-handed/right-handed, daughters/sons configuration suggests that, as well as being separate and different, we combine to make a more comprehensive whole. How we remember works in this way. We amplify each other's worlds. My memories tend to be large, self-dramatising, unreliable – they are easily distracted by auxiliary suggestions (Yes! Yes! That too!), by too much analysis and a morbid compulsion to understand. Dave, on the other hand, has a wonderful, succinct memory for material facts and a sanguine disregard for the kinds of traps I set myself. He remembers the name of our bach neighbours on the Snout, and the moment he says 'Rossel' or 'Russel' (later, we sort out that they were Rousells) I truly believe I can picture the man, rather sandy haired and big, with a greasy beret pulled back over the nape of his neck.

Dave remembers that another family whose father's name sounded like Jock Steneer, or more likely the Rousells, whose bach was closer to the Horne one, included a couple of daughters, three or four years older than us, with whom we used to row across the bay to get ice creams – and the moment he tells me this, I'm sure I remember it. He remembers vomiting out the car window as Chick drove us along the twisty gravel road from Blenheim to Picton, and at once I can smell his sick and see the resigned pallor of his face. He tells me that the Rousells owned not just a launch but a 'classic displacement launch'; impressed by this, I find a memory rising up of a fishing trip in that launch, when someone hooked a big octopus out by the reef at Dieffenbach Point and hauled it up to the boat's gunwale; it pumped water and ink all over us before someone cut it loose.

This is how I know that Dieffenbach Point isn't just the place, or the sign of the place, where I first began to be distinct and at home in myself; it's also 'the place' where I am joined to my brother and what he remembers, which is different from what I remember; and to our mother and father. I imagine that the octopus has by now taken our father's Omega Seamaster watch and our mother's ivory bracelet to a safe place, a lair, where it protects them. And that's where they are.

The artesian well

Not as I encountered it later, but as I remember it, 32 Francis Street, Blenheim, was on the right-hand side of the road as you approached Horton Park. It had a glassed-in sunporch to its right, where you convalesced when you had the mumps or flu. The house was set back from the street across a broad, immaculately mown lawn. There was obviously something about sustaining a beautiful grass nap that obsessed my father – perhaps it was the combination of order, which he loved, and doing stuff outdoors, which he also loved. Many years later, I would watch with admiration as, wearing a disgraceful pair of khaki shorts, he mowed the desiccated grass in front of the apartment he and my mother had in Amman, Jordan, while astonished Jordanian families watched and made comments from neighbouring balconies.

To the right of the house as you faced it from Francis Street was an un-gated driveway which opened across the footpath to the road. In summer, the tar in the footpath, and especially along the edges of the gutter where it joined the road, would get soft and almost melt. I remember the taste of that tar, and its delightful smell and texture. Our grandmother had a method of removing the stuff from our hands with butter. I don't know how, or why, that worked. Nana Horne had other mysterious remedies and arcane approaches to hygiene and sanitation in her repertoire, of which the most fearsome was a pink rubber hose with a squeezable bulb at one end, which was used to introduce a warm, soapy, colon-cleansing enema to her twin grandsons.

Though the driveway down the side of the house was made to accommodate a car, it never did, since there was a single garage to the left of the house on the street-front. This was where the well-used grass catcher was stored, along with various other useful things. It was also where I remember Chick kept his home brew, and where he sampled it with friends. Dave, however, remembers another shed or garage at the end of the right-hand drive where the brewing occurred. He thinks brewing also took place in the mirror-image garage of the house next door: 'The name Joker Hillman springs to mind. Hedge clipping on the Horne side was rewarded with a nod and a wink from Joker, and Dad would disappear.'

I can remember exactly the intonation and shape of the word my mother (Dave thinks grandmother) called out when it was time for our father to leave his lip-smacking cronies and come inside for some reason – 'Al-*beeert*!' I think there was a concrete-mixer in the garage too, but this memory may be specific to one occasion when it was in use there, on the footpath, with a hose running to it from the garden. No doubt there was a pile of builder's mix or sand nearby, so perhaps it was also the time when Dave and I poured sand into the family car's petrol tank. This story was told often, as were other catastrophe anecdotes, including the time we painted the inside walls of a neighbour's wash-house with blue shoe polish. I don't remember the sand-in-petrol-tank incident, or the shoe-polish one, though I'd like to.

When I navigate my way with as much honesty as I can along the seam between what I believe I really do remember and that other class of 'memories' consisting of handed-down family stories, photo-album prompts, or the mnemonics that have been implanted by research or the serendipity of return visits, I discover a special class of memory that seems to defy the distinction between remembered fact and recovered memory. The facts include the basic appearance and layout of the house in Francis Street, with its large back section and a corrugated-iron fence between us and neighbours called Priddle. The Priddles had a parrot which clung with its frightening black claws to the rotary clothesline in their backyard; I remember the sound of its yells, but not what it said. I remember the workshop my father kept across a concrete yard from the back door to the kitchen. I remember the smells of sawdust and the sound of a saw. Years later, when I read Katherine Mansfield's perfectly chosen word 'panting' to describe that sawing sound, I was returned instantly to that workshop. As a bonus, I also remembered the ripe smell of my father's farts, which I associate with various kinds of exertion there.

I remember a large walnut tree at the far end of the back garden, and beneath it the immense, warm, sweet-smelling compost heaps with their piles of minutely chopped clippings from the grass catcher. I remember sticking a garden fork through my foot in or near the compost heap, and the bizarre sequence of allergic reactions to the penicillin shot I was given to ward off tetanus – the rash, the ludicrous swelling and so forth.

I vividly remember the sight of Bobby Moss's backside disappearing urgently through a hole in the hedge at the bottom of the garden where my father cultivated strawberries, and where he'd surprised Bobby in the middle of a raid (we'd just returned from Waikawa Bay); I also remember the taste and smell, unmatched since, of the strawberries.

I remember the feeble pallor of Dave's face after he'd had his tonsils out, and his horrible breath; and the bloodstained shirtfront of the distraught man who'd bowled him off his bike, and Dave's bewildered yells as he was lowered into a bath to be washed so his wounds could be seen (I also remember envying his bravery when he went to the police station with our father to make a statement, returning with a certain smile and Chick's arm around his shoulders).

I remember disliking the corned beef our mother cooked, which tasted of its smell; I disliked it just as much when she persisted with it in the years not long before she died.

I recognise the other kind, the recovered memories, for what they are, because they seldom come with smells or sounds – thus, the pageboying of Norma's bridal train is a blank, wan, two-dimensional event. These memories play in my mind like film sequences without sound; they are incomplete artefacts; they don't make me go hot or cold, or feel anything much – my balls don't retreat in remembered fear, I don't get teary; try as I might, I can't find empathy for those other actors in the moment, not even for my brother.

And then there are the transitional memories, as I think of them: the memories that seem to rise slowly to consciousness and, once there, to build a broad, expandable field of meaning around themselves. Their factual immediacy or accuracy I can't be certain of, but they come accompanied by the most vividly carnal sensations of all.

There are few of these memories. They seem to be the most important ones. I think of them as making their home in my imagination, at once free from indexical truth and at the same time precisely situated – even embedded or embodied – in phenomena. What I've learned about them is that their triggers are primitive and undeniable.

In 1969, at the age of twenty-two, driving out of Colombo towards Kandy in what was then called Ceylon, thirteen years after leaving Dave's and my childhood home up the Karnaphuli River in East Pakistan, a smell of frangipani, dust, cooking spices, shit and dried cow-dung smoke came in the car window on a scorching breeze, and I at once had a memory so vivid it was almost a hallucination of the floral pattern on one of my mother's dresses when we lived in the riverside wilds on the perimeter of the stinking paper mill at Chandraghona. I hadn't seen my mother for several years – she and Chick had been in Cairo and were currently in Amman – but then, all at once, she was in the hot, dusty car with us; or rather, a pattern of shapes and colours that stood for her was in the car.

I think of the imagination as a place of narrative scaffoldings. Here, smells may be represented as colours, thoughts as beats or rhythms, and words as movements. In this space my imagination makes what sense it can of a pleasurable chaos. It's a place of promiscuous sensory mash-ups, fascinating because illicit, illicit because unreliable, unreliable because contingent. Nothing becomes lucid there without having first pushed back against or given in to anarchy. This is the home of play. Facts aren't playful; nor are taste- and odour-free recovered 'memories'. But those transitional memories are invitations to play.

The last time we sat down to talk about our childhood in Blenheim, Dave had no memory at all of the artesian well in our Francis Street backyard. This was a shock, because for me it's one of the few memories that lead a rich, privileged, unpredictable life in my imagination. I know this makes it unreliable – but I also know it's undeniable. The well was to the right of Chick's workshop and just beyond the concrete apron that extended from the kitchen steps. It was set into the lawn by the workshop wall or perhaps the wall of the laundry that adjoined the workshop.

How could Dave not remember the strong, thick, wooden

lid that sealed the well and was meant to be too heavy for kids to move aside – but which we did? The lid was exciting because it signalled not just danger but danger that was specific to small children. As if in defiance of this danger, I once hammered a packet of my father's precious brass boat nails into the lid, which was probably one of his overdone woodwork projects – they tended to be too heavy and not quite square, just like mine.

Though I know it may be my imagination orchestrating such auxiliary effects, I remember the brass nail hammering produced a deep, hollow, echoing sound that was frightening because it was happening in an unseen place, and because it made my stomach heave with a kind of pleasurable terror, as if I was standing on the brink of a cliff or clinging (as I once did) to the upper trunk of the walnut tree. It was dark and cool in the well once the cover was off, and an unfamiliar smell came out of it. It must have been the smell of the water itself, and of the damp brick shaft, and I remember it as having a mineral freshness, unlike the leaf-mouldy smell of the creek at Waikawa; but I think of it as the smell of darkness.

How old would I have been when I first inhaled that darkness and peered down into it? Chick used to lower into the well a wire basket filled with big brown bottles of beer to cool them, and perhaps I first peeped over the edge as he did so, and listened to his warnings about the danger of the well which were no doubt both frightening and tempting. I must have been at least six – just old enough to shift the heavy lid aside – when I gave in to the temptation: 'I' because Dave denies any memory of the well, though in fact it would have taken the two of us to shift the lid (ha!).

I seem to remember (but can't be sure) that I (or we) liberated a frog into the well, or that a frog had somehow got into it, and lived there, happily croaking. This was only one of the reasons for our parents' anger and distress when I (or we) poured a can of drained-off sump oil into the well – which would have killed the frog as well as poisoned the water. It was the possibility of transgression, the terror and seduction of that mineral smell of darkness that made the well and the memory of it potent. But the stinking black sump oil that killed the frog we never saw, only heard, in the water we never saw, only smelled, pushed that illicit anticipation across into something more fearful and incomprehensible, with sorrow and remorse attached: a first inkling of death, perhaps.

It must be absurd to suggest that a five- or six-year-old kid could have that kind of apprehension. Or perhaps not. About sixty years after I poisoned the well at Francis Street, Donna and I went on holiday to Niue in the Pacific. One day we walked through forest on the eastern side of the island to a deep chasm at a place called Vaikona. Spiky pandanus plants grow across razor-sharp formations of coral granite honeycombed with deep caverns and tunnels, some of which run out to the sea or open in huge submarine cracks in the reef. There's a cave surrounded by pandanus, with a dusty lip overlooking a steep slope down to the cave floor and, further in, a pool of fresh artesian water.

The scanty information we had suggested you could go down there using a knotted rope attached to a tree root at the cave entrance. The rope wasn't there, though a rickety sign warning of danger was; but I nearly did scramble down anyway. Not far away, the rhythmic surf drove against a rocky coast, but deep within the cave the chasm's tranquil pool glinted where sunlight reached it through the dark opening. It looked heavenly, but the rope was missing, and so, although I hesitated at the lip for long enough to hear the echo of the surf hammering on rock at the nearby coast, I didn't go down.

Getting back out again was what I should have thought

about, but didn't – until later that night when, hot with fearful sweat, I began to walk towards a mirage of the deep cave pool and the resonant hammering that came from it. And then, as I stood half-awake on the balcony of our room overlooking the sea, I saw a rope of stars that reached the moon gleaming like a pool in the sky, and I climbed back into sleep but couldn't tell if the hammering rhythm I heard there was in the chasm or somewhere else, a place I couldn't return to, no matter how much I wanted that.

What I remembered at that moment on the balcony of our holiday place on Niue, in a state halfway between waking and dreaming, in which images, sounds and smells seemed to pour in and out of each other, was the well next to my father's workshop at Francis Street in the early 1950s. I hadn't thought about it – or the sound of hammering, or the smell of darkness – for sixty years. But it was there. And when I was awake again in the bright Pacific morning, it was as if the transgressive power of my childhood memory had shaped my sixty-year-old glimpse of death. And had done that by reaching out from the imagination-home that had always travelled everywhere with me, into the vivid, pleasurable, particular world of phenomena at the edge of the Vaikona cave.

The shit

I was impressed during one of the remembering-home conversations I had with Dave when he came up with the name of Bobby Moss's sister – Glenys. Perhaps this was the woman about my age who introduced herself to me as Glenys at the 2013 Millenium Gallery reading – but I can't be sure of that. I remembered Bobby's backside beating a hasty retreat through the hedge behind my father's prized strawberry patch; I can remember that as an incident, but can't get a mental picture of Bobby himself, what he looked like, his face, his expression. I get nothing except his fleeing bum, which was in grey serge shorts, and the sound of Chick bellowing. And I can't remember anything at all about Glenys. She's just not in the jigsaw set.

But in trying to find her, and while poking around for her shape among the fragmentary memories of childhood life in Francis Street, I am startled by a memory I haven't gone looking for, haven't expected and don't want – except that, like my memory of the artesian well with its smell of darkness and, later, its reek of defilement, this memory is potent and irresistible. It's irresistible in part because it's been hidden all these years; no doubt it was hidden because it was illicit at some early stage; and no doubt it's irresistible now because it was once forbidden. Here, then, is my chance to summon up again those innocent transgressions that took place within the childhood family home.

This in itself is a seductive idea. It reminds me of the moody frisson that quivers inside Rimbaud's great poem 'Les Poètes de sept ans', in which the introverted child, his soul 'livrée aux répugnances' (given over to abhorrence), lurked in the cool of the latrine, nostrils flared, thinking; or bit the naked bum of the eight-year-old girl who'd jumped on him and then 'Remportait les saveurs de sa peau dans sa chambre' (carried the flavours of her skin to his room). Rimbaud gives his game away in the last two lines of the poem, revealing his adult retrospection, his perverse relish for the precocious brat who:

– seul, et couché sur des pièces de toile
Ecrue, et pressentant violemment la voile!

– which Jeremy Harding has translated as:

He lay in his coarse canvas sheets
Gripped by a premonition of setting sail.

What's going on here? Of course we can never remember exactly, or recreate, or relive the experiences we had as children. Rimbaud looks back at his febrile childhood self, rebellious and hypocritical, furtive and charming, besotted with travel and adventure romances, from the point of view of a precocious seventeen-year-old who has already begun to 'set sail' for the exotic locations that would seduce and destroy him. He's delighted to observe in this child-self the seeds of what he's becoming as a man. No doubt what he sees and writes in his poem is accurate in some way – as is what he writes a couple of years later in 'Mauvais sang' from *Une saison en enfer* (1873): 'Encore tout enfant, j'admirais le forçat intraitable sur qui se referme tojours le bagne . . .' (When I was still a small boy, I admired the unrepentant convict on whom the prison gates would always close . . .)

But what we're also reading is the record of the grown Rimbaud's desire that it should have been like this. And so my memory of what my brother's word 'Glenys' summoned up is likely to be a mixture of what did happen and what I now want to have happened. And what I want to have happened is likely to be coloured by my adult relish of the fact that it was illicit.

Instead of Glenys (or Bobby) Moss, there appears before me a small, wiry, pungent girl with short, black, curly hair and a narrow white face. She was energetic and bony, and the smell I remember is of sweat, and dirt from the summer places we played in, such as the dry, grassed-over storm drain at the back of Horton Park (though there's another more important smell). I don't know who she was but I think she was a year or two older than us. How old were Dave and I then? Younger than Rimbaud's child poet – young enough to have been running around in the fascinating wake of kids a bit older than us.

I remember that her house had an outside dunny – it was behind a door of green-painted vertical tongue-and-groove timber, and it had a latch with a scalloped thumb-piece. It opened off a back veranda by the wash-house. Her mother scolded us when we clustered outside the door while the girl took a shit: she'd be reporting on the shit's progress ('It's coming now!'); we'd be pressing close to the door, and one of us would be trying to open it. Dave and I were hangers-on to some big kids' game, but I for one was enchanted by the sharp stink of shit, which was exciting because it was dirty and forbidden, and because it made the girl's mother angry. I seem to remember (but can't be sure) that she caught us at it more than once; I think she reported the game to our mother and (as seems likely) that we got a few whacks with the back of Linda's tortoiseshell hairbrush as a consequence.

I haven't talked to Dave about this yet, but he, grinning,

remembers the pong of piss-wet woollen shorts drying on the radiator at kindergarten. He remembers a kid who habitually pissed himself. I can't remember either of these things, and perhaps he won't remember the shitting game when I tell him about it; but we both remember what – or that something – happened in the dry ditch at the back of Horton Park. With matter-of-fact good humour, Dave refers to the activities in the dry ditch as 'doctors and nurses'. His equanimity is both sensible and unconvincing. Though I didn't know what the bigger kids were up to, I sensed then (and remember now) that it involved a particular kind and degree of danger and fascination *for them*, and that this was somehow conveyed to us, the childish voyeurs of whatever it was they were so intently clustered around, whatever it was that involved dry, hollow stalks of grass, funny noises and exclamations and, once, a jet of pee that squirted up into the faces of those watching.

Of course my adult brother and I both dismiss these memories as ordinary, even trivial, and certainly typical of most kids. And yet, like the Rimbaud of 'Les Poètes de sept ans', I also want to recover the ignorant thrill of those moments when I knew I'd entered forbidden territory. I also want to (but can't) have some of Dave's memories, such as the time the fish and chip caravan that parked by the Taylor River levee next to Blenheim Primary School caught fire, or a peeper's knothole in the changing sheds behind the school swimming pool.

The thrill of those moments is stretched between the ignorantly sensual childhood home I left when I grew up, full of alluring dangers and sensations, and the knowing home of the senses I inhabit as an adult. I look back from this adult home with a certain kind of longing for the brief, ephemeral, carnal innocence of childhood – and sometimes get, instead, a premonition that has had to wait until now to make sense.

The ball gown

I hesitate to address the question that immediately comes to mind after those memories, at once comical and profound, of the artesian well outside my father's workshop, the shitting game by the green door of a neighbour's dunny, and the obscure experiments in the dry ditch at the back of Horton Park. I hesitate because of the answer that makes the question difficult to ask. Also, the question of *my mother's ball gown* feels inappropriate, or tasteless, in the context of the infantile scatology of those other memories.

But those pungent memories, infused with alluring hints of transgression, are about the moving home of the imagination, and the enduring agency of childhood sensations – especially smell. They are about how the imagination's home travels and relocates with us through time and place, furnished with the sensations of childhood that never quite leave that home. But the memories also tell us about the way we leave the undiscriminating home of childhood sensation for the selective one of adult retrospection.

Why is it that I now suddenly remember the aroma of my mother's ball gown? My question is shaped by the imaginative home we don't leave and the home of childhood sensation that we do. It's trivial to flinch from remembering my mother's Masonic Ball perfume in the company of a polluted well, fresh shit and the piss-reek at the back of the park. Childhood memories don't obey taste prescriptions, and what we learn from them through the distorting lenses of adult perspective won't be about taste either, though it may well be about the idea that knowledge and understanding 'are coeval with Sensation', as John Locke believed.

The three centuries from Locke to contemporary cognitive psychology are littered with arguments reconciling the cultural and the phenomenal. For me it's not an issue – I don't see how what I know and what I understand could fail to be shaped by how I perceive and how I sense; how what I perceive and sense could not, in turn, be shaped by what I already know and understand; and how this virtuous circle could not be articulated by memory, not least the life-script-writing memories of childhood.

As I try to write down what I remember, think and feel about the perfume that accompanied the rustle of our mother's gown into Dave's and my bedroom as she and Chick prepared to leave for the ball, none of the words at my disposal seem to belong in that moment. They don't grasp the space, colour, scale or sound of the moment. It's as though the language I had then and what I have now were divided at that point. There's a kind of silence between then and now, the silence of shock, perhaps.

The language I have now is estranged from the room where our mother and father came in to kiss us goodnight, where we heard the stiffened-fabric sound of the gown, the click of our father's dress shoes; where we smelled the fresh nugget on the shoe leather and, especially, the different perfume our mother wore on such occasions. The language is no longer embodied in my sensibility *then*, on the far side of that silence; nor can I rediscover the words in my memory of the bedroom whose door had creaked open, framing our glamorous mother and father against the light in the hall.

The moment was impressive, I remember that much, and

so does my brother. It was he who remembered that they were going out to the Masonic Ball – I remembered only the awe-inspiring sumptuousness of Linda's gown and the grandness of Chick's long-tailed suit, with his war medals and Masonic regalia. Or perhaps I've back-loaded the regalia from another time and place. Dave remembers that Linda's gown was a purple colour, and was off-the-shoulder. He remembers Chick's 'tails'. When we talked about them, we simultaneously chose the word 'glamorous'.

Why is it that I now remember the aroma of my mother's ball gown?

I have a strong, almost devastating sense of loss, remembering it. Like Dave, I remember being enchanted by the theatrical moment of the farewell. I remember, as he may too, a sense of awe at the transformation that had made our mother and father into those fabulous, dimly lit people. What I also remember, or think I do, is the sense that *they had left themselves.*

And in doing so had left us. They weren't just 'going out' – they'd *gone.* The mother and father I knew didn't look or smell like this. If I was upset that they were going and leaving me (with Nana Horne, and my brother, after all), I was more upset that they'd become strangers. The bedroom I'd been asleep in before the door creaked open and they came in with their sounds and aromas of exotic foreigners was no longer the same. The mother and father who'd always presided over the comforting sameness of our bedroom had gone.

Now, the bedroom was strange, too. It was in a home whose familiar, immutable layout and location had been made strange by the different perfume of Linda's ball gown. These were not the people who lived there, wore the clothes I was familiar with, did the things I understood, spoke the words I was accustomed to hearing; who smelled of cigarettes, perming fluid, workshop farts, two-stroke outboard-motor fuel, corned beef, Veet depilatory, thermette wood smoke, car upholstery, mown grass, Flit insecticide, toothpaste, the compost heap, pikelets, sweat, sawdust, coal briquettes, talcum powder, fried fish, Paine's ice cream, Rawleigh's ointment, oil-of-wintergreen inhaler, the sudsy washing tub, the piece of mutton fat my father rubbed over the tines of the garden fork I rammed through my foot, the hot fabric and steam of ironing in the kitchen, blue-bags, the crusty gluepot, furniture polish, my Plasticine, my bedtime pillow.

There was a time when I began to be aware that I was at home in and with myself – counterweighted with my twin brother; another time when I felt that self might be most at home in what I now call my imagination; and another when vivid sensation furnished the home of imagination and connected it to a world of seductive risks and mysteries. All this was safely enclosed in the wider world-home that had our house, Francis Street, Horton Park, my brother, our Nana, and our mother and father in it.

And then a door closed on all that, leaving a bewildering perfume behind.

'Bye bye. Nighty night. Sweet dreams.'

The missing Taits

Because we saw our parents sporadically after we were ten, and only briefly lived with them again as a family when we were fifteen, there are large gaps in my knowledge of family history. We had cousins in Blenheim, but our uncle Paul Wedde's three children, John, Peter and Margaret, were younger than us and I didn't get to know them until we ended up living in the same street in Wellington in the 1970s. Both Dave and I vaguely remember a combined family picnic at Pelorus Bridge, where either our cousin John sconed me with a rock, or I threw one at him and connected. An alternative scenario is that I scalped Uncle Keele with an inexpertly hurled river stone.

I vividly remember the smell of the bush and the river, and the sounds of birds – but not people. Much of what I can record now comes from what I learned later. Uncle Paul was ten years younger than Chick, and their sister, our Aunty Phyllis, was the oldest. Her daughter, our cousin Norma, whose wedding-dress train we'd lifted as pageboys, was much older than us. Linda's younger brother Keele had one daughter, our cousin Jocelyn, about five years younger than us; we didn't meet her until the 1960s.

There was a middle Wedde brother, Hugh Lancelot, three years younger than Chick, whom the family never talked about. Towards the end of his life, my father owned up to an old guilt – that he hadn't looked out for his younger brother, whose catastrophic infatuation with a woman drove him to suicide. Hugh was only twenty-two when he shot himself in the back room of the office where he worked with the woman. I got the impression the family had shelved Hugh Lancelot under disgrace as well as grief, but his Tennysonian middle name retains the wistful trace of his father Albert Augustus Wedde's hopes for him – A.A. Wedde was a respected school principal as well as a composer and excellent cricketer who, it's said, once clouted a six out of the Basin Reserve in Wellington, smashing the stained-glass window of a church over the road.

These disparities and disconnects reflect the fact that we were born when our mother and father were thirty-six and forty-one respectively. We grew up in a thinly stretched-out family within which we had little or no contact that I can remember. And then we left when Dave and I were seven.

Linda and Chick used to say that their leaving Blenheim, the two grandmothers and (eventually) their twins was frowned on by the rest of the family, some of whom also thought the escapees had given themselves airs. That distanced us, too. We were taken on a meet-the-family tour of New Zealand when we came back from England in 1961. Tongue-tied, under-socialised, with Pommie accents, used to being on our best behaviour and in our best clothes when we stayed with people, we struck pity into the heart of one some-kind-of-cousin called, I think, Geraldine, whom I remember as gangling and racy (she smoked), whose summary of our situation was probably accurate: 'Jesus – you poor little buggers!' That's all I remember, but Dave's recall is more substantial, so 'Geraldine' obviously made an impression on us. He thinks she may not have been a cousin, but the daughter of a family friend, Lewis Fitch, who worked for the Christchurch *Press*, and that she later became a psychiatrist in the Royal New Zealand Navy – where, no doubt, the diagnostic 'poor little buggers' came in handy.

We weren't poor in any practical sense, but that's not what she meant. Though Chick had earlier 'lost everything' in a West Indian banking collapse, he'd subsequently worked at the highest levels of United Nations Development Corporation secondments for long enough to have bought a modest two-bedroom house in Auckland and kept us in private schools in England for five years. In terms of the 'betterment' only dreamed of by his contemporaries in Blenheim, he'd done well by his twins. Footloose as a young man, he had begun to gain professional accounting qualifications as a soldier only during the war. For him, education was his personal near-miss, and he equated it strongly with social and professional standing; he never saw the estrangement of his children from the rich narratives of family as anything other than a gainful trade-off.

In his last years Chick tried to tell me family stories, or to remember them – for example, his memories of old Heinrich August drinking schnapps and reciting Goethe's *Faust* in bed – but his heart wasn't really in it, and my own interest came too late. And I think my mother concurred, though in her old age she confessed to having had guilty doubts from time to time about the dislocated life she'd agreed for her children.

We didn't get to know family, or much about them, when we were little, though I remember a vague sense of connections in Marlborough – out at Spring Creek and Tua Marina, where a family known as the Hastilows farmed; the big house with banisters and a grandfather clock where our cousin Norma Robinson lived up under the eroded, sheep-nibbled hills at Lake Timara in the Waihopai Valley; the backyard at Uncle Paul's where I seem to remember he cooled bottles of home brew in covered laundry tubs.

The gap between the dissociated, diasporic life I'd been given when we left Blenheim, and the congenial narrative of family life and history, was also one that I cultivated, somewhat resentfully, for some years. I blamed my mother and father for the dislocation. By the time I wanted to close the gap, which was about the time I stopped feeling deprived of family and started to admire what my parents had done, it was almost too late. Having grown up without stories, the effort to find them was more ethnographic than social.

What the sorrowful future psychiatrist saw as 'poor' was probably her tongue-tied, Pommie-ish, maybe-cousins' estrangement from the give-and-take, yarn-swapping, leg-pulling entanglement of family; and this was what I immediately envied when in 1975 I met up with my cousins John, Peter and Margaret in Maidavale Road, Wellington. They were, briefly, sharing a house there, and this magnified the sense I got from them of continuity and connection through their lives. They knew relatives, and school and university friends, and they had stories to tell about the family's comings and goings, the scandals, the business and love affairs; they'd played sport with team-mates they still partied with; they spoke in joking code about an inner circle of relatives I barely knew and couldn't place anywhere in the social geography of my own life. I was torn between envy of that richly social milieu, with its stories, its ability to cultivate humour and extroversion, its mixture of tolerance and piss-taking, and grateful relief for the escape hatch our mother and father had opened.

Looking back across that broad but (for me) thinly peopled expanse of family, with here and there a familiar face and here and there a story or object (the Hornes' black iron kettle) and here and there a romantic figure I'd apotheosised (my great-grandfather, the sailor Heinrich August), I encounter a large vacant space. This is where my maternal grandmother Aggie Horne's maiden name resides. The fact that I know almost nothing about the Scottish Taits – even less than I know about any other limb of the family tree – seems to stand for that dislocation from the larger home of family that I've both celebrated and mourned most of my life.

And so I spend a pleasantly vicarious morning browsing the Tait genealogy forum online. A few minimal threads tracking the Tait name and family reveals that it had three historical entrepôts from which its members spread promiscuously around the globe. One was in the north-east of England in what was called Northumbria, a much fought-over territory on the border of Scotland and England, which was part of the Danelaw Viking expansion in the ninth century. Reverse migrations to Finland produced Taits, Teits, Teetts, Trittis and Teittinen families there; but the name's Viking origin was probably a combination of the given or nickname from Norse 'titr', meaning cheerful (I am suspicious of the convenient phonetic resemblance of 'titr' to 'titter'), and the word for a certain kind of mercenary soldier (which is more convincing).

A second major entrepôt was also on the Borders along the River Tweed, where 'Red' Taits owned lands around Pirn and Tweeddale in Innerleithen; this was perhaps where my ancestors came from, having moved to Dundee on the Firth of Tay. There's a Tait Lane in Dundee, and the name has often been associated with medicine, as well as with fishing and seafaring.

The third entrepôt was in the Shetland and Orkney Islands, where the Norse or Viking connection has been well documented in records of land ownership. The Shetland Taits divided into two rival factions according to hair colour, the Black Taits and the Red Taits (the Reds moved to mainland Scotland) – which caused some confusion among

Tait genealogy forum members, since there are also black Taits in Alabama descended from emancipated slaves who took the name of their former slave-owner, himself probably descended from one Colonel Tait, stationed on the Coosa in 1778.

There are many pretenders to a Tait family crest, but my favourite is one with blue birds on it and the travel-weary motto 'Toujours le même' – which hardly does justice to the diversification of Scottish Taits across the globe along sea routes opened up by mercantilism, main-chance enterprise, lack or loss of opportunity at home, Industrial Revolution skill sets, mercenary willingness, British empire-building and, it would seem, a perverse (and cheerful) desire to be anywhere else.

I feel at home here – as I do when browsing the stories of restless Weddes and Hornes. The ones I'm descended from were the ones who *left*. It's an impulse I recognise as I sample the stories of these people who may or may not have been directly connected to me.

Some Tait men sought their fortunes in the fur trade with or in competition with the Hudson's Bay Company in what became Canada, a nation replete with Scots-descended Taits. Many had wives back in Scotland but took First Nation wives while trapping and trading. The resulting Metis children included Taits who, as well as enriching and extending the meaning of 'Red' Tait, subsequently complicated things by marrying French Metis.

Taits went to Ireland (one became a famous bishop there), and some came back again; others moved on from Ireland to Auckland, New Zealand, along the familiar narrative track of a Catholic–Protestant marriage that was unacceptable to relatives in the old country. I don't know what became of those ones, though they are 'closer to home' than some prosperous

Taits in Oporto, Portugal – the 'Casa Tait' is still there.

I found a Tait family in Argentina whose origins were in Inverness, and so perhaps remotely connected to the Taits that came to New Zealand. I can't reasonably claim the (Black) Shetland Taits whose descendants, including Sir Frank Tait, were theatre impresarios in Melbourne. They promoted Dame Nellie Melba, and made and acted in Australia's first feature film, *The Story of the Kelly Gang* (1906), written and directed by Charles Tait. Producers included John and Nevin Tait; the film starred Elizabeth and John Tait, and is recorded in the UNESCO Memory of the World Register as the first full-length feature ever made.

Another Australian Tait, whether 'Red' or 'Black' I don't know, was the Sydney cartoonist William Tait, whose work I know. Nor can I claim Robert G. Tait, captain of the *Duchess of Argyle*, which sailed from Greenock in 1842 with emigrants for New Zealand, or his brother William Tait, a master mariner of London, because they were English, not Scottish. However, William's son Alex emigrated to Auckland in 1861 and died there in 1923 aged ninety-four, leaving behind five daughters and contributing to the great Tait narrative mash-up.

Along this irresponsible digression I note the ubiquity of my grandmother's name, Agnes. No doubt it was a commonplace Caledonian favourite, but the Taits were especially fond of it and often seem to have grafted it through their family trees from grandmother to granddaughter and quite often from great-grandmother to great-granddaughter – which gives the impression they preferred the long view to the homely one, and stretched-out, far-horizon narratives to domestic ones. The markers of their world views seem to have been receding horizons and improbable fortunes, not neighbourhood fences and pensions. Despite the energetic participation of a few Tait genealogists in the online forum, most of the traces they're looking for seem to have faded without regretful backward glances; most of the wandering, cheerfully mercenary Taits, whether Red or Black, seem to have been content to disappear without trace into their unpredictable futures.

A few achieved historical notoriety and survive in sensational stories. My favourite is David Tait, to whom I feel an instant brotherly attraction. This David was involved in the notorious Fort Mims Massacre on 30 August 1813 during the Creek Civil War in Alabama. At the start of this conflict, frightened settlers, including mixed-blood Creeks north of Mobile, sought refuge in Fort Mims on the Alabama River. Led by one Peter McQueen and his cousin by marriage William 'Red Eagle' Weatherford, the Red Sticks faction of Creeks had been armed by the Spanish in Florida. They were successfully ambushed at the Battle of Burnt Corn by a force whose leader, the mixed-race Creek captain Dixon Bailey, thereby lined himself up for return-bout vengeance. 'Red Eagle' Weatherford was especially keen to have Bailey's scalp. Unfortunately, given the complicated intermarriages that had taken place between Creek and settlers along the Alabama, Tensaw and Mobile rivers, Red Eagle's brother and several of his sisters, as well as his half-brother David Tait, were among those taking shelter in Fort Mims. Red Eagle's sister, Hannah McNac, and her sons were with his war party, but her Scots husband, described in John Simpson Graham's 1923 *History of Clarke County* as 'a true friend of the Americans', was among the 500 massacred at Fort Mims, though it's not recorded if his scalp was one of the 250 taken that day. Nor do we know if David Tait lost his – but in any case, the Tait blood as well as the Tait name adopted by emancipated slaves had already flowed into complex tributaries from David's father, the soldier adventurer Colonel Tait, who had been stationed at the Hickory Ground on the Coosa in 1778.

There's something feverish and over-complicated about this narrative (which I would like to be part of my own story – which I feel at home in) with its meandering, swampy tributaries the Coosa, Alabama, Mobile and Tenshaw rivers, and its entangled bloodlines and conflicts. I'm drawn to its narrative chaos and ambiguous, transgressive, melodramatic storylines much as I was to the stories that enmeshed me when I was seven. I'm reminded again of Rimbaud's skulking seven-year-old poet, 'writing romances about life in the great desert where ravished Liberty shone, forests, suns, riverbanks, savannas' – or reading 'his endlessly absorbing romance full of heavy ochre skies and flooded forests, flowers of flesh deployed in star-pitted woods, vertigo, collapse, disarray and pity!' No wonder Bobby and Glenys Moss and my own brother sometimes left me to my convoluted play-acting in the Francis Street asparagus patch – but that's not what I now remember with a familiar thrill.

What I remember is the ecstasy of *being inside* stories, and especially of reading them, which both Dave and I began to do early. I remember that what I didn't understand in Robert Louis Stevenson's *Kidnapped* and *Treasure Island* was part of their fascination. Linda read us *The Jungle Books* by Rudyard Kipling – I've lost my copy of Book One with a 'love from' inscription by her on the inside cover. Only a few years ago, I guiltily returned to my brother his similarly inscribed Book Two, which I must have pinched fifty years ago. Mowgli was a bigger force in my childhood than any cousin. Only Dave was more important.

Perhaps our rootless childhood deprived us of family stories. Perhaps my brief, enjoyable excursion into the dispersed Tait narrative has involved a hedged bet – it almost involved family, but did so from a distance, and via improbable stories.

Maybe that's why I enjoyed it as much as I did.

It seems to me that I was more than compensated for any family deprivation by the stories I read, and by the fact that I would soon be reading them not in Francis Street, Blenheim, in the familiar family home within its perimeter of park, school, town baths, Paine's ice cream and the Sounds, but in a small, bare, concrete house above the cholera-infected Karnaphuli River, where snakes came in through the bathroom drains during the monsoon, and where Mowgli was if anything more plausible than the cousins we'd left behind, at least to my mind.

It's possible, too, that this narrative and its successors replaced family – or that imagination replaced intimacy. It seems both disenchanted and accurate to propose, as Donna does, that I like *the idea of* home because it's a place I come back to, rather than a place I stay in. The shadow that falls from this gentle admonition is that perhaps I like the idea of family in the same way.

The distempered pup

We came back down the Karnaphuli River from the Rajah's palace above Kaptai to find our little puppy Tiddles was dead. My brother's memory is that we came back from an overnight stay in Chittagong, where we'd probably gone while the puppy he remembers as Tweedles was put down.

'Rajah's Palace' was what we called the place I remember as a sprawling compound of rain-stained buildings with a rectangular ornamental water tank the size of a swimming pool in the interior courtyard. The pool was full of pea-soupy, turbid water and dead leaves. I think we'd been led to expect more, because I was disappointed by the un-splendid nature of the place. But my disappointment was dispelled when the 'Rajah' gave Dave and me Box Brownie cameras.

I remember him as an urbane man with nicely combed hair. It's possible, however, that this person belongs somewhere else in the story of our time in East Pakistan. I think we had tea and very sweet cakes, served next to the scummy pool by an elderly woman in a white sari edged with blue. She, too, may have drifted into this episode from elsewhere. I do remember the taste and smell of rose petals – I think the cakes had rose petals scattered on them, and rosewater as well.

I have no idea why this man and his old palace were up the river there, a long boat trip from the nearest city, Chittagong. Nor do I know why we were visiting him and his family, or with whom, aside from our mother. I don't remember my father being there, so it must have been Linda, taken there for a day trip by one of her new friends from the mill.

Dave remembers that Linda collected epiphyte orchids on the way, and that the driver of the Willy's jeep, whose name was Jan, climbed up a tree to get them. Perhaps we stayed longer than a day – I can't remember. Perhaps the Rajah's compound has gone now, submerged by the lake created by the Kaptai dam, built by an American company whose commissariat dispensed luxuries such as the peanut butter which Dave remembers Tiddles, or Tweedles, was fond of; work began on the dam a year or two before we left Chandraghona. It's also possible that the Rajah wasn't Bengali, but a member of the old Hill Tribe aristocracy, probably Chakma, in the Rangamati region. An ethnography of the Hill Tracts published in 2001 documents the submersion of the old *rajbari* or mansion in the newly created Kaptai reservoir in 1961 – perhaps this was the one we'd visited.

When I went back up the Karnaphuli in 2005, I stopped at a tea and picnic garden a few kilometres upriver from the mill, crossed the river in one of the oar-creaking sampans I remembered from my childhood, and went for a walk in an old, rustling tea plantation there. Perhaps that's what the Rajah was doing up the river – growing tea. Or perhaps he was harvesting the introduced plantation teak over towards the Hill Tracts; it has now mostly gone, along with the vast forests of bamboo where wild elephants and tigers used to live – the bamboo was taken out to make paper at the Chandraghona mill where Chick had come to work. Or perhaps the 'palace' was a jungle hunting lodge – another anachronism now, since the animals have all gone as well.

From the time of our visit to the Rajah, whichever of us wasn't taking the snap usually appears in it, holding their camera. The Box Brownie had a strap on top which your fingers fitted under, and a small round window in which a number appeared when you wound the film on for your next shot. When a roll of film finished, it was satisfying to hear its tail-end tear free of the winding-on sprockets inside – I could imagine it tucking itself away inside the yellow and black cylinder in which the negative film was delivered to Studio Mohib at Chandraghona.

The viewfinder was on the top and you peered down into it – to my mind, the world of the printed photographs was always disconcertingly upright, whereas the world I viewed with my Box Brownie was read like a book, as if what was out there could be transposed into a story with pictures. Often, these picture-stories had animals and pets in them – the doomed puppy Tiddles, a dead snake with our flinching feet standing back from it, a ferocious turkey-gobbler viewed from a safe distance, a baby leopard cub that we had as a pet for a mysteriously short time, a monkey on a long leash whose chattering grimace I was scared of, and which used to piss on us when it got agitated – there's a picture of our friend Billy McKenzie holding the monkey on his knee while it pulls his nose.

There are numerous photographs of us riding on elephants. There we are at Sitapahar in Kaptai – Dave's almost very correctly punctuated caption on the back of the photograph reads, 'Peter, Geraldine, Ian, and I riding an elephant at Sitapahar. (all the children are not visible.)'; at Kaziranga in Assam, where the elephant is almost submerged in a lotus swamp; in various anonymous, scrubby landscapes; later, at Kandy in Ceylon.

My mental viewfinder to this tilting world also had the black-and-white illustrations from Kipling's *Jungle Books* in it. The menacing tiger Shere Khan, known as Lungri or the Lame One, thrust his huge snarling head into the cave where the infant Mowgli was playing with his new wolf brothers, and Raksha, Mowgli's adoptive wolf mother (or was it Father Wolf?) bared her teeth at him and drove him away. Later, the grown boy Mowgli drove the tiger off with a burning branch. Later still, he conspired with Grey Brother, his wolf sibling from the Seonee Pack, to trap Shere Khan in a narrow gorge, where he was trampled to death by the buffalos herded by Mowgli – I loved the picture of Mowgli skinning the dead tiger while Grey Brother pinned the terrified village hunter, Buldeo, to the ground.

I longed to have a knife like Mowgli's (we did get sheath-knives), and to speak to and understand animals. Also, Mowgli was fearless, and he knew better than the village grown-ups, especially Buldeo. These were powerful fantasies, and I think they probably went upriver with me the day we visited the Rajah's old palace. Perhaps the narrative of Mowgli's comings and goings from wolf and village homes, his exiles, abductions and returns, was also beginning to grow in my imagination. It certainly took up residence there later on.

One reason I was disappointed by the decaying, water-stained palace was because it fell short of the Cold Lairs, the mighty ruins Mowgli was abducted to by the chattering Bandar-log monkeys. I loved it when Mowgli placated the hissing cobras in the Cold Lairs' ruined summer house by uttering the snakes' Master Word. I loved even more the scene in which the great python Kaa smashed through into the summer house and rescued Mowgli, and then hypnotised the Bandar-log with his hunger dance – but not Mowgli, who was immune to it. I loved that he was immune, and could get his protectors, the bear Baloo and the panther Bagheera, away from Kaa's weaving spell.

There's a before and after the Rajah's Palace. In the before, Dave and I don't have our cameras, so it must have been our father who took the photographs of us with our new pet puppy Tiddles. I remember the sour smell of the puppy's peed-on tummy, which was soft and almost hairless. Dave and I are sitting with our mother on the outside steps of the bare, semi-detached, two-storey concrete house on a hill above the river – our first home at Chandraghona. You got to it along a river-bank road that crossed tributary streams on hair-raising twin-track bridges. The plastered steps and ground-floor veranda were painted red and polished frequently by the mysterious man known as the 'bearer', who lived in a cubby under the stairs to the upper floor of the house where the bedrooms opened on to a balcony. The stairs went up from the lower veranda and so the bedrooms were accessible from the road outside the house.

Dave and I are wearing identical striped T-shirts in one of the puppy photographs, and short-sleeved shirts in two others, so our time with Tiddles must have gone on for several days or even weeks before the trip upriver to the palace. Linda has a precautionary look as the puppy tries to nip us – I imagine she'd have been worried about germs, which were a major preoccupation early on in our years by the brown river.

I thought about germs while listening to Linda read us the story of 'Mowgli's Brothers', imagining that the wolf cave was full of them – but that Mowgli was impervious to germs much as he was to Kaa's hypnotic hunger dance. I guess what appealed were Mowgli's special powers, as well as his fearlessness. I also liked his scornful attitude to the village people who were both afraid of the jungle and prone to germs, like the cholera victims we were warned about during the yearly 'cholera season'. Mowgli didn't get cholera, even though he drank the same water and ate the same food as the wolves. And though the puppy Dave and I shared as a pet was barely weaned when we got him, I'm sure I cast him as my own personal Grey Brother and built myself asparagus-patch-type stories in which we conquered the fearful forces of the jungle around us.

There are also two photographs of Dave and me on the upper balcony of the house with the bedroom doors opening behind us and the outside stairs in the background. In one, we're sitting at a cane table with our crookedly smiling father. I'm holding a book and have my finger marking where I've got to. In the second photo we're sitting with our mother, but in this one I've gone back to reading the book.

Perhaps it was my fantasy of impervious power, Mowgli-scorn for stupid humans, and a blurring of boundaries between adventures in books and others in the jungly bush along the river that led me to chuck clods of dry clay at the bearded loony who passed below Dave's and my lair above the river road. He was dressed in rags, and walked along muttering and gesticulating. He yelled at us when the clods connected, and we fled home with the puppy.

At night we slept with the doors to the upper veranda open, to let the cool air in. The yapping puppy woke me up, and I saw the loony we'd chucked clods at silhouetted in the open door of the bedroom. He moved quickly towards us with a large stick. But the puppy flew at him, yelping furiously, and grabbed him by the arm. Then the bearer appeared and collared the man. I think he pretty much threw him down the outside stairs – in any case, we never saw the madman again. The puppy was the hero of the night, but I woke up the next morning with the guilty secret of the clod-chucking, and worse, with my terror at the sight of the man rushing into our room.

What did I do with the terror? Folded it back under the story in which I was unafraid, confronting danger with my Grey Brother. And then, when we got back from the Rajah's

Palace, we were told that Tiddles had had to be killed because he'd caught distemper and was going mad. Grey Brother had succumbed to germs.

It's about this time that I remember sensing something was going wrong in the first house we lived in, the one with the outside stairs and Bengali neighbours in the other half of the semi-detached. Whereas, for a time, Dave's and my activities had been nervously monitored for germs, the dangerous river, snakes and whatever lurked in the jungly bush, we seemed all at once to have almost complete freedom – the sort we'd had back in Blenheim.

I remember sneaking out one night with Dave to meet up with the kids, Peter and Geraldine Bowers, who lived in a similar semi-detached concrete house on the hill across the valley from us. Their mother was a stately Burmese woman called Elsie, their father a Scots brigadier in the East Pakistan Rifles and head of security at the mill – Dave remembers that he was only ever called Brigadier. It was dark and hot, and there was a rustling pile of dead night insects under the light by the outside stairs. When we got to the Bowers' house, we tried to throw pebbles against the kids' bedroom window. I don't remember if we met up with them – probably not; in any case, we made our way back across the valley on the dusty, dark, concrete road and returned to bed undetected. But in the morning we were told that a panther's paw prints had been seen in the dust by the valley road, that it had probably been hunting goats or chickens among the riverside houses, and that we needed to be careful where we went. Of course we both believed the panther had been stalking us, which wasn't improbable.

The panther scare didn't stop us from expanding our territory. We watched featherless-necked vultures sticking their heads up the arses of dead cows and dragging their guts out. Once, running through the scrub, we saw what looked like two desirable club-shaped sticks standing up – but then we saw that they were cobras, and ran screaming for the road. There was construction work going on in the cleared valley below the houses, and railway tracks had been laid for heavy steel buggies to take out waste and bricks – we used to get the empty buggies rolling and then jump on.

We ran around the edge of the forbidden river and played on the huge rafts of bamboo that were floated down to the paper mill. The rafts had caretakers living on them in little bamboo shelters – sometimes the men tried to shoo us off, but we ignored them. Once we found a decayed corpse trapped in a raft. We were told that in the 'cholera season' bodies often turned up in them – it was probably a scare story, though there was a holding pen for the rafts where the rubbish they trapped could be removed and sent back out to the river channel. I saw all this again when I went back in 2005, though there was now very little bamboo coming down the river. I also met a very old man, a former night watchman at the mill, who remembered Dave and me running around the place fifty years earlier, 'like two little goats with white hair'.

In photos from that time we're often shirtless, with sun-bleached hair and dark tans – and Dave's splendid teeth almost always bared in a broad grin. We made ourselves sick trying to smoke 'beeries', and we lit forbidden fires in the concrete monsoon drains at the back of the house. We picked our way through the messes of liquid human shit in the latrine gulley used by construction workers. We tried to fly fighting kites, made bamboo bows and arrows, and went pretty much feral. We took photographs with our Box Brownies.

We were meant to be doing Correspondence School lessons with our mother, and we did, up to a point – mostly art and reading, in my case; Dave remembers learning to write longhand – 'joined-up writing'. There's a photograph of us being supervised by Linda in the bare, sunny room with glaring, uncurtained windows where we worked at opposite ends of a table. Dave seems to be running his finger down a sheet of text, and his open mouth suggests he is reading from it. Linda has a similar sheet in front of her and might be following the same text. I seem to be ignoring them while trying to thread string through something. It all looks peaceful and organised. But along the way something changed, and it was in the schoolroom that I first became aware of this.

When Dave and I compare notes about our home in Blenheim, we mostly remembered the extent of our territory. At six and seven years old we biked all over the place – once as far as the Hastilows' farm out at Tua Marina. They rang home to come and get us. We both remember the whey pipe from the dairy that fed the squealing Hastilow pigs; and the slaughter of the pigs and the way they were bled for black-pudding sausages. A pig's bladder was blown up like a football – I can remember the smell of the thing we kicked around in the back paddock. We remember tossing live bootlace eels to the hysterical chickens which skewered them and gulped them down while they sprinted away from the pursuing flock.

Back in town, we tried to spear eels by the sewer outlet into the Taylor or Opawa River. We hung out at the aviary with its incongruous monkeys, went on regular schedules to the roller-skating rink, biked to the public baths where we had swimming lessons (Dave thinks it was the school baths), hurled acorns at the wooden clothespeg Jesus-and-Mary crèche at Sunday school, ate tar, sniffed shit, trooped around in a kind of gang.

We biked up into the Wither Hills where Dave was once ambushed by a rival gang, one of whom fired an arrow into his mouth – he pedalled home stoically, bleeding like a pig. There was Horton Park with its various attractions – the swings from which we leapt with optimistic parachutes, the dry storm-water ditch with its interesting experiments. Dave, tapping into his early passion for aircraft, remembers that we planned to make a boat out of discarded aeroplane fuel tanks from Woodbourne Air Force base, and we ran free during summers at Waikawa Bay.

Reminiscing about all this, we both agree that 'home' was more a territory with vague borders than the house we lived in. This territory was full of changing activities and events rather than fixed objects. What seems to have characterised 'home' for us was a persistent probing of its extent, a desire to move further and further from the house in Francis Street. We didn't want a safe home-house – or we took that for granted; what we wanted was anything different and exciting, across the edge of the known world.

Were our parents negligent? I don't think so – we were probably typical of small-town kids in the early 1950s, expected to be outside when not at school, nearly always unsupervised, occasionally getting told off or dobbed in by neighbours for some misdemeanour or other, but also well known to them, and looked out for. But Dave and I were also twin brothers, and we amplified each other's opportunities to stretch our territory.

So when I think about the two white-haired little goats going feral in Chandraghona, it's as though we simply began at some point to behave as we always had back in our expandable 'home' territory in Blenheim, which had only a provisional centre in the house where we lived, and where there were hazards other than snakes, germs and panthers;

and as though our mother, in particular, either stopped worrying about us and left us to be at home in the way we always had – or she lost the will to worry.

The photographs of us leaving our first home in Blenheim are suffused with pride and happiness. Our mother and father are smiling broadly. We are quite dressed up, as if for a formal outing, Chick in a suit and Linda in a stylish camelhair coat. Dave and I seem to be in best clothes, as if in acknowledgement of the need to mark the occasion for posterity. But neither of us can remember being told anything about 'East Pakistan' where we were going. I don't think our parents were any too clear either. Of course they knew where the country was, and must have located the city of Chittagong on a map; but I suspect they didn't know anything about the reality of an in-development industrial location the best part of a day's trip up the Karnaphuli River to the Rangamati district in a wild zone of giant bamboo forests close to the tribal Chittagong Hill Tracts on the borderland between Burma, India and what is now Bangladesh.

The paper mill at Chandraghona was one of three or four economic modernisation projects initiated in the early 1950s by a government quango called the Pakistan Industrial Development Corporation. They advertised internationally for someone to establish financial management and accountable shipping systems for the mill, and I suspect that Chick, egged on by Linda, came across it more or less at random in a professional gazette.

I remember (though Dave doesn't) a moment when we were on holiday at Lake Wanaka, sitting by the lake and grizzling (me) about itchy 'duck rash', and a grinning Chick walked towards us waving a telegram. That was when he heard he'd got the job. That's what they were dressed up for and smiling about next to the TEAL DC6 that would take us to Sydney; after that we flew to Darwin, then Singapore, then Calcutta, and finally to Chittagong. Dave vomited resignedly the whole way – his introduction to the motion-sickness problem that would plague his lifelong passion for flying. We both threw up into a gutter in Calcutta, watched by an interested crowd. We saw our first bandage-swathed leper when Chick herded us onto a crowded airport bus in Chittagong.

Then there are photos, taken by him, of us on the boat with Linda, heading upriver. The formal clothes have gone, Linda's too – she looks incredibly happy in a sun frock and dark glasses. There was no lavatory on the boat, and it may have been on this trip that she impressed me by peeing into an empty biscuit tin and then hurling it over the side. But we went up and down to Chittagong quite a lot – once getting stranded on a sand-bar and finishing the home trip in a sampan – so this could have been another time.

Neither Dave nor I can be sure about the sequence of events around our departure from Blenheim. At some point we all flew to Wellington and stayed with Chick's sister and Uncle Norman, on their farm at South Karori. This was probably to say goodbye, but may also have been where we caught the ferry to Christchurch, to get on the plane to East Pakistan.

Dave astonishes me by remembering that the plane to Wellington, which took off from the Bleinheim Aero Club, was a 'Miles Gemini twin engine, low wing, with tail fins on the tail plane. Bulbous nose'. But then he also remembers the family car that took us on a picnic to Pelorus Bridge and on our South Island holiday that included Wanaka – it was a Ford V8 with running boards; and he remembers that the outboard motors for the clinker dinghy in Waikawa were, in succession, an Anzani, a Johnson (which leapt from the back of the dinghy and sank) and, finally, a Seagull.

At the South Karori farm, we both remember being shown how to tickle trout, and how to give a fiercely tugging lamb a bottle of milk. Only I remember being told off for whacking into a tree with a hatchet, so perhaps only I did that. It seems possible there was tension in the farewell, as it left Aunty Phyllis with the responsibility for our Wedde grandmother.

But what I remember most vividly is going to the pictures with Linda and Chick, and seeing the brand new 1954 release *Three Coins in the Fountain*, with Dorothy McGuire and Clifton Webb. I didn't understand the story, but I thought Linda looked a bit like Dorothy McGuire, and Chick sang the theme song on the way home (a baritone with 'rounded vowels'), though he didn't look much like Clifton Webb, who had straight, rather thin lips and no moustache. In some way, even allowing for the possibility that subsequently I may have wanted it to be so, the film, with its exotic, incomprehensible romance, cast some kind of spell over my experience of leaving New Zealand. Not really understanding the film's story was probably part of that.

Dave remembers the film trip differently. In his version, we went to town on the Karori tram with Nana Horne. He doesn't remember Chick being there at all. So it's also possible that I picked up something from our parents. I think leaving New Zealand was a romantic adventure for them, and for Chick a chance to return with his adored Lindy to a world he'd tasted in Egypt, Palestine and Italy during the war. In photographs early on at Chandraghona, or on the riverboat, Linda has a thrilled Dorothy McGuire look, and Chick looks resourceful and pleased.

But in a later Box Brownie snap of Linda on the untidy bank of the Karnaphuli River, her expression is introverted, her head tilted forward a little, her gaze fixed on something by her feet, or on nothing in particular; the ivory bracelet is loose on her thin left forearm. She was always slim, but now she looks drawn and unwell. She's sitting on a driftwood log next to a picnic hamper and wearing the same patterned sun frock as in the happy riverboat picture. That frock appears in another photograph, also melancholy, of her standing in strongly dappled sunlight in a thicket of bamboo, with her twins gazing nervously in opposite directions, while she has that sad, not-seeing-anything-in-particular expression.

This was the patterned frock I remembered years later when the roadside smells of burning cow dung and hot dust entered the car window on the way out of Colombo. Is it possible that I remembered the pattern of my mother's sun frock because it marked an important moment when her happiness left her; when the adventure of the journey to Chandraghona lost out to the loneliness and difficulty of her life there – when the *Three Coins in the Fountain* romance ended up on the germy, crappy banks of the Karnaphuli? Why would I so vividly remember *that* pattern, if not because I associated it with something memorable but incomprehensible, such as my mother's uncharacteristic misery – because I wanted her to take it off and not wear it, because she was unhappy in it, in the same way I later wanted her to take off the ivory bracelet I associated with her dying?

In another sad photograph, this one taken by Dave's Box Brownie, she, Chick and I are standing next to the bush swimming hole near the Baptist hospital and leper refuge run by Dr Bottoms. This time Linda's wearing a swimsuit. Chick is wearing a T-shirt and shorts, I'm in togs, and we're all barefoot. My Box Brownie hangs by its strap in my left hand. Both Linda and Chick look too thin. His resourceful, slightly leery grin is anxious in this photograph, even a little fierce. Once again, Linda has the same looking-at-nothing expression, her head turned slightly to one side and tilted downward, her eyelids lowered, what could almost have become a smile, if she'd wanted it to, stopped by a tightening or numbness around her mouth.

The controlled resignation and grief in her body language and expression is shocking to me now, but not surprising, because I remember that something changed around the time we came back from the Rajah's palace, when our puppy died, when we got our cameras. Remembering this, I now see in the swimming-hole photograph taken by Dave how tenderly Chick's hand is curled around Lindy's bare left shoulder, how tentatively she's touching mine, and how my father's expression, which could almost seem peevish at first glance, reveals a deep unease. So does the way I'm standing – looking dolefully down, with both my parents appearing anxious to reassure me with their touches.

There are two other photographs from our time in the first house at Chandraghona, both of them featuring Linda's attempts to bring a garden to life there. The photos are black-and-white, so it's not easy to identify the flowers; but in one of them she, Dave and I are sitting on the front steps, next to a crestfallen bed of what look like parched marigolds. We have kites with the two-handled reels that skilful kite-fighters used to manipulate their weapons in blistering convections above the roofs of the houses. Linda's keeping to the shade; next to her are some boxes of what look like gardening supplies, or seedlings. In the distance beyond a bamboo lattice, at the margin of our Bengali neighbour's section, some kind of hedged, flowering shrubs stand out against the far, scorched hillside.

I remember the effort and anguish of her desire to make a garden in non-existent topsoil where, if the plants didn't wither, they were eaten by hard-shelled, munching beetles. Later, when we moved to the second house on a hill above the first one, she established a wonderful garden and planted trees, including the plum tree whose fruit I ate when I came back fifty years later. But in the second plant photograph taken at the first house, what look like zinnias and some kind of thick-stemmed, orchid-like gladioli have been staked up in earthenware pots on the upstairs veranda. They look like Linda's frustrated, last-ditch attempts to make a home she cared about there, or a home with some attribute that she'd made and cared for, that sustained the romance of her and Chick's adventure. The pot plants at least look healthy, but their diminished scale seems to capture the sick frustration I sensed in her when I was a child.

We spent diligent time each day on the Correspondence School lessons sent from New Zealand. We practised writing, we read a lot, and painted pictures with the poster paints that came with the Correspondence kits. And then one day Linda suddenly got to her feet and rushed from the room. I heard her say, 'I feel sick!' in a funny voice. Then the sound of her vomiting. Then she pulled down the bamboo blinds in her and Chick's room, and went to bed. I don't remember what happened after that, except that she stayed in her darkened room for days. She probably had one of the tummy bugs that we all caught. But there was more to it than that. She was forty-five or forty-six – perhaps she was also menopausal.

It was around this time, when our mother was staying in her darkened room, that Dave and I were let go in a way that was at once confident and an admission of defeat. Leaving her home in small-town New Zealand was an enormous shift for Linda – far more than for us. Though she'd resented her mother, she no longer had Aggie to help with us. The social life she'd loved in Blenheim was gone. Her husband was off building his team at the mill – a time, as I discovered when I went back there, of huge challenges for him. She struggled with her restless boys during Correspondence School hours and, she told me later, confronted again her own curtailed education. After she died, I found notebooks recording her efforts to learn French, a postcard sent to a friend in which she despaired of keeping up with the exercises we were set by the German tutor later hired by the mill, and notes on the flowering plants and shrubs of South Asia – I still have her large botanical compendium for the region.

Still, our mother, with characteristic no-bother determination, pushed herself through what I now believe was both a depression and a period of physical weakness, and emerged into the life she would lead with enjoyment, esprit and courage – though perhaps not the one she'd first envisaged when her embarkation photograph was taken next to the DC6 in Christchurch. This was the optimistic picture of a complete family, the Blenheim and Sounds unit about to be lifted into the air and put down somewhere else, intact, but inside an envelope of liberation, romance and adventure. After the 'I feel sick!' incident, she absolved herself of some responsibility for us, and at the same time committed herself to what she could make of the place and the future that opened from it.

Though she never talked about it when, later, we reminisced about those years, I think her depression and the realignment of her hopes were connected to her old disappointment at being made to leave school early. Having finally, in a vehicle of romantic hope and opportunity, got out of the place in which that disappointment had nagged at her, she confronted her responsibility for the fact that she might be depriving her own children of education – not just because she'd taken us out of school, but also because she didn't feel up to teaching us. And it was always a tender point with Chick, who'd narrowly missed defaulting on his schoolteacher father's intellectual ambitions.

Four things became inevitable then. A teacher was hired for the gang of management kids who'd accumulated at the mill. The likelihood that Dave and I would sooner or later be sent to boarding school was established. Our mother and father would increasingly turn to each other and sustain their lifelong adventure together in homes without their children. And their children would live in provisional homes until they grew up and made their own.

When I look back I can see how these trajectories are prefigured in the image of my mother's misery on the banks of the Karnaphuli River. I don't believe she wanted to 'go home'. She wanted to find a way to go on. Her air of thoughtful misery doesn't appear in photographs after that brief time, and that suggests she found the way.

'Penthouse-like'

A couple of years after arriving in Chandraghona we moved into a simple, four-room, brick-and-plaster house in a cluster of four or five others, on a scraped-bare hilltop across the valley from our first home. Establishing this 'compound', as such clusters were called, had involved building an access road on the inland side of the ridge above the river. Before concrete paving and storm culverts were added, the road was prone to monsoon flooding and became an exciting quagmire through which slithered the company's clapped-out army surplus 4WD Willys jeeps.

In the valley near a cinema, there was a brickworks like those I saw again in 2005. It was here that the concrete-mix aggregate for the roading was produced. A steep road was cut up the side of the hill to the houses, skirting a large tree – about the only one left standing. It was still there when I went back, and was the landmark that guided me to the hilltop house we'd moved to between the end of 1955 and early 1956.

Through a blur of unexpected tears, the first thing I noticed was the ancient plum tree, heavy with small tart fruit, that Linda had planted, along with many other varieties, fifty years earlier. The next thing that jolted a specific memory awake was the house's monsoon and cyclone protection. The house sat on a crumbling concrete pad with a splash-rim high enough to stop rain from reaching the bottoms of the doors. There were deep storm-water drains all around it, and a slightly tilted roof designed to shed water directly to the drains, without guttering. I remembered the sheets of runoff that used to roar down from the roof when storms struck, and the driven water that used to get under the doors despite the flood-sill outside. Once, during a big cyclone, we'd crouched scared but thrilled by a window, watching the lightning flash and crash between the houses, and seen a pile of bricks lifted one by one and flipped into the road by the wind.

But the aspect of storm protection that affected me the most that day I went back was the protective concrete cowling jutting from the water-stained wall above the double window to Dave's and my bedroom. It was there to prevent water from the roof, or wind-driven at the wall, from hitting the windows directly. I remember that it mostly failed when the rainstorms were at their heaviest. By 2005, the crumbling, exposed brickwork around the windows, and above the flood-sill of the ground-level concrete plate, suggested these protective features had been failing for a long time.

What affected me, though, wasn't the memory of storms or the dispiriting state of our old house, but a quote, 'with your hat penthouse-like o'er the shop of your eyes,' from Act III, Scene 1, of Shakespeare's *Love's Labour's Lost* and a speech by Armado's witty page, Moth:

> No, my complete master: but to jig off a tune at the tongue's end, canary to it with your feet, humour it with turning up your eyelids, sigh a note and sing a note, sometime through the throat, as if you swallowed love with singing love, sometime through the nose, as if you snuffed up love by smelling love; with your hat penthouse-like o'er the shop of your eyes; with your arms crossed on your thin-belly doublet like a rabbit on a spit; or your hands in your pocket like a man after the old painting; and keep not too long in one tune, but a snip and away. These are complements, these are

> humours; these betray nice wenches, that would be betrayed without these; and make them men of note – do you note me? – that most are affected to these.

Of course I didn't remember much of this as I stood covertly weeping in front of Dave's and my old bedroom window. What I thought I remembered was in fact some kind of mashed-up quote with the metaphor 'penthouse lids' in it – which did, however, guide me to what Robert Lübker had been talking to us about in the hot schoolroom with its sun-glare bamboo blinds down in 1956. I remembered that, in his gently pedantic way, he'd taken his half-dozen heat-dazed kids through the cognitive philology of metaphors.

Herr Professor (Professor Professor) Lübker was the second teacher to come up the Karnaphuli River to the paper mill at Chandraghona. The first, a youngish Swiss man called Herzig (I think that was his surname), is to be thanked sincerely for teaching his motley class pretty good French and German by immersion, but nothing else. I have a photograph of him shinning up a coconut palm in his skimpy shorts, and another of him up a big tree with Dave, me and another kid wedged precariously in the forks of branches. A liking for climbing trees wasn't his only eccentricity. Towards the end of his increasingly erratic classes, which took place in a stifling schoolroom set up with the teacher's desk and chair on a slightly raised platform in front of the kids, our lower vantage point allowed us to see him slipping his cock out the leg of his shorts and jerking off. This was, coincidentally, and owing nothing to the poor man's example, about the time Dave and I discovered how to do it ourselves. I think he was just going crazy with loneliness, but even so his ability to keep a straight face while he got himself off under the desk may have been why he was sent down the river. We were told that he'd gone mad, and was last seen wandering around Calcutta with his cardboard suitcase.

Robert Lübker and his wife Magdalena were never in any danger of going crazy in remote foreign places. Ever since retiring from academic life (he published on the syntax of English verbs in their finite forms, among other things), he and Magdalena had regularly set off to travel, live and work in hard-to-get-to places. They wore frugal clothes with amazing sandals, ate all local food, and had bleached-out knapsacks that I knew were somehow rebellious, though they would both have been in their late fifties and were very correct in their manners. They were also punctilious in their politics (though their son, who I think was called Hans, and who taught us the rudiments of Latin when he visited, expressed ideas about discipline that made us uneasy). They refused to have a cook or 'bearer', though Magdalena relented to the extent of employing a young woman to help with the cleaning.

In 1995, while travelling in Germany for Te Papa, I visited Robert in Hamburg. His beloved Magdalena had recently died, he was ninety years old, but we walked steadily around the city, he in yet another pair of amazing sandals, while he expounded on the city's mercantile history and architecture, delivered a shrewd critique of Walter Abish's 1980 novel *How German Is It* (*Wie deutsch ist es*), and ate a lunch of fresh asparagus with a glass or two each of Riesling. We knew we'd never see each other again. He stood waving to me as my train left the station – I could see that he was weeping, as was I, but in his case he'd had his carefully folded handkerchief ready in advance.

As I remembered from my childhood time with him, he managed to be at once kind and formally remote. He was very fond of Linda, and asked me to send him a photograph of her. I suspect that he and Magdalena contributed to her exhaustion and subsequent death after she made her last visit to them in Hamburg in 1986 – they took her on long, arduous car trips with many pedagogic visits to interesting sites, and long, bracing walks along the sea-dykes in Baltic gales; her letters home recorded these with mixed affection and dismay.

For years I'd received his yearly 'reports', which were scrupulous accounts of his and Magdalena's travel around remote parts of Africa or the Middle East, combined with his reading or, more often, re-reading programme, a critical review of the German idealist philosopher Fichte or something else, and his latest philological thoughts. That some of the books had been lugged around in a bleached knapsack, and that the careful pages of his reports typed back in Germany were intangibly infused with dust or tropical storms, was what made them special if, sometimes, barely readable. They were weirdly complicated, mostly as a result of Robert's obsession with clarity and scholarly objectivity, which played stubbornly against his chin-jutting appetite for extreme excursions and the unreliable narrative points of view they afforded him.

If the Swiss teacher's method was involuntary language immersion, Robert's was deliberate immersion in textual analysis. He liked to do this with Shakespeare most of all. On the day he explained how metaphors worked, he took us all outside to look at the windows of the house he and Magdalena lived in, where our schoolroom was. The windows were storm-protected by the same rectangular concrete cowlings as ours – the ones that made me burst into tears fifty years later.

Carefully, pedantically, he explained the magical mechanics of the word 'like': how the word 'penthouse' combined an architectural feature (a jutting-out Elizabethan window-roof) with an item of human apparel (a hat jutting out over the eyes), but cunningly did so while transforming the eyes under the hat into shop windows – which, however, weren't quite, or just, shop windows. They were now *something else*, at once windows and eyes, and yet not just a combination of the two. And what did it mean to make the human head like a building and the eyes in it like windows? What was in the house? What kind of life was being lived there? Were the windows full of things people might want to buy? Were these things thoughts? Were the eye-windows display spaces? What was there to see in them? Were they the eyes of the text looking into our reading eyes?

Dry and exact to the point of obstinacy, it was Robert Lübker's explanation of what was going on in 'penthouse-like o'er the shop of your eyes' that, in an almost frightening way, expanded the imaginative home in which I lived – where what was out there in the world, and what was in my head as stories, both merged and exaggerated each other. What I understood as magic was the possibility that the process Herr Lübker had unlocked could produce effects and objects that ordinary things and their names could never match.

What I now saw, and was hypnotised by, as if by the great python Kaa's hunger dance, was the existence of another plane of reality – not the porously adjacent domains of story and real world, but a third one, in which special arrangements of words could bring into being things that had never existed before. These things were entirely real to me, even if barely perceived and fragmentary, and at the same time they were like ghosts or monsters. They began to haunt the home I lived in – both the house and the other one in my head.

Creature from the Black Lagoon

Soon after we moved to the new house on the hill, we went on a family trip to what I remember was called Chimbuk, a hilltop village in the Hill Tracts inhabited by tribal Mru people. We crossed the Karnaphuli River on a vehicle barge, and then drove some distance in one of the mill's Willys jeeps up into the steep hills. After that we had to get out and walk a long way on a track that went sometimes through forest and at other times up the sides of slash-and-burn hillsides. It was incredibly hot, and we'd been told we had to ration our water because the streams weren't to be trusted. At the village there was a bamboo guest house on stilts, and Dave and I played underneath it with some of the Mru kids.

This was where I finally saw Mowgli in the flesh and understood that he could be real at the same time as in Kipling's *Jungle Book*, but that neither of these was quite the same as the Mowgli in my head, who was also me – that 'like' magic.

The hill-tribe Mowgli was one of the lean, muscular, top-knotted Mru men in loincloths that didn't cover their bums. The women wore little woven aprons and were bare breasted. At evening, some of the men played elaborate bamboo pipes that stuck up above their heads in clusters. Dave and I took snaps of them and their tall pipes silhouetted against a spectacular sunset thickened with burn-off smoke. Later, they drank what we were told was rice beer out of long straws poked into calabashes, and sang and laughed. There were lots of flea-bitten, curly-tailed pi-dogs, which howled and yipped during the night. We slept in the guest house on hard bamboo stretchers like the one I'd have near Bandarban above the Sangu River in 2005.

Though we were curious visitors to this strange place, I don't remember feeling different or scared. My inner Mowgli was alive and well, and I was protected by the belief that in some way this was recognised both by the kids we played with on the Mru hilltop and by the tough, stringy men with their long scrub-clearing machetes.

Walking back down to the jeep the next day, I got so hot and thirsty that I gulped huge swallows of forbidden water from the stream we stopped to cool off in. I also got too close to the edge of a waterfall and fell down it, skinning my arse on rocks and landing in a deep pool at the bottom. This was the first time I'd felt real terror in our East Pakistan home territory – much worse than the time the madman came into our bedroom to avenge our clod-chucking.

The pool was deep and dark, and full of floating leaves on which huge, viciously biting red ants were swarming. I fought my way up through the black water that immediately seethed with pythons, slimy gnashing fish and an unknown horror; I broke the surface, screaming loudly, and began to get bitten all over by the red ants. I'd torn a decent amount of skin off my arse, lost some fingernails on the way down and was covered in ant bites; but it was the horror of the deep pool and its imagined monsters that stayed with me. For days afterwards I'd wake up with a sensation like choking, unable to remember the dream I'd been having, but in a cold sweat of dread.

It was around this time that I wrote my first poem. All I remember about the poem is that it had biting red ants in it and some kind of refrain about the ruins of a lost city being overgrown by bitter vines.

And the bitter Rangoon Creeper covers it all!

I have a very dim memory of 'Rangoon Creeper', possibly because it was something our mother tried to cultivate, along with profuse bougainvillea and swarming jasmines that became overrun with munching beetles, and flowering shrubs that Dave thinks were hibiscus from which we collected jars full of the ravenous insects for a bounty; they gave off an acrid stink when squashed.

Down in the valley below the management bungalows on the hill where we lived, there was a settlement of paper-mill houses with a transport hub, a bazaar and the newly built cinema near the brickworks. Though we went there several times, the only film I remember is *Creature from the Black Lagoon*, the 1954 monster horror film directed by Jack Arnold. The Creature was the Gill-man, so obviously a human in a fish-suit that I knew there was no reason to be scared of him. But I was – and not just scared to the point of clutching and shrieking like the rest of the audience, but terrified to the point of trauma. The film's lurid effects spilled out into the night's monsoon deluge – rain crashing on the roof, explosions of thunder.

That frightening effect explained so unfrighteningly by Robert Lübker, whereby something that had never existed before could become a real neither-one-thing-nor-the-other, and my horrifying immersion in the squirmy pool under the Chimbuk waterfall, somehow combined with the Gill-man to send me running in an icy chill of fear and panic into the makeshift cinema lobby, where my father found me with my teeth chattering, refusing to go back in. He finally persuaded me to watch bits of the film from up in the projection box, where I could catch glimpses of the action through the holes in the wall and avoid seeing anything by moving my head just a little.

Dave watched the whole movie with enjoyment and told me bits of the complete story later, after which he went soundly to sleep – though he says he still gets gooseflesh thinking about the scene where the clawed webbed hand rises out of the river, clutches at the bank and scrapes back into the water, leaving deep scratches.

But I couldn't sleep, or was too scared to, because *there was something under the bed.* It had escaped from the Black Lagoon which was also the Chimbuk pool, and stayed under my bed for months, even compressing itself into one of my shoes. A couple of years later it migrated to the spiderwebby darkness around the back of the Markwells' house where we spent school holidays in England. Going around there at night to fill up the coal scuttle, I knew that never seeing the thing in the darkness – even when I whipped my head around really quickly to look behind me – proved only that it was fiendishly clever, and therefore that it existed.

I look back now at this frightened child and think it was after Chimbuk and *Creature from the Black Lagoon* that I lost something like my inner Mowgli – secure, invincible, with a few special powers – who allowed me to feel at home in different places, even when they were scarily different. Though I'd sometimes had bouts of the night horrors (the wardrobe in our bedroom back in Francis Street), they'd never amounted to much. Now, there was danger and difference everywhere, all the time. Our Siamese cat Sammy went feral and showed his terrible, hissing face at me when I crawled into some scrub to persuade him to come home. A green bootlace of a snake which Dave accurately ophiologises as a Whip Viper scared the living daylights out of me when I encountered it dangling under the kitchen-garden bean trellis – our neighbour Mr McKenzie, the Scottish chief engineer at the mill, rushed over with a double-barrelled shotgun and blew the bean trellis to smithereens but missed the snake, which should have been funny and cathartic but wasn't. The gardener, whose name (Dave's memory again) was Sultan, then clobbered the thing without fuss.

Worst of all, one hot night I went to have a shit in the bathroom, and a snake that had been coiled around inside the cool toilet bowl rose up between my legs. I ran shrieking across the concrete floor, the chill of which remained reptilian long afterwards and made me want to sprint or tiptoe across it. My father went into the bathroom and killed the snake with a golf club, but that didn't make me feel any safer. Once, I'd gloried in my special relationship with my protector, the great python Kaa; now, at my most vulnerable, I was at the mercy of a snake in the dunny.

And it was about then that I began to write obsessively, secretly, with a conflicted sense of shame and a desire to impress. Impress whom? That wasn't clear – my mother and father in the first instance; but, beyond them, the shadowy, impersonal constituency that had just then come into being across the gap that had opened between me and the ones who seemed fearlessly at home in what they did and where they were, in how they appeared, in how they talked to each other, in how they looked me in the face and grinned, unimpressed or unpersuaded by the fibs and stories I was making up in order to close the gap.

I was writing stories, which was hardly surprising, given the large number of them I read – a core sample would include *The Wind in the Willows*, *The Water-Babies*, *Cuddlepot and Snugglepie*, all the 'Famous Five' books, all the 'Biggles', abridged versions of *The Three Musketeers* and *The Man in the Iron Mask*; illustrated editions of *Robinson Crusoe*, *The Swiss Family Robinson*, *Gulliver's Travels* and *The First Men in the Moon; Lorna Doone*, *The Adventures of Tom Sawyer* and *Huckleberry Finn*; Classic Comic versions of *The Count of Monte Cristo, The Last of the Mohicans*, *A Tale of Two Cities* and *The Hunchback of Notre Dame*; a variety of books plucked from the book-club editions mailed to my father, including *Seven Years in Tibet* by Heinrich Harrer, especially a description, which I barely understood, of arcane brain surgery to make a 'third eye'.

In the early throes of sexual curiosity, I pored over some passages in a steamy swashbuckler set in Louisiana in which a young woman overheats and takes a cooling night-time bath in a large, moonlit barrel of water, watched by a panting adventurer who soon slips in with her. In a few more years I'd be writing single words such as 'thigh' or 'breast' on single sheets of paper: they were all I needed to bring on paroxysms of lust.

But more often, and from the very beginning, I was writing poems, even though I'd come across very little poetry apart from my father's Masefieldian rowing chant, my mother's volume of Tennyson, and a 1907 edition of Robert Browning's complete works with my grandfather Wedde's signature ('AA Wedde') on the fly leaf (I also have an 1894 edition of *Boswell's Life of Johnson*, which was his 1896 Wellington College 'General Work' Prize). We had Robert Louis Stevenson's *A Child's Garden of Verses*, which I think I read more or less by accident because I was obsessed with Stevenson's stories and novels, especially *Treasure Island* and *Kidnapped*. But I didn't like Stevenson's poems much. I liked Tennyson's 'The Charge of the Light Brigade', which I also remember Chick reading aloud with rhythmic gusto; I remember ploughing uncomprehendingly through page after page of 'The Princess' and poring over the shivery words in 'Maud':

> I remember the time, for the roots of my hair were stirred
> By a shuffled step, by a dead weight trail'd, by a whisper'd
> fright,
> And my pulses closed their gates with a shock on my heart as
> I heard
> The shrill-edged shriek of a mother divide the shuddering
> night.

In my grandfather's lushly padded and leather-bound volume of Browning, I galloped through 'How They Brought the Good News from Ghent to Aix', got lost in 'Childe Roland to the Dark Tower Came', but groped blindly through the tangles of 'Sordello' with a weird kind of pleasure.

It was *not* understanding everything, or not easily, that made the occasional words and sentences I *did* get the meaning of seem vivid and shivery, as if the outlines and fragments of the world the words were showing me weren't things I could possibly know already and recognise. It was as though I was seeing them for the first time, or I was the first person to see them. They were from somewhere else, 'penthouse-like', or like the Gill-man; the stories they lit up in flashes and glimpses weren't connected to the language I heard around me every day. In a way it was like reading the French we were by then getting quite good at, but not good enough to be at home with.

I liked how poems could tangle up the narrative, make me unsure where I was in time and place, and with whom, unsure about who was seeing or saying. I enjoyed long books like *The Swiss Family Robinson* (Linda had her brother's copy, inscribed in meticulous, spidery copperplate, 'H.K. Horne, Francis Street, Blenheim') – I remember the illustrations, which is how I know my parents took some of their books with them from Blenheim. But I speed-read the Robinsons to get to the interesting bits, which mostly involved the sons being allowed to have guns – the story didn't interest me much and it was years before I made the connection with *Robinson Crusoe*, a story I did love.

The sceptic in me scoffs at the idea of a coherent convergence of effects that got me writing as a kid. But when I came back to Bangladesh in 2005 I felt strongly a combination of disturbing memories, great happiness and familiar hollowness – a space I longed to fill, and an impulse that could do that. Back around 1957, I wrote a ballad about brave Captain Oates who, uttering the words 'I may be some time', left the tent he was sharing with doomed Captain Scott and went out into the blizzard to have a pee, freezing himself to death via his cock in the process. Chick gave me a perfunctory spanking for this effort, on account of my disrespect (unintended) for such a hero; secretly I suspected he was both amused and proud. It was too late to care, anyway. I couldn't stop doing it.

What were the conditions that produced this obsession, which I called 'writing poems', without really knowing what I was doing? Then, I didn't know why any more than what, and neither mattered. Now I sense it's been a thread that keeps on unspooling through my life, and I have to follow it back through a maze of digressions if I'm to find again those homes which 'writing poems' made real in some way. Perhaps it progressed from the earliest 'asparagus-patch' dramas I expected others to act out with me, to the shit-type scenarios, to the 'penthouse' magic – and then, after the Black Lagoon, to a sense of emptiness that had to be filled. 'Writing poems' both filled that emptiness and increased it. The poems signalled the fact that I was *homesick*, and *that* was something

I hoped to semaphore, somehow, in code.

Many of the reasons for my unhappiness were simple. Around the time of the Black Lagoon my eyesight began to deteriorate and I was fitted with owlish glasses by Dr Bottoms at the Chandraghona Hospital. I had my crowded teeth fitted with a wrenching apparatus of wire and rubber bands by the glamorous dentist wife of the mill's German personnel manager (his favourite pastime was rounding up stray pi-dogs and shooting them) – I felt faint the time I looked down her front as she bent over me and I saw the pinkish outline of a nipple. I developed a painful kind of osteochondrosis in the heels of my feet and had to stay in an improvised wheelchair, and the resulting lack of exercise, plus surging hormones, made me fat.

The wheelchair, which consisted of bicycle wheels and a customised office chair, meant I got dog shit on my hands when I whizzed around after the other kids for whom pushing me too fast had been a short-lived novelty. What made things worse was knowing that we had a cook in the house who, if asked, would whip up another batch of toast. I remember him muttering curses under his breath. I also began to raid the pantry to gobble spoonfuls of peanut butter and drinking chocolate bought from the American stores at the Kaptai dam. A kind of morbid self-pity began to set in. I must have been bossy and obnoxious.

I look back on myself at ten years of age with mixed pity and impatience. Instead of the 'white-haired little goat' with the fearless Mowgli-within, I see a fat, temporarily disabled, snaggle-toothed, myopic kid who'd taken to ordering the servants around, and who spent increasing amounts of furtive time in Dave's and my bedroom. I suspect our parents thought I was jerking off in there (often I was). But mostly I was writing stuff. I just had to keep doing it, and hiding it, at the same time flaunting my secret life that was halfway between a jeer and a boast.

Now I think I was magicking the fear embodied in Gill-man-type spooks under the bed, the ones that had begun to materialise about the time I stopped feeling at home in the world the white-haired little goats had always run around in freely and without fear. The only way to deal to the spooks seemed to be through voodoo channels opened up by Robert Lübker's gently pedantic explanation of the alchemical word 'like'.

The lie

In 1976 Alan Brunton and I started a small tabloid paper called *Spleen* – the name was at once a gesture towards the unforgiving scorn of Charles Baudelaire's *Le Spleen de Paris* prose poems, and an announcement that we intended to make trouble. Other would-be troublemakers, notably Martin Edmond, soon came on board. For all its posturing, *Spleen* was intended seriously, but we also had a lot of fun with it before exhausting the good will of its financial supporters a year and eight issues later.

In one issue, I reviewed a new collection by the poet Vincent O'Sullivan. These days I get on well with Vincent and like him a lot, but my review gave him good reason not to like me – and indeed he took *Spleen* to the Press Council, which exacted an apology from its editors. The offending review consisted of a running list of 'like' constructions from the poems, with a final gratuitously splenetic exclamation, 'Ah, fuck it!' Some weeks after the Press Council complaint, I met Vince at a literary function of some kind. My friend the poet Bill Manhire made a polite show of 'introducing' us to each other, and then walked off to watch what might happen from a distance, a droll smile on his face. Vince and I stood opposite each other for some minutes. I remember that we both resorted to default tics – I fiddled with my bottom lip, while he tweaked his chin. Eventually we gave up.

I now look back on this comical moment with mixed chagrin and renewed interest. Though the final line of my 'review' was gratuitously splenetic, the critical point being made wasn't gratuitous; but it was excessive – why? What I'd reacted to in Vincent's poems was what seemed at the time like a take-for-granted attitude to metaphor, a comfortable homeliness with the likening of one thing to another. These metaphors were too *easy*, I thought; if they weren't going to call up something distinct, one of those disturbing third terms that hinted at another plane of existence, then what was the point?

I remembered this event – it popped back into view – just as I was going to start writing about that miserable time in my childhood in East Pakistan when I was immobilised by self-pity and fear. When I was happy, with my head in a book, or my imagination in an adventure that Dave and I made up as we ran across the bamboo rafts on the dangerous river, or threw stones at the gut-tugging vultures, it was *making myself up* that let me into those transforming places where I could be at home in another identity, at once myself and someone stronger and more powerful.

Before Robert Lübker, it was simple. All I had to do was play and the transformations would happen. After Robert Lübker, it got more complicated, but also more interesting, because the playing included some degree of consciousness of what 'liking' could do. But then the magic broke down. 'Liking' was no longer about play but had become worried; it was how I reached across or tried to fill the gap between where I felt separated from home and the people who seemed to have no trouble being there. They included my brother, and our mother and father, but also the kids we played with. And vague, loudly talking crowds of happy people I didn't know, like those we saw at big celebrations where sporting events and feasts took place (I remember an immense pilau being cooked over a slow, aromatic fire in a large marquee). It was at this point that I became a compulsive liar.

It was while I was trying to remember the details of a particularly egregious lie that I remembered, instead, the review of Vincent O'Sullivan's poems. I suppose that was because I expected so much of what I can now call metaphors. There was a time in my childhood when 'likes' were my magic; they transformed me. But sometimes the 'likes' were also the moments at which my magic broke down and I saw myself as others did: as a joke.

When I went back to Chandraghona in 2005, I walked through the garden that had once been the property of the paper mill's general manager, a genial but tough Swiss man called Hans Meyer. The Meyers had a small swimming pool built on a promontory above the river, and at set times and for limited spells the hilltop kids were allowed to swim there. In 2005 it was dry and full of trash; lizards were stuck to its walls; the concrete floor had cracked and there were tree roots festooning the mildewed sides. But I remembered vividly the pleasure of swimming in the pool, and feeling physically liberated. Because I was having trouble walking, the pool was one place where I didn't feel separate from the others – where, because I was a good swimmer, I even felt special.

I remember standing on the edge of the pool in blisteringly hot sunshine, feeling the water dry quickly on my skin, swelling with physical pride and pleasure, at which point one of the other kids – I think it was Billy McKenzie, but can't be sure – reached across and jiggled my by-then substantial tits, meanwhile making a sucking sound and baring his teeth.

I wheeled this humiliation back to our house where, when Linda lost her temper and told me to stop sulking and do something or other she'd asked me to, I threw myself out of my improvised wheelchair on to the polished red plaster floor, shrieking and sobbing, and crawled towards her on my hands and knees, dragging my bandaged ankles behind me. My mother picked me up – or helped me to climb up – and sat me on her lap, where I wept loudly into her neck and gasped out my lie.

I should feel sorry for the fat kid with sore heels who, while watching his mother's reaction closely, bellowed out his all-too-plausible account of why his life wasn't worth living. My mother was capable of taking a sceptical view of such performances, and she'd seen a few already; but this one got to her. She may not have believed that I wanted to die; she may have seen that my performance was good enough evidence of my unhappiness. In any case, she too began to weep, and we clung to each other, sobbing, while she stroked my hair and murmured, 'There, there . . .' – the peculiar choice of words that worked for me then, even though what I wanted was to be 'here, here'.

I still remember the shame that poisoned my happiness. I knew that what I'd done was a lie, that I'd watched myself do it, and that I'd rejoiced in the impact it had on my mother. I should feel sorry for this little imposter – but I can't, because what I'm mostly left with is the guilt that stabbed me when, over the next few days, I saw my mother look at me with a small, sad, conspiratorial smile – and when, over the next few years, I heard myself telling the lie again in one way or another.

I'd cheated her – so that when I encounter metaphors that are easy, confident performances, the miserable little liar in me flinches. He wants something paradoxical or even impossible, at once lucid and truthful to things as they are, but also truthful about the inevitable unreliability of any narrator who *likens*.

I think that bitter, childish homunculus seeded my young man's preference for perverse narrators – those in the writings of Burroughs, Gaddis and Houellebecq, for example. Perhaps it explains the impact on me in my peevish twenties of Melville's realisation that he had to write a novel *that would fail* (*Moby Dick*). It still accounts for my impatience with disingenuous narratives in which exposition masquerades as character; my awe at Conrad's ability to construct an impeccable armature for his narrators' points of view; Mansfield's delicacy with *style indirect libre*; my admiration for the unswerving rhetorical scepticism of great thriller writers such as Elmore Leonard; my enjoyment of perverse books such as those composed by Oulipo magicians like Georges Perec.

A couple of years ago I was talking to the American essayist and translator Eliot Weinberger about an American poet, a distinguished professor within the creative writing department of a large urban university, who seemed to me to be *performing* in an open-shirted, bucolic, somewhat Frostian tradition – plain-spoken with pessimistic undertones. I didn't buy it. Eliot, whose default is a kind of scathing equanimity, observed that yes, really, did we need yet another poem about changing the storm-shutters?

The lie I gasped into my mother's neck after dragging myself towards her across the floor was my induction into bad faith. I don't believe for a moment that Vincent O'Sullivan was guilty of that in the book I reviewed splenetically, goaded by the inner brat that had supplanted my inner Mowgli, any more than the American poet professor was necessarily guilty of bad faith when he wrote about shovelling snow or burning a pile of autumn leaves.

I don't renounce my sceptical inner brat – what would be the point? – and anyway, he has his critical uses. But what I really confront at those moments when the brat gets in my ear is the fact that I've doomed myself to look askance at most of what I write, in case it's a reprise of the moment I was helped on to my mother's lap and knew I'd betrayed her.

Great Uncle Fritz

How does memory lie? Or rather, what kind of truth does memory promise? Does it make any sense to treat one of my ancestors, my great-uncle Frederic Alexander Wedde, known by the family as Fritz, as the divining rod through which some kind of memory is recovered or encouraged to flow into the present where I'm thinking about home? What 'home' could Fritz possibly tell me about? Almost nothing is known about his own, though the family has generated a collective romance about him ending up in Mexico. I know I've hopelessly romanced several of my forebears about whom I know little outside of the sketchy family record – my great-grandfather Heinrich August and his wife Maria Josephine Catharina Reepen (or Riepen, or Repen), for example.

My father actually remembered his grandfather Heinrich August, but he never mentioned his grandmother Maria, whom he would only have met when he was an infant. On the face of it, Maria seems an unlikely match for a low-ranking, runaway merchant mariner. For that matter, it's not clear why she was emigrating to New Zealand where, as far as I know, she had no family or other connections. It seems her parents had died, and two of her sisters, Charlotte and Dora, also emigrated, though to Australia not New Zealand.

According to her descendant Bill Whitmore, whose mother was Freda Whitmore (née Wedde), and who of course also has Heinrich August as his great-grandfather, the Reepens can be traced back to Cordt Reepen (1613–1700), who lived in Wedehorn in the Bremen district of north-west Germany. Maria's father Peter was a master joiner in Kiel, Schleswig Holstein. He and his wife Elisabeth had ten children; Maria was the eighth. It seems that the Reepens were well connected in musical circles – Brahms was a distant relative, Maria's sister Sophie 'cut some ice as a soprano in the operatic world' and, reports Bill, 'a cousin Klaus Groth was a poet, who is commemorated by a bronze statue in Kiel'. It seems Groth (1819–99) reawakened interest in 'Plattdüütsch' (Low German) dialect poetry.

Heinrich August and Maria married in 1876, had eight children and lived in Bute Street in Wellington. Maria left in 1910 to live with two sons and a daughter on a land settlement farm at Kaitieke in the Ruapehu district. In 1896 Maria seems to have been living in Maarama Crescent, Wellington, and in 1901 Heinrich seems to have been living in Nairn Street, but whether they had parted before 1910 isn't clear – probably not. Maria's address is in the Electoral Rolls, which may show a 'live-in' employment and does show she'd registered to vote after the 1893 Electoral Bill was passed. Heinrich moved to Blenheim to live with his son Albert Augustus and daughter-in-law Mabel (née Thwaites) in York Terrace sometime between 1910 and 1915, when he died of pneumonia after falling into a river – there's a suggestion he was pushed by someone who didn't like the German surname.

My father was born in Wellington in 1906 and would have been about four when his grandfather, the old seaman, came to live with them in Blenheim. He would have been seven when Heinrich died. The memory I have of Heinrich is my father's childish one – the old man getting shickered and reciting poetry in German – as well as the collective family one – Heinrich jumping ship in Wellington, in pursuit of Maria Reepen – both of which I've embellished and written about from time to time.

The few records I've subsequently found or been sent suggest that his arrival may not have been as romantic as this, but was no less dramatic. It seems likely that Heinrich, aged twenty-eight, arrived in Sydney as a cook-steward on the brig *Robin Hood* from one of the French ports of Poitou-Charentes. He later deserted from the *Lammershagen*, which arrived in Wellington in July 1875, presumably having shipped from Sydney. The fact that he turned up again in Wellington on 7 February 1876 on the passenger list of the *Stormbird* from Whanganui suggests that he made himself scarce up-country between July 1875 and February 1876. In August 1876 he married Maria Reepen in Wellington – she had sailed from Hamburg to Wellington on the *Shakespeare*, arriving on 23 January that year.

This amalgam of inherited memory, romance and fact-checking has become one of those ambiguous mental and language objects that drift somewhere between wilful fiction and the sparse record upon which fiction thrives. But about Great Uncle Fritz, the most enigmatic of all the Weddes, nothing is tied even that loosely to what any member of the family can say with certainty. The portal that opens from the family's story of Fritz leads into a territory almost devoid of factual armature.

But of course this is why Fritz is a powerful talisman. He represents what no one will know for certain and therefore what stories will grow from, as if from a rich host of what-might-have-been – from unreliable *liking* – like the missing Taits, those not-quite ancestors who populated the steaming, exotic narratives of half-caste 'Red' Taits involved in the Creek Civil War in Alabama, that place where my imagination is at home even if my genes are not. Except that Fritz's story is marginally less a fiction than the 'Red' Taits' seductive digression, and it's in the tantalising scraps of information about him that the cells of narrative begin to split and multiply.

In February 1970, when Rose and I were living in Amman, Jordan, and where my father was posted with the UNDP, civil war broke out between Jordanian Hashemite forces and Palestinian *fedayeen.* Many foreigners left the city; the Red Cross evacuated the women and children of foreign workers. Rose and my mother were flown to Cyprus. Chick and I stayed behind – in my case because I had a job and badly needed to get the money I was owed, and because I'd illegally bought a Commer van registered in the UK, and needed to get it out of the country before it was commandeered by the *fedayeen* or impounded by Jordanian authorities.

While the fighting continued, Chick and I barricaded ourselves on the ground floor of the apartment building he and Linda lived in. We had some basic food supplies, limited amounts of bottled water and gas for cooking, and a case of whisky. It was under these enforced conditions, and with no good reason not to pour a nerve-calming drink whenever we felt like it, that my father and I talked to each other at length for the first time in our lives. We were in a kind of theatrical, staged condition; the power went on and off; the crack and rattle of automatic gunfire echoed ambiguously around the hills and valleys of the city; the bigger explosions of artillery and mortars intermittently shook the window panes behind their closed drapes.

Perhaps not surprisingly given these prompts, Chick talked about his experiences in Egypt and Palestine during the war. He'd never done so before and never did again. Now, I can connect the relish and affection with which he reminisced in

1970 to the photograph I have of him in uniform on the eve of his embarkation thirty years earlier. In the photograph, a lean, tanned Chick with sergeant's stripes on his sleeve is sitting on the veranda balustrade at 32 Francis Street. He's got that hard stare that often seems to have spooked people, but also a suppressed grin. His booted feet are dangling above the ground, as if he's already left. Like many men of his generation, he was about to go overseas for the first time. In general he seems to have had what was called a 'good war'. He saw minimal action and was mostly involved in quartermastering at training camps – Camp Maadi near Cairo, and in Italy – resource management work that was a kind of pre-echo of what he would go on to do in the travelling years to come.

The little black-and-white snaps of Maadi, Cairo and Jerusalem that he annotated meticulously in a photo album I now have, as well his collection of hand-coloured postcards of Italy, seemed to segue into the thousands of 35mm colour slides he went on to take during the years when he and Linda travelled from job to job. He and I were in a kind of time warp for the few days we talked and drank in the dim concrete room on Jebel Amman – Chick seemed to be half there, and half back in khaki in a black-and-white snapshot landscape with tents, desert dugouts and his 'corner of Cubicle N.Z.S. of I.', with what looks like a double photo-portrait of my mother next to his camp stretcher. This may be the one I now have, a diptych pocketbook leather folder with photographs of Linda in a high-necked, striped costume. Her handwritten note on the back of one reads, 'This should remind you of the Sounds, dear. Look at the mouth – just like a cod!'

But Chick's snaps are also of fine modernist buildings in tree-lined streets at Maadi, the Barrage Gardens in Cairo, Heliopolis, the Cheops pyramid at sunset, feluccas on the

Nile at sunset, the golf links and racecourse at Gezira, the Dead Sea, street scenes in Bethlehem, the Damascus Gate in Old Jerusalem, archaeological sites at Memphis and Sakkara, camels and camel-herders on the way to Alexandria, the French Gardens at Ismailia, and King Farouk's private yacht at anchor.

My father appears in many of the snaps, presumably taken to be sent home. Often, too, he's been photographed with his brothers-in-arms. In August and September 1942, Chick was photographed with three of his mates astride motorbikes in a desert landscape – the airy caption reads 'cycle trip'. In another, he's been photographed with the 'Marlborough Sgts.', N. Waters, R. Gee, J. Best, G. Robinson, B. Harrison and 'yours truly'. There are pyramids in the background.

Listening to my father reminisce, I got the impression that when he returned from the war to the stone balustrade at Francis Street, his feet never quite found the ground again; his attention to the present was redirected towards a possible future by memories of his years away at the war. It was as though memory became the subversive agent that relocated him in the bunkered room of the apartment building on Jebel Amman thirty-five years later. It was in this theatrical space of gunfire, reminiscence and a few drinks too many that Chick first mentioned his Uncle Fritz – as if Fritz was, at that moment of ambiguously layered time, the ideal character through which to utter an unreliable narrative, an unstable but tantalising kind of truth.

Fritz, he told me, had been believed by some in the family to be missing presumed dead in World War I, though his name never showed up on the rolls of honour. Somehow, despite having a distinctly German name, it was thought that he'd managed to go to the war in Europe with the New Zealand Expeditionary Forces. Once there, some members of the family believed, he'd deserted with a quantity of valuable *matériel* and joined the other side. Then, he'd repeated the manoeuvre and disappeared for something like forty years, until he re-emerged in Mexico, where (the story continued) he'd been a mercenary soldier in the Mexican Revolution and subsequently the Mexican Civil War, was pensioned off, accumulated substantial wealth, and spent his last years living in an observatory across the Rio Grande border from the town of Eagle Pass, Texas; his cosmological and astronomical interests were apparently complemented by an orphanage he maintained on the ground floor of his observatory.

Accompanied by the intermittent gunfire of the Jordanian–Palestinian civil war, my father's memory default to the first great adventure of his own wandering life, and tumblers of frugally watered Scotch, the ripping yarn of Fritz easily overrode my scepticism and lodged in my adult imagination as tenaciously as Mowgli once had in my childish one. It was a story I *could* both believe enough and incorporate in another narrative, the one in which my father and I were at home together in a shared history of wanderlust and adventure.

When Linda and Chick had finally returned to New Zealand and my father was no longer working, I used to go up to Auckland from Wellington as often as I could, sometimes with Carlos when he was little, and sometimes by myself. Chick would often come to meet me at the airport. He seemed to be in good shape, and had begun to respond to my questions about the family – which I was asking less out of real curiosity than because I sensed that time was running out, that my mother's and father's memory time was getting short. Chick drove extremely slowly from the airport; an increasingly impatient queue of cars would bank up behind him. Among the stories he told me as grimacing, honking drivers tore past his oblivious profile, two stood out: the romance of Heinrich August and Maria Reepen jumping ship together in Wellington Harbour; and the story of 'Great Uncle Fritz', which I'd first heard fragments of during the time Chick and I were holed up in Amman.

As it turns out, the romantic story of Heinrich and Maria coming ashore together is highly contestable, but the likely facts make little difference to the big salients of their narrative. One way or another, they came ashore together or separately in 1875 (Heinrich certainly jumped ship), married in 1876 and raised a large family in Wellington. He was employed by the Wellington Harbour Board as pilot for sailing ships, but made himself scarce when ships under German flag entered the port. His and Maria's children were exceptionally successful at school, the boys (Herman, Fritz, Herbert, Wilhelm, Reinhold and Albert) at Wellington College and the girls (Bertha and Freda) at Wellington Girls' College; five of the eight won school scholarships and were duxes. The sisters were among the first women in New Zealand to go to university. Freda went on to teach in Napier, Pahiatua and Whangarei.

The story of Fritz is another matter. The basic factual record disappeared or dissolved into family myth early, not long after 1905, and was recovered only in fragments when the missing-presumed-dead prodigal made contact with the family in the mid-1950s from somewhere within administrative reach of Torreon, Coahuila, Mexico. Fritz is described as a surveyor, civil engineer, mining engineer and astronomer; the last attribute begins to shift him towards improbability.

I have a copy of a photograph of the Wedde siblings. The oldest, Reinhold (known as Ren or Dick), was born in 1877, the youngest, Herbert, in 1889. My grandfather Albert, and Fritz, were numbers five and six respectively. In the photograph, Reinhold's hair has begun to recede a little; the youngest, Herbert, looks to be in his mid- to late teens; my grandfather looks strikingly like my father in his twenties. I'd say the photograph was taken somewhere around 1905 when my grandfather was in his mid-twenties. My father would have been a year old. Fritz would have been about twenty-one.

This rough and ready exercise in genealogical geometry inaugurates a seductive opportunity, an opening between minimal facts and the beginnings of a narrative veering already into fiction. Though Fritz is only, let's say, twenty-one in this photograph, four years younger than my grandfather and seven or eight years younger than Ren, there's a sternness and implacability in his expression that set him apart – he looks older than the others not so much in years as in temperament. This isn't easy for him to do – all the siblings have the direct look and wry expression I've come to think of as typical Wedde, and they are all handsome and well turned out. But Fritz alone has a resisting look, an impatience – his mouth has a faintly derisive or mocking twist; he alone looks as if he'd just as soon be elsewhere, and will be, once the photographer's finished with them all. It's like the expression I see on my father's face in the snapshot taken when he swung his feet above the ground while sitting on the balustrade at the front of Aggie Horne's house in Francis Street just days before he left for Egypt in 1940.

I don't know which member of the family Fritz dropped his bombshell letter on in the 1950s, when he announced that he was still alive, living in Mexico, was intestate, and looking to find out the names and locations of his relations, the likely inheritors of his estate. Some family members seem to have begun a disordered quest for what soon became a fabled

fortune. When my father died, I found among his papers a file of correspondence with lawyers in San Francisco and Dunedin, and a bank in Eagle Pass, Texas, which showed that in the 1960s he'd taken on the apparently thankless task of coordinating the family's quest, tracking down and arranging for the distribution of the by-then-deceased Fritz's assets.

Fritz's initial letter, which doesn't survive as far as I know, seems to have been addressed to his relatives in the King Country. Dorothy Bennett, a granddaughter of Fritz's sister Bertha, subsequently began a correspondence with the British Vice-Consul in Torreon. Chick's file, filled mostly with his own patient, meticulous and economical letters to the various agents involved, also contained one to Dorothy from S. Dutton-Pegram, the British Vice-Consul who, with rueful asperity, included the following aside in his letter: 'It appears that I am, under an Anglo-American Treaty, the person who has to try and administer the estates of British subjects who die intestate and I can only say that, as far as I am concerned, I most assuredly hope that I never have another.' This letter, dated 3 November 1958, also contains a P.S. in which the dry, and to my ear Conradian, Dutton-Pegram adds a killer last paragraph: 'As regards the Will, two or three friends of his have told me that he mentioned to them his intention of making a Will, but on being informed that it would cost about $10.00 Dls., he replied:- "I think I'll let it go!"'

Over the years that Chick managed the affair, some of the proceeds from the sale of Fritz's assorted stocks and shares were distributed, in dribs and drabs, to his nephews and nieces – but clearly the agents in Eagle Pass, Texas, in Torreon, Mexico, and in San Francisco didn't or couldn't clean out the safe, except perhaps (it was hinted) into their own pockets. My father's efforts, increasingly irritated though never impolite, petered out in the early 1970s soon after he'd left Lusaka, Zambia, having not had his UN contract there renewed; he stayed on for a while working for the Zambia Printing Company until about 1968 and had, I think, begun to lose heart in general, not just in respect of the quest for Fritz's silver ingots. Dave went on a South Island trip with Chick in late 1968 – he'd 'retired' but was restless. The fabled fortune didn't amount to much, but the thought that it might yet produce a surprise jackpot still lingers here and there among Fritz's great-nieces and -nephews.

For me, though, the jackpot is by this stage interesting only as a kind of fiction – the mirage of a silver mine or hidden treasure that has driven so many exotic and fabled expeditions. It's the kind of Rider Haggard *King Solomon's Mines* story that consumed me when I was a kid; I saw the 1950 movie version with Deborah Kerr and Stewart Granger, and I had the Classic Comic. Later, it would be Joseph Conrad's *Nostromo* that utterly mesmerised me, not least because I knew that Conrad had only ever seen the literal, the *truthful* landscape of his South American location from a distance, at sea.

In Fritz's story, it's the elusiveness of the treasure, not its factual truth, which is compelling; it's the drollness of the Conradian British Vice-Consul's remark about Fritz's friends' anecdote, when my great-uncle dismissed the need to make a will – 'I think I'll let it go!' Who were these friends? What were they doing in Torreon, Mexico? What was Fritz's connection to the bank in Eagle Pass, Texas? Who was the 'common-law wife' Fritz was alleged to have had? What was he doing in Mexico, and why did he have an 'observatory'? Did he really get pensioned off as a soldier in the Mexican Civil War?

Recently, my second cousin Sam Robinson sent me an email which only adds to the fictional seductiveness of whatever we characterise as the memory of Fritz. From what Sam remembers of conversations with his late grandmother, Chick's sister Phyllis Rabone, Fritz travelled a lot, including in the Malay states as a mining engineer. Sam also unearthed some immigration records at Ellis Island in New York. According to these, 'Wedde, Frederick Alexander; Ethnicity: New Zealand, English; last place of residence: Kiel, Germany; Age: 26; Marital Status: S', arrived in the USA aboard the *President Lincoln* from Hamburg on 26 May 1910. Sam's email contains much immigration-record information about the ship, including that it was sunk in the Atlantic by a German U-boat on 31 April 1918, which somehow seems to locate Fritz's voyage at a timely point in the history that, in one version, has him slipping across to the German lines with something of value – clearly, that particular 'memory' can be discarded, though the question remains: where was Fritz between 1910 and 1918? The Mexican Revolution led by Francisco I. Madero started in 1910, which provides a shapely but entirely speculative milestone to Fritz's chronology. Between about 1905 and 1910 he was in Malaya, he was in Germany – where else? There seems to be an almost hyperbolic instability in the sequencing of events in Fritz's life.

According to Sam's research, there's another Ellis Island immigration entry for 'Wedde, Frederik', which corresponds exactly to the *President Lincoln* records, except that it has Fritz arriving two days later, on 28 May 1910, aboard the *Amerika*. This entry, too, is accompanied by detailed accounts of the ship's provenance and fate. Sam concludes, 'Somehow I feel I know more about the ships he travelled on than about Fritz himself. Odd the cards that history can deal one's life.' By now, it seems entirely plausible and appropriate that even the official memory of Fritz arriving in America could be unstable, offering different versions of the truth.

Recently, I caught up again with my cousin Norma – Sam's mother – in Blenheim. She said she thought she had some letters of Fritz's. It turned out that she didn't have any letters, but she did send me a typed page on yellowed, foxed paper, dated '1st. June 1957', with a footnoted address at 'Apartado Postal 113, Torreon,/Coahuila Mexico', and signed (in type) 'F A Wedde'.

At first, the typed signature confused me, since the initials are also my father's. Very like my father's kind of succinct prose is the statement at the end of the sheet: 'Please keep this paper as it may be of interest sometime in the future.' While I have to conclude that the 'F A Wedde' refers to my great-uncle Frederick Alexander Wedde, not to my father Frederick Albert Wedde, the two identities seem to overlap, and I remain unsure as to whether the page is a transcript made by my father with his plea-to-posterity appended, or whether the whole thing comes from Fritz, with its final sentence reaching forward to a moment when someone – me, for example – might read it.

The text itself, however, is the only object to which I can attach Fritz in any material way. He wrote it in June 1957, not long before he died. These are his own words. I'm not surprised that they seem to emanate from the top floor of 'an observatory' somewhere near Torreon, in the state of Coahuila, Mexico, whose border with the USA runs for 512 kilometres along the Rio Grande – the truth of this seems satisfactory and even appropriate, given the content of the document.

A NEW HYPOTHESIS OR THEORY OF THE UNIVERSE

Many years ago the English scientist, Dalton, gave the world of science the Atomic Theory, all chemical elements consisted of atoms the smallest particle of an element that could enter into chemical combination with atoms of other elements. With most elements the atoms combine together forming a molecule of two atoms. This theory is now known to be correct. Dalton did not make the error of stating that the atom was the smallest indivisible particle of an element. We now know that atoms consist of protons and electrons and perhaps others. I deal only with these two. Protons and electrons are bound together with enormous energy and the release of this energy is the enormous power of the atomic bomb. The proton is electrically positive and its mass is about 2000 times that of the electron, the negative electric particle. Our universe is an electric universe and where protons are found in this universe galaxies are in the process of formation, or have been formed in former eons of time. What exists between the galaxies, between the stars which form them and nebulae, masses of gases which are seen in our own Milky Way? My hypothesis is this; these enormous spaces are filled with electrons, negative particles of electricity which repel each other and by so doing in the vicinity of the solid or gaseous bodies like the sun and the planets are the cause of gravitation which these bodies seem to possess. Light from the farthest stars reaches us with the same speed as an electric current travels through a copper wire. The electron alone without the mass of a proton about which it revolves cannot reach a body consisting of elements, protons and electrons bound together by atomic force. Thus the hypothetical 'Ether' of former scientists is nothing but a universal mass of electrons which pervades all space. Such is the medium which carries light throughout the universe.

This is a far more compelling last will and testament than any notarised redistribution of assets could ever have been. It bequeaths us an actual fragment of Fritz's thought, which he had *somewhere* – in whatever constituted his home then. In this home he was reading, thinking and looking at the heavens. His thought has expansive scope, and yet is particular; it is at once speculative and confident of facts. I want to imagine that he discussed these thoughts with his friends in Coahuila, who heard him disparage the necessity for a will and reported this as a joke to the British Vice-Consul, Fritz's grudging but amused conduit to his descendants half a world away. But I don't need to do this – to imagine a conversation punctuated by shots of tequila perhaps (though I already have). The fiction that is generated by the energy of this text seems to travel at the same speed as the fact of its utterance.

What I will permit myself, however, is the phantom of my father's typed signature on this yellowing sheet of paper: not a possessive presence, just a companionable one. I can imagine Chick and his Uncle Fritz sitting with a bottle of whisky between them in the shuttered room on Jebel Amman; I can imagine overhearing their exchanges of memory. My great-uncle, his nephew, his nephew's son – what passes between us across time and space? There are perhaps spaces between us like those between the astronomical bodies Fritz looked at from his 'observatory' – traversed by memory, as if by light, within a compound energy-field of fiction and truth.

More poignant in the end than such dubious metaphors are a couple of simple facts noted in the Vice-Consul's letter. There were only two claims against the estate of Frederick Alexander Wedde at the time of his death: one a doctor's bill for \$600; the other from 'the Spaniard who rented him his room and who insists that he even advanced him money and that he is owed by the estate, altogether, less than \$200.000

Dls'. The grammar is slippery here, but I want to assume the 'he' who advanced the money was Fritz, because we know he had money and owed 'less than' an amount. The other grammatical option, of course, is that Fritz was just as stingy with his rent as with paying for a will to be drawn up.

He was about seventy-three when he died; he was sick when he contacted his distant family; and he owed rent on 'his room'. If I locate his succinct atomic treatise within the vectors of these minimal facts, I can almost say I know where his home was at the end of his life. And I have his last words: 'Please keep this paper as it may be of interest sometime in the future.'

The plums

My twin brother and I were born twenty minutes apart in a race I used to claim to have won but which Dave did. As if by Great Uncle Fritz's gravitational force field of negative and positive energy, we were pulled together and apart by 'the thing we held up between us' – the other's thumb, the stupendous fish, our cousin's bridal train. We went through our childhood days as if joined by an elastic rope, so that when one drew away from the other the pull between us increased.

Under Marlborough's hot sun on the scratchy grass of Horton Park, overtaking each other on bikes, hauling back on our individual oars in Bertie's dinghy, making our way to and from school, rattling sticks along corrugated-iron or paling fences, in cosy adjoining beds at night, in the gone-to-seed asparagus patch, the dry ditch by the culvert, the mushroomy paddock at the back of the Hastilow farm with its rumour of a bull, in the linotype shop at the *Marlborough Express* where Chick melted down lead scraps to make fishing sinkers, by the green dial of the radio in 'the front room' at Francis Street – we were together all the time. I know this, even though my memory-picture of the physical space Dave would have occupied doesn't always have Dave in it. When I envisage Dave, it's always Dave's big smile that I see, the one Dave's still got. I don't have a pronoun for that smile: it's Dave's. When I attach a pronoun to it, *him*, the smile moves *over there*, away from *we* and *us*.

People often remark, as if challenging us to contradict them, that it must have been amazing to have grown up as a twin, 'with that kind of *special* relationship'. They imply, with a hint of envious longing, that Dave and I, though not identical twins, must have had some kind of psychic connection. Perhaps we did, whatever that might mean – and however I might know it, or have known it when I saw it. But the truth is that my awareness of my brother, and I'm sure his of me, was almost peripheral. We just were there with each other, that was all. It was so obvious, you didn't notice it. It's not even possible for me to say I loved my brother when we were kids – that was an awareness that could mean anything only after we'd grown up and lived apart. Now, I know I adore my brother, though we've never lived close to each other as adults, and our kids – my sons, his daughters – barely know each other.

Despite my shooting him in the thigh, Dave and I were even closer during the years when we lived by the Karnaphuli River, and ran feral in the scrub or along the river banks, and later, horsed around in the compound on the hill with the kids who turned up in Chandraghona a bit after us. We were constant companions in the environs of the mill, and on the holiday expeditions our parents began to organise more and more often, setting the enjoyable pattern of their lives – to the Kaziranga wildlife park in Assam, where we rode on elephants through tall cane thickets and lotus-clogged swamps, and saw a rhinoceros; to Puri on the east coast of the Bay of Bengal, where we saw a great many temples; to Shimla hill station in the Himalayas, where I rode around on a stout, stubborn pony because of my sore heels; to Darjeeling, where Chick photographed us with Sherpa Tenzing, with whom he had a mysterious friendship, and where we saw Mount Everest fuming wind-blown snow in the distance; to Dhaka and Calcutta; and quite often down the river to Chittagong, where we sometimes went out to the beach at Patenga, or prowled the bazaar with our mother, who'd begun to accumulate textiles. And it was in Chittagong that we were measured up for the English-style schoolboy outfits (jacket and pants) that were a sign of things to come.

Once we got to England and went to school there, Dave and I were thrown together by default, because we didn't have a family home to go to in the holidays. But in fact we'd already begun to draw apart, back up the river at Chandraghona. I know this because he wasn't unhappy and I was – see how that pronoun *he* peels away and goes over there, beyond the conjoining tug of what always drew us back together; *over there* is where I saw Dave's sunny smile, with the others. It began to be that way.

I felt it when I went back there. It was strange and a bit sad to be standing alone in front of our old house and looking at the mildewed *penthouse-like* storm ledge above our bedroom window; Dave should have been there, *we* should have been there. But he wasn't; we weren't. He wasn't, because he didn't want to be there. He didn't want to be there because he had no reason to go back. I wanted to be there because I had a reason: to revisit the last home in which Dave and I had been that supple, elastic, indivisible *we*; the home we'd left on trajectories that then began to warp apart; the home in which I'd begun, for a time, to be *homesick*.

So I went back by myself – knowing I was no longer that unhappy kid and hadn't been for most of my life, knowing that the memories I had or might recover would be different from the experiences they'd originally stored, but confident that something would happen when I got there and went up the big brown river to the home I remembered with a confusing mixture of bliss and grief.

In the chaotic crowd that mobbed the Biman Bangladesh check-in counters at the airport in Kuala Lumpur were large numbers of transient workers returning to Dhaka with outsize items such as plasma TV screens. A smiling Bangladeshi man, with that characteristic combination of friendliness and importunity, seized my small bag and entreated me to give him my passport and ticket.

'We pass it!'

That was when I arrived back. The privileged child who'd grown up in the compound of mostly expatriate senior management at the paper mill, and who, in the final stages of his time there, had begun to boss the servants around, hesitated suspiciously.

'Is quicker, no?' The man smiled, wagging his head from side to side.

It was. The bag, passport and ticket were passed over the milling crowd; the passport and a boarding pass returned soon after.

Bangladesh is a desperate place whose situation can make it dangerous. But it's also a place in which innumerable intricate networks link transactions, enterprises, social exchanges, relationships. Watching my bag and passport being passed hand to hand over the heads of the crowd, I thought with a pang how isolated we must have been as kids. Leaving aside those holiday excursions with our parents, our contact with the world beyond the compound and the surroundings we played in was limited to occasional trips to buy shoes at the Bata shop in the Chandraghona bazaar – where Dave remembers he dropped and never recovered the ('.177-calibre') trophy slug recently extracted from his thigh. Even if I could have, I didn't want to go back to the world of the petulant, over-fed child I'd become by the time we left the house on the hill; but the memory of him demanding more toast – '*Juldi juldi*!' – 'Quickly, quickly!' – came back to taunt me often over the next weeks.

Something else happened at the KL check-in. My new friend asked me where I came from. When I said New Zealand, he wanted to know if I knew the cricketer Stephen Fleming – 'Everybody admire him!' And then, why I was going to Bangladesh? I told him I planned to visit the place I'd lived in as a kid in the 1950s – I wanted to see it again, and understand it better. It was the first week in February. I had a visa for three weeks and planned to extend it for another three once I arrived.

'*Ekushey*,' said the man. 'You will be there. *Shohid Dibosh*.'

I didn't know what *Ekushey* was, or *Shohid Dibosh*, and that astonished and dismayed him. How could I have been in Bangladesh in the 1950s and not know what *Ekushey* was? It was when the language martyrs would be commemorated, on 21 February. *Shohid Dibosh* was Martyrs' Day.

I didn't know who the 'language martyrs' were. I knew a little bit about the Baul poets and hoped to hear them. But not the martyrs.

My friend was losing interest in me. 'You will find out,' he told me, with a sad head-wag. 'There will be *hartal*, but you must see.'

I knew what *hartal* meant. It was a general strike, often accompanied by violent demonstrations. Some were scheduled about the time I was arriving. I'd read the Travel Alerts.

'And what do you do?' asked the man as I edged away with my passport and boarding pass.

'I'm a writer,' I told him.

He put a respectful hand on my laptop case. And what do I write?

I'd been there before. I took the easy way out.

'I'm a poet.'

It wasn't the easy way out. As I understood his pained expression, to be a poet in Bangladesh was something – but a poet who didn't know about *Ekushey* (a cricket lover who didn't know about Stephen Fleming)?

Preparing to go to Bangladesh, I'd wanted to find someone who would have known my father, perhaps a member of the young team he recruited at the mill. I had black-and-white photographs of them from my father's albums – young men, in their late teens or early twenties, smiling and eager, like the man at the airport in KL. After months of unsuccessful inquiries to Bangladesh's press bureau, the Parjatan Tourist Corporation, the labyrinthine bureaucracy in which the history of the old Pakistan Industrial Development Corporation is now buried, and the British High Commission in Dhaka, I finally made contact with an extraordinary woman, Lina Chowdhury.

As luck would have it, Lina was the niece of one of my father's team between 1954 and 1958. She worked as a liaison officer at the British High Commission and was an activist with a special interest in women's rights and the issues of forced marriages and child prostitution. Much of her work, I learned, involved disabusing journalists bent on exposing the exploitation of young women in the garment-industry sweats. She'd take the journalists downriver to the floating brothels at Barisal on the Kirtankhola River, and let them see for themselves how the child prostitutes fared there: might it not be better to support the sweats, where young women could earn social value as well as money for their families, where they could avoid being married and having children at fifteen and sixteen, while people like Lina lobbied for good insurance schemes and safe working conditions?

She got in touch with me because she'd heard on the

grapevine that a journalist from New Zealand wanted to go up the Karnaphuli to the paper mill at Chandraghona where his father had worked when the mill first went into production in the early 1950s. The Rangamati area around the mill was pretty much closed off to foreigners. There had been 'trouble' there as a result of ongoing armed conflict between indigenous tribes and Bengali settlers in the Hill Tracts to the east; and gun-running between Bandarban in the hills and Kaptai where the dam had flooded vast areas of tribal land. But the 'trouble' also related to the mill itself. It had become a sensitive site after it was included in the WHO list of 'catastrophic' pollution zones – and, as I was to discover, because of skimming, stand-over and payroll-padding by *dacoit*, as they were usually called in the Bangladesh press: gangsters of various persuasions, some political, some religious and some (as at Chandraghona) associated with unions. Access to the mill was forbidden, especially to those on journalist visas.

As she told me later, Lina was in a quandary. While not wishing to whitewash the problems of Bangladesh, and least of all the sweats, she was sick of dealing with journalists arriving with fixed agendas to expose corruption, labour exploitation, the endemic bombings, assassinations and violent political *hartal*, and especially the country's spectacular urban poverty. But she was also the devoted niece and intellectual companion of the elderly Mr R.D. Qureshi who, as a young man of twenty-six, had joined my father's team and was trained by him to be the Accounts Manager for marketing and shipping paper from the port at Chittagong.

The mill had a long history of 'trouble' – it was rumoured to have been built so far upriver from Chittagong in order to have access to non-union labour. As Mr Qureshi put it in a letter he wrote me after we'd made contact, 'Common laws of the country did not apply in the Hill Tracts, governed by special laws, so that formation of labour unions could be kept at bay.' This may or may not have been true – it's also possible the mill was sited to be upriver of tidal salination, which would have wrecked the pulping machinery ingesting rafts of bamboo. But soon after Mr Qureshi and the Wedde family from New Zealand arrived at the mill, there was a violent uprising of workers, in the course of which a number of managers were killed; the unrest wasn't just a labour matter, but was also due to conflict between Urdu-speaking Pakistani bosses and foremen, and Bangla locals. The tension that would lead to the War of Liberation in 1971 was already building from its inciting incident on 21 February 1952, when students were killed by police during a pro-Bangla-language demonstration in Dhaka – the *Ekushey* moment I'd never heard about as a kid. All we knew about the riots at the mill back in 1954 was that for a few days some of 'the Brigadier's men' were posted about the place with .303 rifles, and we had to stay inside.

Nor had I ever heard of or bothered to find out about the huge popular impact of the Language Movement's rallying text, the poem *Kadte Ashini Fashir Dabi Niye Ashechi* ('I have come not to mourn but to appeal for hanging'), by the Chittagong writer and activist Mahbub Ul Alam Choudhury, whose funeral on 10 November 2007 was a national event; or the song 'Amar Bhaier Rokte Rangano' ('My brothers' blood splattered') by Abdul Gaffar Choudhury, which is still sung every year at the *probhat feri*, or barefoot march, by hundreds of thousands to the Shaheed Minar martyrs' memorial in Dhaka on *Ekushey*; or the great Bengali rebel poet and Tagore disciple Kazi Nazrul Islam, whose 1922 poem *Bidrohi* ('Rebellion') became the anthem of the Bangladesh War of Liberation in 1971.

On 21 February 2005, I had *Ekushey* lunch with Mr Qureshi and his extended family. Qureshi was now retired, a seventy-seven-year-old *haji,* long-bearded, moustache-less, exquisitely courteous and very funny. As well as writing regular newspaper columns on popular music and film, he'd written a travel guide to the holy Muslim sites of Turkey. His name revealed that he was descended from the Arab Islamic missionaries who came to the Sylet region from Mecca 700 years ago. He remembered my father with affection and gave me back a letter Chick had written to him, congratulating him on his marriage in 1959. In return, I gave him a black-and-white photograph from my father's vast collection: it showed the youthful, goateed R.D. Qureshi with my father and a number of the other trainees. We sat in Mr. Qureshi's living room after exchanging these gifts, and shared the same box of tissues. Qureshi claimed it was his pipe-smoking that made his eyes water; we both knew better.

Later in the day, I walked from my guest house along to a nearby traffic island to get a rickshaw across to the Shaheed Minar demonstrations, and passed a guy with a little bicycle-tyre repair shop. He'd made a papier-mâché model of the Shaheed Minar memorial, using what Mr Qureshi had earlier told me was a copy of a Bangla newspaper with Kazi Nazrul Islam's famous poem in it. This was partly out of respect for the language martyrs, but also as insurance against the Awami League enforcers who were policing the general strike during the holiday. As the Bangladeshi historian Rafiuddin Ahmed put it, Bangladesh never believes anything until there is a poet to articulate it. And the authorities know this: Mahbub Ul Alam Choudhury's poem, which had been printed clandestinely, was banned by the government, which issued a warrant for Choudhury's arrest; he fled disguised in a woman's *burqa* and remained in hiding for several months.

It's difficult for a poet accustomed to a low-key poetry culture such as New Zealand's to comprehend the public scale and historical significance of poetry in Bengal. The nearest I'd come to it was in 1969–70, in the Middle East, where the poems of the Palestinian Mahmoud Darwish were broadcast to attentive audiences on breakfast radio, fed the rhetoric of popular political protest and at the same time underwrote the cultural credibility of high-level diplomacy.

Over the next month, as I began to learn about these things, it was as if I stepped a little way beyond the wall of privilege and ignorance that had surrounded me as a kid, and which I'd been content to live in up to the moment when I surrendered my passport and bag to the crowd at the Biman Bangladesh check-in counter – a moment denoting privilege articulated from below by hospitality, rather than from above by power. I was in a culture where private, introspective expression seemed like an oxymoron; where it was absurd to imagine any *writer* being unaware of 21 February as International Mother Language Day, and only slightly less absurd to imagine a writer with a history in Bangladesh being ignorant of the origins of International Mother Language Day in the Bangla Language Movement. Fifty years after beginning to become a writer, I re-encountered the perfect diagram of my childhood introspection: another kind of privileged compound; a home I had to leave again in order to understand what it had shut out.

Lina wanted to discourage me from going up to the Rangamati region and the mill. But she knew that her uncle and I had to meet, and that Mr Qureshi would conspire to help me. I didn't tell her I intended to go to the Hill Tracts as well. There were reports of foreigners being abducted there, and of armed confrontations between the army and tribal rebels. But behind these were blithe Parjatan promotions targeting Bengali holidaymakers, with excursions to the cool hills and to water sports on Kaptai Lake.

It was late at night when I arrived in Dhaka, and outside the airport an enthusiastic demonstration was underway behind a high security fence. Various competing loudspeakers were haranguing the mob, which was shouting at armed security forces, some of whose uniforms I would later recognise as belonging to the notorious RAB, or Rapid Action Brigade, most often involved in what the Bangladeshi press daintily called 'crossfire'. What sounded like old-fashioned cherry-bomb firecrackers went off; some red smoke bombs blurred the lighting along the security fence; paper bags of flour were biffed over the fence and burst harmlessly near the security guys, who looked bored and sullen. The crowd resembled those you see at cricket matches in the subcontinent.

When I got to the guest house I was staying in, I asked its manager, Parveen Prodhan, what the demonstration was about. Over the next few weeks I came to be in awe of her, and of her sidekick Justina Biswas. Their supply of information was phenomenal, as was their combination of entrepreneurialism and charm.

'Was nothing,' said Parveen airily, adding, 'but *hartal* going to happen on fourteen and fifteen, better to stay here. Very good lunch. Cheap.'

I soon began to find out what 'was nothing' meant. Like the language of Bangla poetry, Bangla political activism and the demonstrations that express it are at once dramatic and commonplace.

On 9 February 2005, the day after I arrived, 30,000 male workers from eight jute mills in the Kulna-Jessore industrial belt formed a human chain in bare feet and sleeveless undershirts. All were carrying empty earthenware plates. A similar human chain had been formed the day before at

Rajghat, in Jessore's Abhoynagar *upazila*, or administrative district. In Dhaka, the opposition party Awami League's supporters, unofficially led by Asma Kibria, widow of the assassinated former Awami League finance minister Shah A.M.S. Kibria, repeatedly formed human chains, holding kilometres-long banners inscribed with poems. So did those silently protesting at the ongoing killings of journalists, especially after the death from bombing of the Khulna journalist Sheikh Belalludin on 11 February.

Such peaceful demonstrations don't rule out rioting. The ordinariness of violent unrest was captured in a Dhaka *Daily Star* newspaper headline following the first day of the two-day *hartal* on 14 and 15 February – the days Parveen had suggested I spend having affordable lunch at her place: 'Street show-off ends without confrontation'.

In fact, fifteen people were injured in Tangail; BNP activists ransacked the Awami League's Bogra office where they set fire to papers and burned the portraits of Bangabandhu Sheikh Mujibur Rahman (the Father of the Nation) and the woman leader of the Awami League opposition, the phenomenally energetic Sheikh Hasina. The 'without confrontation' included ten people injured in Moulvibazar; 10,000 extra security forces mobilised in the capital; bombs thrown at a railway crossing, a bus stop, and near Golap Shah Mazar in Gulistan. Numerous police baton-charges were reported off-handedly in the press. Baton-wielding police tried to arrest women picketers at Russell Square in Dhaka but were beaten back by Awami League leaders, and Awami League women activists were forced by police to parade blindfolded and tied together with rope through the streets at Meer Hazirbagh. On the second day of this *hartal* non-event, a Valentine's Day crowd at Dhaka University was hit by four bombs, with sixteen people injured and a subsequent student strike. The bombs were left in potato-chip packets and went off when trampled.

I kept my head down during *hartals* and once took lunchtime refuge in a kebab shop after an explosion nearby. It was probably a large firework intended to frighten, but people cleared out quickly into adjoining side streets. The kebab shop was pretending to be closed by keeping its lights turned off, but its owner served me delicious fiery chicken with *bhaji* and gave me a box of rose-scented tissues. A couple of loud fireworks also went off the day I attended the *Ekushey* rally at the Shaheed Minar; an estimated million people were there, and the explosions hardly registered. They weren't reported in the press.

During all this, I went through various processes of getting (or not getting) official bits of paper giving me access to the Rangamati region, to the mill itself and to the insurgent Chittagong Hill Tracts. Later, I forked out extra cash for obscurely sourced documents from the local *upazila* official in Chandraghona allowing me to be there after I'd already spent the day with members of the paper mill's management. Like the disturbances, these arrangements seemed both crazy and organised.

I kept count of the rising number of 'cross-fire' killings in shoot-outs between political cadres, *dacoit* gangsters and the RAB (in the region of 350 killed in my first couple of weeks there). I talked to different kinds of people, including aid workers and corporate textile consultants, retired state bureaucrats from the days of the Language Martyrs in 1952 and the Freedom Fighters in 1971, and I collected accounts of extraordinary probity and patriotism, and of massive corruption.

I planned to write an article about all this, and I talked myself into believing I was doing research for my 'home' book – filling in the world beyond the compound of my childhood home. But what I began to notice on a daily basis was something different; something I remembered. The vivid memory of sweeping and sorting was what opened the door to my childhood home at Chandraghona.

In Bangladesh, sweeping is an art form every bit as ubiquitous as demonstrating or poetry. Even in slums built on and out of the refuse of the cities, among the *bushti* shelters along the railway, on the road to Narayanganj, in the garbage heaps on the road to Comilla – in fact, surviving on the resources of the dumps – there are clear margins where the swept human space ends.

Everywhere things are sorted, stacked, piled and arranged: bamboo bundled and graded by diameters, new-season bricks (brickmaking in Bangladesh is seasonal because of the rains), stooks of thatch, cowpats. Chaotic in motion, the rickshaws somehow always end up with front wheels aligned when waiting in rows. Things are bundled, basketed and bagged; the baskets are themselves patterned and stacked, or arranged in rows. The bags are recycled and endlessly rewashed: from trains, you see jute gunny-sacks and their more contemporary synthetic-fibre cousins drying in rows by village ponds and city canals.

The kids selling freshly scraped and sliced carrots and cucumbers along the roadsides and by city parks and traffic roundabouts have arranged them in circular patterns on wide bamboo trays; when a customer buys some, the carrot wheel is rearranged. Elaborately symmetrical, giant flower arrangements being taken home in rickshaws on Valentine's Day, despite the *hartal*; marigolds and zinnias on the *Saraswati puja* which combines rites for the Hindu goddess of knowledge with the traditional Bangladeshi spring festival; the immense arrangements of flowers at the Shaheed Minar memorial for

Ekushey Language Martyrs Day. The beautifully patterned spatial and communal orderliness of the rice paddies; the frugal symmetry and serial construction of my airy, creaking, all-bamboo house-on-stilts high above the Sangu River in the smoky Chittagong Hill Tracts.

'We must clean the path,' wrote Rubana Huq, a forceful businesswoman and social entrepreneur. Huq's industry was textiles and clothing, and she was writing in the *Daily Star* about the need to identify Bangladesh's economic niche in the face of the giant sweats of China, India's cooption of the high fashion market and the advance of automation. 'Clean the path' is a brilliantly apt exhortation to a culture whose genius is to do that every day in a million small ways. It is a clever, patriotic but not nationalist appeal to Bengal's history as '*Shonar*' – golden, once the richest country in the world (Marco Polo said so), where whole new principalities of absurdly fertile silt, the *char* islands of the great delta, will materialise after the monsoon floods and are likely to disappear along with their transient populations without ever being captured in a census. Bengal, once the world's leader in textiles and weaving, always the world's only supplier of jute, was consigned to the ranks of 'Least Developed Nations' by nineteenth-century British textile tariffs and the colonial administration's political and religious divisiveness.

'We must clean the path' is also a brilliant way of eliding everyday sweeping and ordering with the million-times-repeated 2-thaka (8 NZ cents) transactions that constitute the exact and frugal social logic of Bangladesh's survivalist culture.

My father, an optimist by nature and an instinctive collectivist in his economic practice, always spoke affectionately of the social warmth and enterprise of the small-business cultures he worked with, while pouring angry scorn on their inevitable nepotisms, back-handers and grifting. In noticing all this, it was as though I finally stepped out of the circumscribed compound home of my childhood in that place, where the sound of sweeping had always begun early, along with the smell of water sprinkled on dust. I was able to look at it not just through the emotional lens of memory, but with a sense of liberation and understanding.

Parveen Prodhan, the manager of my little guest house in Dhaka, was a good paradigm of the world beyond my cloistered childhood home. Shrewd, efficient and constantly inventing commercial opportunities, her dazzling smile usually signalled a bright, value-adding idea.

'Not to worry, no need to pack, pay half rate, nobody is going in only me,' was her suggestion when I left with a small shoulder-bag to catch the train to Chittagong, and wanted to store the rest of my stuff and save on the room. To read that smile as an outrageous invitation to bargain would have been a big mistake. 'Is your home away from home, isn't it, Mr Ian?'

Yes, it was, and when I came back a couple of weeks later with a grubby, recycled synthetic-fibre poultry-food bag full of overflow stuff from Chandraghona and Bandarban, there was a fresh packet of tissues in my little room, my laundered socks were tied together with pink thread and labelled 'Mr. Ian', and there was a fresh micro-cake of rose-extract soap next to the thundering cold-water shower. It was a good deal; what's more she knew I could afford it, since, though I travelled and lived ridiculously cheaply, I was a millionaire in the real terms of on-the-street benchmark Tk2 transactions.

I think it was a desire to 'sweep the path' – to find Parveen's kind of order and value in the chaotic and emotional circumstances of my return to Chandraghona – that prompted me to lay out five objects on the worn table in my Chittagong hotel room. I didn't know what to do with them. I'd laid them out there, and they were asking me for a ritual response – some kind of large meaning out of modest or even trivial components, like the shapely fan of peeled carrot sticks on the woven cane platter of the kid who ran along beside your rickshaw. I felt emotional about the objects on the table, and half-arsed shy at the same time – as you can when alone in a room which someone may enter unexpectedly and catch you stifling your sobs. Not for the first time that day, I'd had to sponge up tears with Bangladesh's ubiquitous tissues.

The last time I'd been handed a tissue was earlier in the day in the archive of the ruinous paper mill at Chandraghona, a time warp of mid-1950s optimistic industrialisation and modernisation that looked ghoulishly prescient when held up against its 'developing nations' ideological successor in 2005. Here, in a dim room whose paper files of company records and old-fashioned photo albums were themselves museum artefacts, I'd seen a faded black-and-white photograph of my ghostly father in an eager crowd of people on the banks of the Karnaphuli River, in what was then East Pakistan, in 1954.

As I'd sniffled modestly into my rose-scented tissues, I'd also seen, beyond the archive's window, yellow, rusting, 44-gallon drums of chlorine gas spilling from the broken-down brick entrance to a warehouse. The gas was used in the pulp-bleaching process: it was modern technology in 1954; now it's banned almost everywhere. It had been a by-product of the rayon mill nearby, but the rayon mill closed down and now the paper mill had to import its chlorine gas, which diminished its already minimal economic viability. Out the window I'd also seen the armed guard in his watchtower by the mill perimeter lean his ancient .303 rifle against the wall of his lookout and climb down for midday *namaz*. The imam was calling from the mill's mosque, and everyone with me in the archives room politely took their leave and left me with my ghostly father and my pink, tear-soaked tissues.

Earlier, I'd looked at well-preserved pulp rollers, the very best in their day, 1953, the year the mill was commissioned. Some of them were working perfectly – the great machines looked like museum specimens of industrial revolution, with grease-nipples and shining brass handles. Down the end of the production line, where the pulp emerged as paper and was guillotined into sheets, were men with racing hands and strangely lifted elbows who could count bales of 500 or 1,000 sheets with fingers that repetition had made infallible; they were intricately callused from a million paper-cuts.

Finally, getting a grip on myself, I rearranged the objects on the Chittagong hotel table so they'd fit in a landscape-format photograph, and I took their picture. The flash and the bare room's single fluorescent light gave the picture a faded look, like the photographs in the archive. I'd been calling this 'research' for weeks, but it was really an emotional solution. I needed to stop these things from becoming as ephemeral as they really were and had been fifty years ago, when the tree that the plums in the photograph had come from was planted by my mother in the bare red dirt at the front of our new house on the hill above the Karnaphuli River.

The resulting photograph was a peculiar kind of still-life. Equally peculiar was a portrait-format photograph of a narrow doorway obscured by a grubby rayon curtain, with the sign 'Room No.1' above it, which I'd taken earlier in the day. Room No.1 had been Dave's and my bedroom, and our mother had planted the plum tree outside it.

Though not as neat as the Bangladeshi genius for organising objects would have made it, my clumsy still-life was a small homage to that frugal genius and the hope it kept transmitting to me while I was there – hope that I might understand more than I deserved, and that I might lay the petulant, unhappy, introspective ghost of myself at age ten.

The door's curtain was drawn out of modesty. It was both somebody's bedroom and decrepit. It was also – I would subsequently find out – the site of a labour union scam. The union was standing over the mill's management, and obliging it to over-staff and accommodate non-working families in company houses. Notwithstanding its rich secret life, including its time as the bedroom door Dave and I had closed obediently in order to make our nocturnal exit by the window, the door was another clue. Its sign's odd precision (there was, after all, only one other door, which had been our parents' bedroom door) shows how that cultural habit of systematic neatness can also generate loony bureaucratic pedantry, with proliferating signatures, stamps, baksheesh and fee-skimming. Its appearance of bureaucratic probity may conceal a scam. It can be at once frugal and the generator of surreally organised chaos. It was this that had both delighted and enraged my father many years ago. At *Ekushey* lunch back in Dhaka, Mr Qureshi had hinted politely that Chick had hospital-passed his crusade against Chittagong dockside ticket-clipping to the young Qureshi, who'd then, at some peril, had to confront 'miscreants', including local politicians and gangsters.

The still-life objects on the table in the Chittagong hotel room included four plums from the fifty-year-old tree. After photographing them, I ate them, one by one, and flicked the stones out the window into a small garden next to the hotel. Perhaps they'd germinate there. They'd been collected by M.D. Humayunkabir Huron, who cooked at a Thai restaurant in Chittagong and night-portered the desk at my hotel. He'd agreed to come as an interpreter on my trip from Chittagong to Chandraghona (we had to drive in his nephew's car as the river was now too silted for boats), and when we got back to the hotel in the early hours of the following morning he gave me the plums, washed and wrapped in a tissue (of course).

The other objects included a carefully unenthusiastic 'Permission of Visit' letter in English from Kazi Manower Hossain, the Deputy Chief of Personnel (R&T) 'For Chief of Personnel', Bangladesh Chemical Industries Corporation. Though the head office in Dhaka would have struggled to find a lower order of management willing to risk committing this unconvincing 'permission' to paper under the corporation's letterhead, I knew the lengths that my ally, Mr Qureshi, had had to go to in order to obtain it. I knew he'd been rebuffed humiliatingly several times, but had finally got the corporation's Secretary to fix it. I didn't ask what kind of debt he might have incurred; he wouldn't have told me, anyway. The letter arrived dramatically in a taxi the night before I was to get the early-morning train to Chittagong. Mr Qureshi rang me at the guest house around midnight to make sure it had reached me.

'Give my regards to the desk,' he said dryly over the phone, referring to the photograph of him and my father in the room of heavy teak desks where they worked; my father's was inlaid with a large brass KPM plaque. He clearly didn't rate my chances of meeting the person who now sat behind it.

The letter was cautiously cc'd to Managing Director, Karnaphuli Paper Mills Ltd., Chandraghona, Rangamati. It allowed me to present myself for permission to enter the mill site for one day only between 09-2-04 and 24-2-05.

Huron's teenage nephew drove at breakneck speed along the truck-clogged road from Chittagong to Chandraghona – the road hadn't been there when we lived up the river in the 1950s. From time to time, when I could get my eyes off the road and the Bangla pop-music-blaring buses that tore towards us, I caught glimpses of the river. I began to enter a strange time warp. I recognised the red-flowered trees everywhere – 'cotton trees', said Huron; a bazaar street of colourful cushions; the narrow side road to Chandraghona paved with reddish, brick-chip cement, another colour from my childhood.

Supported by Huron's voluble spiels, the letter was good enough to get us past one army and two police checkpoints; the police looked at me sceptically and asked to see my camera. We arrived at the mill. Beyond the high, crumbling walls, topped by razor wire and eaten into by ancient tree roots, I could see the familiar and not-familiar vista of rusted and collapsing industrial rooftops, the remains of the original Alvar Aalto 'Finnish father of modernism' buildings. My grown-up eyes could see it for what it was, the literal, almost banal wreck of the 1950s dream of modernity that had also commissioned the Louis Khan parliament buildings at Sher-e-Bangla Nagar in Dhaka, but at the same time a strange, anachronistic orienteering was taking place in my mind.

The river was over to my right, somewhere; the mill in front; there was a road that skirted the crumbling perimeter wall and descended into a shallow valley. I knew we had to drive along there, and that we would find some hills rising between us and the river. Halfway up one of these hills would be a large, isolated tree with a steep road going under it to the summit. That was where I had to go: the 'penthouse-like' window ledge was there.

Somewhere around the bottom of the hill there would be some two-storey, semi-detached houses; we used to live in one of them when we first arrived, when we were confined to the house during the 'troubles'. Also at the bottom of the hill would be Robert and Magdalena Lübker's house with the schoolroom. The brown river with its slow bamboo rafts would be flowing between the hills which, on the far side, rose towards the Hill Tracts.

The letter wrangled by Mr Qureshi got the plausible Huron through the heavily guarded gate of the mill for long enough to ring the general manager and make it face-savingly impossible for him to turn us away – though, needless to say, he hadn't seen a copy of the letter. But Mir Muzaffar Ali was a very nice man; and even nicer once he'd come to the conclusion that I wasn't a journalist but a sentimental traveller. We had tea and biscuits, and I showed him the album of my father's photographs that I'd brought with me. He knew of Mr Qureshi, not just because of his long career with successive incarnations of the old Pakistan Development Corporation, but on account of his articles on popular music and film. Remembering Mr Qureshi's droll 'Give my regards to the desk', I noticed that it was still there, in the room where I was having tea with Mr Ali – I seemed to have stepped into the photograph of my father with his trainee team.

The third object on the table in my Chittagong hotel room was a multi-stamped and -signed permission in Bangla which Huron had procured under duress from an official of Rangamati *upazila* in Chandraghona. For Tk100, this impressive piece of paper did give me permission to be there from the inside, as it were. It at least gave us permission to have lunch at the KPM guest house on the hilltop where our old house was crumbling away, since the manager of the guest house, who turned out to be a functionary of the labour union, would not serve it until he knew we were allowed to be there and were not journalists sniffing after the housing scam which had transformed Dave's and my old bedroom into Room No.1.

The fourth item was a receipt for the lunch, signed by the union guy running the guest house. There were three people having lunch: me, Huron and Jahangir Alam, the General Manager of Administration and Personnel at the mill. We had a curry potato and dhal soup, curried river fish (presumably from upriver of the mill's toxic discharge), curried goat, mixed vegetable *bhaji*, and sweet *mushti dhoy* with chai to finish.

Mr Alam was great company. He'd escorted me around the mill and introduced me to the chief chemist, Dr Kshudiram Bhowmick, who showed me the R&D lab of ancient pipettes and wooden benches. When I asked him, he cheerfully agreed that the mill still used chlorine gas in its processes; Mr Alam gave me a sharp look, but then agreed somewhat hesitantly to take me to the archives, where I saw the energetic ghost of my father walking pugnaciously forward with the crowd of young men. It was Mr Alam who passed me tissues there; he in turn had been handed them to give me by the woman chemist whose idea it was to get out the huge old photo albums in the archive; she'd smacked them to make the silverfish run from the pages. In the album I also saw Dave and me at a crowded public event commemorating something – there were gymnasts and contortionists, and I remembered the marquee where the cook had been preparing the enormous *pilau* I've spent my life trying to repeat. In the photograph, my plump face is bisected by owlish glasses; I have my mouth sullenly clamped shut on the German teeth braces.

After *namaz* prayers were finished, Huron, his nephew and I, with Mr Alam riding shotgun, drove up a completely familiar (but much smaller) road around a hairpin bend that was like a comforting fold in my mind, but now overgrown with immense, unfamiliar trees, and arrived on a hilltop with our old house straight ahead. The mill's general manager Hans Meyer had once stepped out into the road with an upraised hand to stop my father speeding around the hairpin in one of the company's clapped-out jeeps – 'Too fast, Mr

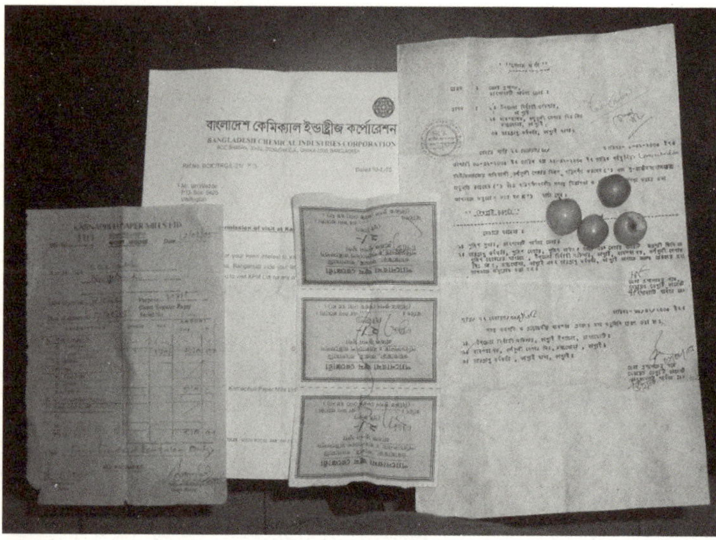
বাংলাদেশ কেমিক্যাল ইন্ডাস্ট্রীজ কর্পোরেশন
BANGLADESH CHEMICAL INDUSTRIES CORPORATION

Wedde!' Dave and I had been whooping with excitement, but we shut up as Chick, red-faced, and cursing under his breath, attempted a hill start with no handbrake while Meyer looked on. The trees my mother had planted were grown up and huge – some of the ones I walked through may even have replaced hers. But I remembered the out-of-control bougainvillea, the mynah birds and crows that were busy underneath the trees; and the plum tree I knew at once was Linda's.

Mr Alam was boarding in our old house, in the room once occupied by my parents, and he went back to his family in Chittagong each Thursday night, returning to work on Sunday. He was moved by my fifty-nine-year-old's retro-pilgrimage, and at the same time nervous, I realised later, of the house's present secret. I saw him being harangued by the mill's union rep outside the general manager's offices, but he was making the man laugh and everybody greeted him affectionately as we did the rounds of the mill's crumbling buildings. I imagine he was telling the union guy that I was a harmless sentimentalist who wanted to shed tears over his long-ago childhood.

He introduced me to some very old men who had known, or who claimed to remember, my father. My father was an energetic man who liked to talk to people. He walked fast. He was a kind man. He looked hard at people and scared them. He had two little boys, white-haired ones – they ran around all over the place like little goats, with no shirts on.

And since we were now completely legal as a result of the impressive *upazila* permission, Mr Alam and I obtained the fifth item, which was four Tk2 tickets to the Boroi Chari picnic tea garden between Chandraghona and the Kaptai dam. Here, listening to Bengali pop songs blasting out over the coloured plastic chairs and tables, we drank sweet tea, nibbled on even sweeter *andosha*, and then went out on the river in the same kind of beautifully curved double-ender sampan with a creaking scull-oar at the stern that had plied the huge brown river of my childhood.

'This is your Karnaphuli,' said Huron, and took a photo of me in the bow of the boat, with Mr Alam's jug ear sticking in from the left. I have a look on my face halfway between sooky and bewildered, as if I'd like to ask Huron to pass the tissues again but can't quite work out why, specifically, this time, I feel the way I do.

We went for a walk in the tea plantation across the river. Looking back, I could see the mill's smoke rising into a humid sunset. We were going to give Mr Alam a lift back to his family in Chittagong, and I knew he was keen to go. But he didn't rush me. He, Huron and Huron's nephew stood on the river bank by the waiting sampan; I dithered for a while among the tea bushes. A bird was singing in the big shade trees above the plantation. It was a bulbul – I remembered its name partly because of a song Chick used to sing in Chandraghona when we were kids, one he'd learned in the Army: 'Abdul Abulbul Amir'.

> The sons of the Prophet are brave men and bold
> And quite unaccustomed to fear.
> But the bravest by far in the ranks of the Shah
> Was Abdul Abulbul Amir.

I was moved as much by my companions' courteous sympathy and patience as by the photograph that had given me such a shock in the ruined paper mill's archive – my father, his bent smile and intense gaze, always going somewhere else.

The blanket

In the course of talking to Mr Alam and his boss Muzaffar Ali, I'd found out that another of my father's team from the 1950s was still alive – Mr K.R. Qurim. Mr Qureshi had talked about him back in Dhaka, but he'd lost touch and hadn't seen him for years. The enterprising Huron spent half an hour on the phone at the guest house where we had lunch, and tracked Mr Qurim down. We drove at high speed past swerving headlights and through crescendos of passing horns, and arrived back at Chittagong around ten at night.

We dropped Mr Alam off at his family home, and then went in search of Mr Qurim's address. His house was in an old part of Chittagong, in a maze of narrow streets on a low hillside. It was by now the hour before midnight, and the street was busy and crowded with roadside food stalls. Most of them seemed to be playing competing music through tinny speakers. Huron went to check we'd found the right place, and then came back to get me.

We took our shoes off at the street door, which opened directly into a small reception room. Mr Qurim was here to greet us – a short, bespectacled, beaming *haji* with the white, moustache-less beard. We shook hands formally, and then he uttered a cry halfway between a laugh and a sob, and clutched me in a close embrace.

'Mr Wedde!'

I wasn't sure if he was embracing me or my father.

Then we sat side by side on a sofa and began to talk. There were religious texts in frames on the wall, some wooden folk-art birds, embroidered flower arrangements and some photographs of Mr Qurim's family. He lived alone, with a maid to clean and cook for him. His wife had died long ago, and his children were in America and Kuwait. One daughter was a doctor, the other a businesswoman. One of his sons was also in business, the other taught in a university.

Unprompted, Huron went out to the car and returned with the album of my father's photographs. We looked at them – Mr Qurim remembered all the people by name. He asked cautiously about his old friend Mr Qureshi, who'd become important and influential before retiring; I got the impression this had required some political skills which Mr Qurim treated with silent deference and a show of ordering tea.

Looking at the photographs of the mill in its glory days, he began to circle an idea. Wasn't I now about the age my father had been when he worked at the mill? No, I said – he'd have been forty-eight when we arrived there; I was now fifty-nine. Ah, said Mr Qurim, but even so he would have been old enough to be the father of the young men he taught. Qureshi, myself and the others! And so he was – he was like a father to us!

We were drinking tea and eating biscuits. Mr Qurim suddenly put his cup down with a clatter and seized my hand.

'When did he die, your father? Excuse me for asking?'

'About twenty years ago.'

'And your mother? With the smile?'

'A few years later.'

'And they remained happy together?'

I told Mr Qurim the story of Chick making lunch three times in a row because, having taken Linda's and my sandwich plates from the garden back to the kitchen to wash up, he forgot that he'd just made lunch and did it all over again.

'That was his record – three times.'

'Of course you and your mother ate it all.'

'Yes we did. And my mother thanked him and gave him a kiss each time.'

'And this happened often?'

'Only once that I know of. But I think his mind was beginning to get tired.'

'He had a very excellent mind, your father. Exceptional. Make no mistake!' Mr Qurim gripped my hand. 'You know, Qureshi and I are fundamentalists. Because of your father.'

I must have looked startled, because Mr Qurim went to great lengths to explain his joke. He lamented the takeover of religious *madrasa* schools by 'fanatics'; he complained about the activities of armed Bangla Bhai Islamic militants and, in the same breath, the violence of Bangladesh's various communist cadres – the PBSP, the CPEB 'Red Flag'; he poured scorn on the corrupt ruling Bangladesh National Party.

I had the eerie feeling that Mr Qurim was talking to my dead father through me. It was as though he was giving my father an account of himself. I was in a fog of anachronistic patronage and paternalism, lit by flashes of Mr Qurim's courtesy. Another tray of tea arrived, and Mr Qurim dismissed his weary maid – it was by now about two in the morning. Huron was struggling to stay awake. The racket of traffic and music in the street outside had died down. I guessed Huron's nephew would be asleep in the back of the car.

'A fundamentalist,' explained Mr Qurim, 'believes in the fundaments. Truth, kindness, honesty. This is not simple.'

I was beginning to get it. Mr Qurim was apologising to me for aspects of life in Bangladesh that he knew my father would have disliked. Rather than agree with him (or my father), I told him how much I admired the social patterning and order

I saw around me; I quoted Rubana Huq's exhortation, 'We must clean the path.'

'This is exactly what your father would have said!' exclaimed Mr Qurim with delight.

There was no escape – I'd become my father, only ten years older. The man who was projecting himself as my son was nearly twenty years older than me. It was time to leave.

Outside on the road, the old man held on to my hand. 'I won't let you go!'

We embraced. I promised to send a copy of the photograph of us that Huron had taken in the small, plain room with its pictures of Mr Qurim's prosperous, modern children and the *hajj* texts that commemorated his two pilgrimages to Mecca. In the photograph, Mr Qurim is beaming and wide awake; I look knackered, and I seem to be suppressing a phantom twist in my smile.

Mr Qurim was wiping his eyes with one of those pink, rose-scented tissues. 'Your father was my guru,' he said as I got into the car. It was one of his twinkly jokes, but he also meant it.

Back in my hotel room, my eyelids sandpapery with tiredness and road dust, I set up my small shrine of objects: the plums Huron had handed me when we parted, the Tk100 *upazila* document, lunch receipt and picnic-garden tickets. Then I had a good cry. Earlier, in the mill's archive, where herds of silverfish had fled from the huge album's pages, I'd photographed the image of my father advancing purposefully with the crowd of eager young men. I brought it up on the screen of my camera. There he was, my father, transformed into a cloudy spectre by the camera's flash. The lovely old man I'd just visited was about the age my father had been when he died. Mr Qurim was almost old enough to be my father; yet he'd addressed that impatient fundamentalist, my father, through me, his fifty-nine-year-old son.

I took my shrine photograph and then ate the plums. I envied Mr Qurim and Mr Qureshi their time with my father, whom they wouldn't have known as Chick; but I didn't envy them his pep-talks on 'fundaments' or 'essentials'. I'd spent much of my life trying to find ways to complicate those, or move past the stubborn non-negotiables that Chick would get peeved about, some of which sheeted back to his subaltern relish for what he called 'rounded vowels', low-level residual patronising racism, and his shoulder-chip about education and betterment. I'd spent even more of my life trying to cultivate the irresponsible, contingent, illicit likings of my imagination – partly to rebel, but also to find a way of being at home in myself and in the places where I was living.

I'd also spent quite a bit of my childhood trying to understand why, in contrast to Mr Qurim's affectionate memory of Mr Wedde, Chick at some fundamental level hadn't wanted to be a father at all. Recently, I found among his papers a yellowed, water-stained, handwritten 'Address of Farewell to Mr. F.A. Wedde, B.Com., F.R.A. (NZ), F.C.I.S., Chief Accountant, K.P.M. Ltd., Chandraghona', dated 'Feby 17, 1958'. This must relate to the farewell lunch I remember, of which some black-and-white photographs survive. Two-thirds of the way through the beautiful calligraphy of the presentation address, I read the following careful sentences: 'We have seen you occasionally working late hours in the Office at the cost of your family attachment. This had apparently been possible due to Mrs. Wedde whose inspiration towards your endeavour can not be ignored and we offer our note of felicitations to her.'

Love that is compromised by conditions has to find a way to be unconditional, and I'd got there with my father many years before returning to Bangladesh – many years before his death, for that matter. Now I remember his blue eyes which, after he'd had a few drinks, my mother used to call 'pee-holes in the snow'; they often watered when he looked at Lindy. I remember his snail's-pace, mostly inaccurate family stories; his gentle groans when I massaged his sore back in the months before he died. But it was meeting Mr Qurim and seeing my father's camera-flashed ghost in the Karnaphuli paper mill's archive that gave me the measure of the gap between sensing that Chick didn't really want to be a father and loving him anyway.

In some way, I was measuring this gap in my mind the following morning on the way to Bandarban in the Hill Tracts, or puzzling over the way a sense of grief or loss had suddenly transformed into relief about the time I'd photographed the little assemblage of objects in my Chittagong hotel room. After taking the photograph, I'd slept soundly for a couple of hours, and then had woken up feeling blissfully happy, with the pi-dogs yipping in the street outside, and echoes of the dawn *muezzin* calling to prayer across the city.

In Dhaka, I'd organised a lift to Bandarban through an agent called Hasan Mansur, who ran tours to the coastal Sundarban mangrove forests, 'domain of the legendary Royal Bengal Tiger'; his son and daughter had a television and film facilities business for wildlife projects. For the equivalent of $US42 I had a permit to enter the Hill Tracts, a lift there and back to Chittagong, and three nights in a bamboo house above the Sangu River. Hasan ran his business from an office on the first floor of the bazaar at the traffic island near my guest house; I made the arrangements there during the *hartal* of 14 and 15 February as enforcers on scooters and in rickshaws emblazoned with slogans circulated through the mostly empty streets, shouting through loud-hailers. Hasan was unperturbed – he made it clear he had his fix in. Besides, he said, as a journalist, wasn't I looking for a good story? His own brother had been abducted by tribespeople in the Hill Tracts.

'Cost a lot of money to get him back. Grade A1 experience for a journalist – give you a real story!'

I got the impression his brother had been in unwise proximity to certain commercial activities in the region. The newspapers had been full of the ongoing skirmishes in the hills – a 'tribal man', Ongthoyaiching Marma, had been arrested in Bandarban on 13 February with two AK-47 rifles and 150 rounds – he was selling the weapons to a Chittagong middleman, Nurul Islam, whose clients weren't specified. There were reports filtering out from Bandarban that the Mru were organising armed resistance to the construction of an eco-park on 5,500 acres of Mru communal land. A Mru rally had been held at Empu Para, thirty-six kilometres from Bandarban. They were protesting the likely eviction of 700 Mru families if the Bangladesh government implemented plans to build the park in Sadar, Roangchhari, Ruma and Lama *upazilas.*

Of course, this was the story I should have been looking for, not the one about the late-middle-aged man who'd woken up feeling absurdly happy, had said goodbye to Mohammed Humayunkabir Huron over a cup of tea, and driven off across the river towards a childhood memory of woodsmoke-hazed sunset and lanky Mowgli-men playing bamboo pan-pipes.

In the jeep that constituted my lift were two aid workers from Dhaka, Lucy Jenks and Janet Raynor; they'd driven overnight from Dhaka, and were tired and fed up, not least when my 'permit' from Hasan Mansur turned out to be worthless. The command post at the Hill Tracts crossing was formidable: there was a fortified lookout with a flag up on the hill, sandbagged gun emplacements by the road, a concrete pillbox, and a heavy metal beam across the road. My worthless piece of paper went up the hill with my passport, and came back down again accompanied by the day's list of authorisations. I wasn't on it. Lucy and Janet had the stiff-necked deportment of people close to making a radical suggestion. But, in the euphoria of the previous day at the mill, my mood was invincible. The name on my piece of paper was the same as the one in my passport – and see? The signature there is the same as the one I've just entered on the authorisation sheet. And Tk100 for your patience. The lieutenant who'd walked down the hill with the authorisation sheet gave me a look between amused and indignant. Then he went away again with my passport.

When he came back, he gave me the passport and a receipt in Bangla with numerous stamps. Mr Mansur's driver translated what he said. As I left the country, I was to give this document to the passport control. If I didn't, I would be arrested. If I'd done anything I wasn't supposed to, I'd also be arrested when they received the piece of paper. The driver kept a straight face. And thank you, they will buy some cold Coca-Cola with the money.

I didn't bother trying to unravel the logic of the multi-stamped piece of paper. Some days later, when I did hand it to the official at passport control, he threw it in the bin without looking. That didn't surprise me. It had done its work. It was just another talismanic object, like the *upazila* permission of the day before which had allowed Huron, Mr Alam and me to be where we already were, have lunch and then go out on the river of my childhood; and like the 'Permission of Visit' letter in English from Kazi Manower Hossain, the Deputy Chief of Personnel (R&T) 'For Chief of Personnel', Bangladesh Chemical Industries Corporation, which had allowed me to meet the ghost of my father face to face in a place I was forbidden to enter, while the mill's staff were at *namaz* and the broken-down perimeter fence was unguarded.

Despite my euphoria, many of the photographs I'd taken of the mill are hellish. Almost obscured by stinking smoke, the old wreck looms behind huge rotting stacks of sap-wood timber; yellow chlorine-gas drums spill from a broken brick warehouse; turgid scum swirls downstream from the mill's pulping discharge. I'd taken the pictures while Mr Alam wasn't looking – or else with him in them, smiling dutifully, and with something harmless in the background. These images were on a memory chip I'd removed from my camera in the guest-house washroom, replacing it with another on which I then photographed the tea garden, river, bamboo rafts, Mr Qurim, and my hotel-room still-life. Soon to join these were picturesque images of my little creaking bamboo house above the Sangu River, my bamboo-slat bed with its mosquito net, misty views of the forested hills across the river, and photogenic canoes stacked with produce arriving for the market at Bandarban.

To the hellish chip I added images of military watch-towers on hilltops, the military cellphone-jamming installation, and a Danish teak reforestation project in the Manza Reserve which appeared to have a significant military presence associated with it. Military convoys ground up and down the hill. Army helicopters clattered overhead a couple of times a day. There was a deforested saddle up the road from where I was staying where the cellphone jammer didn't work; there was a sign saying this was an authorised telephoning site, and a steady stream of motorbikes went up there from the village below, watched by a command post on a hill.

Janet Raynor told me that when she worked in Chittagong they used to hear the covered freight trains grinding out of the city marshalling yards at night under army escort with loads of illegally felled teak. NDFB (National Democratic Front of Bodoland) cadres were reported to be active in Bhutan, resisting Indian security forces in the north-east, and they were said to have links with tribal cadres on the Bangladesh side. An Ericsson engineer had been kidnapped near Bandarban the week before. The cadres' common foe on both sides of the India–Bangladesh border was Bengali settlers operating under the protection of government forces, both Indian and Bangladeshi.

One day, I went for a tramp with a Mru guide called Raoul, whose village abutted the Manza Reserve. We walked through a desolate landscape of cut-over scrub above the Sangu; there were no animals – Raoul said they'd all been eaten long ago, even the monkeys; the snakes, too, he said, but I think he was pulling my leg. Besides, there was nowhere for them to live.

And the forest? Wasn't it being replanted? In answer, Raoul pointed to burn-off smoke rising from hillsides downriver. We hired a canoe to take us down to the landing at Bandarban; on the way we passed the burn-off hillsides. These were Bengali settlers, not slash-and-burn tribal people. They'd rigged loudspeakers by the burn-off and were blasting Bangla pop songs across the river. Even by Bangladeshi standards, the volume was aggressive. The implication was clear: despite the occasional plantation project such as the Danish one up the hill, much of the former giant bamboo and teak forest was being left fallow for Bengali settlement. There was a large military cantonment in Bandarban; the tension between Bengali and tribal people in the town was low key but obvious. In the street outside the walled *madrasa*, an elderly *mullah* was walking along accompanied by a young man carrying an AK47.

Back in Dhaka, talking to Mr Qureshi about this, I encountered a standard strain of Bengali prejudice: the tribal people were primitive; Bengali settlement since the War of Liberation in 1971 was part of an inevitable programme of rural expansion and patriotic reward. Mr Qureshi was one of the most urbane and civilised men I'd ever met, but his discreet racism no longer surprised me. Like his old friend Mr Qurim, he mocked the 'fundamentalist' *mullahs* who were radicalising and in some cases militarising the *madrasa*. But his disapproval of my trip to the Hill Tracts was clear, if subtle – as was his impatience with armed indigenous resistance.

The disdain of Justina and Parveen back at my little Dhaka guest house was theatrical by comparison. The recycled poultry-food bag in which I'd brought back a woven blanket from the Mru village near the Manza Reserve was ordered from the room by Parveen while she held her nose with one hand and wagged a disapproving finger at me with the other.

The blanket, too, offended her. It wasn't new, but smelled of the baby who'd been wrapped in it. More offensive to Parveen than the baby's smell, however, was the object's cultural significance. Why was I buying this low-value, primitive rubbish? Why not new fabric from Aarong chain, superior quality? Beautiful saris for my wife? Beautiful *nakshi kantha*, if I want village craft? Don't I know famous poem by Jasmuddin, about *nakshi kantha*?

'At least we are washing?'

But I took the blanket to my room unwashed. It wasn't in the least dirty, just a bit faded, with one edge unravelling, and with a faint aroma of baby and wood smoke. The woollen yarn was thick and soft, the weave loose, with faded natural-dye stripes in reds, browns, greys and blues. It was large enough just to cover a double bed. I didn't want the bright new ones that were being rattled together on looms for the market in

Bandarban. I especially didn't want one of the woven Bible satchels the Baptist missionaries had got the people making. I wanted something that would reach back into the emotional place I'd been allowed to re-enter. I wanted another talisman, a passport to the happiness I'd felt when I woke up after visiting the mill and Mr Qurim. The young Mru woman whose baby was wrapped in the blanket was surprised, and so was Raoul, when I said I'd buy *that one.* But she was happy to sell it. She wanted Tk250 – about five New Zealand dollars. I gave her Tk300 and still felt like a cheat.

It was too hot to sleep under the blanket, but I kept it across the end of my guest-house bed, and on the chair when I was writing. Every day, when I came back to my room, the blanket had been banished to the cupboard where my suitcase was stored. Parveen and Justina made jokes about it – 'How was your blanket today?' 'Are you missing your blanket?'

But the blanket's magic was impervious. It was better than a memory. It was much better than the tangled narrative that had knotted up my brain and made me lurch from tears to bliss the day I went back to our old house at Chandraghona. Its supple weave and the soft symmetry of its stripes were more important than the grim images I'd collected on my furtive camera-chip – and more honest, too. What's more, it had a nice smell. The blanket told me that what I'd gone there to find had nothing to do with writing up the 'situation', camouflaging my incoherent need under practical, investigative activity, note-taking, interviewing, press-clipping, *research* . . . all I'd really wanted was the simple comfort of coming to terms with a leave-taking – a leaving-home that had happened when I was beginning to leave childhood. Later, the blanket was on our bed in the Wellington home Donna and I occasionally shared with our grown-up, transient boys. These days it's with us in Auckland and it still reads well; it's simple.

The YHA hostel guide

I have an image of my brother Dave crouching on his knees at the edge of a low table, writing with his left hand while brushing the back of his right-hand thumb to and fro across his lips. I associate this image also with a mean-spirited Youth Hostel Association warden who'd jeered at our attempts to cook dinner, and who'd also made snide comments about Dave's preferred way of writing his postcards. It's an image that mirrors the sadness I rediscovered and comforted when I visited the old mill at Chandraghona in 2005.

But of course I'm only guessing that some of the sadness might belong to Dave. When we talk about the time we spent in England as kids, he's mostly blithe, as I'd expect him to be. If he was ever sad about the life we led away from our mother and father, it can't have amounted to much, or was at best transient. Or he managed to shove it down into a deep place it couldn't get out of. Perhaps what I see when I look at the image of him writing a postcard to our mother and father is just my own sadness – which, too, was intermittent and, towards the end of our years in England, largely over and done with. But still, the image remains potent because of its sadness; and I can't believe that some of that wasn't Dave's, though his equanimity overrode it in the end.

I guess that at some level my Bandarban blanket was an atavistic sign of comfort. Comfort was what I took from it as an adult, even as that made me grin; but it also tapped back into the place where powerful, transitional, ambiguous memories reside. The one that first rose up in the presence of the blanket was of Dave in the unfriendly youth hostel, which I think may have been at Bellever in the middle of Dartmoor, a conveniently bleak place for melancholy to gather, like the damp mist we'd ridden our bikes through to get there – melancholy not least because it was chilly and off-season, and we were the only ones to emerge from the mist and ask for a place to stay.

But before I run with this compelling memory – before I take the sentimental bait it offers – I have to ask myself Parveen's and Justina's merrily sceptical question, 'How was your blanket today?', because the pleasure I got from it was as much about acquisition as comfort. What I acquired when I bought the blanket from the Mru woman with the small, astonished baby wasn't just a way to resolve my confused sadness; I also acquired an object I thought was beautiful, which I wanted to *have*; and which I got. And how to measure the gap, or the overlap, between desire and absence is never easy. Nor is it easy now to do so in respect of the poignant image I have of my 'cack-handed' brother in the common room of the chilly hostel, writing his postcard home (only it wasn't), as the YHA guy passed with a sneer and Dave went ahead with an activity that had its own pleasure – a chance to show off, perhaps: 'Look where we are!' – while simulataneously comforting himself with the involuntary gesture that was only a short distance from sucking his thumb.

Whatever it was he felt then, it's still clear to me that I felt defensive on his behalf, intimidated and humiliated by the YHA prick in the Boy Scoutish outfit – and, not too far under the surface of my own triumph at our adventure, uneasy with the thought that this was also a good way for our school-holiday minders to get shot of us for a week or two.

But this is how it was. The situation we were in, where we saw our parents at most every couple of years, and lived in the provisional homes of boarding school and school-holiday guardians – a couple called Reg and Peggy Markwell – was both desirable and lacking. As Dave reminds me when I get maudlin about our situation, Reg and Peggy took on 'a couple of "different", even misfit kids belonging to people they barely knew', and gave them a home where he at least felt welcome and cared for. It delivered freedoms and adventures, and a kind of inverse *Swiss Family Robinson* narrative: Look, we could boast to our parents, how well we're doing on our castaway island! But such satisfactions, and even the fun of riding around unsupervised from hostel to hostel, carried with them, like the shadows of us pedalling along, the implication of homelessness; sadness; loneliness; the absence of a place that amounted to more than a bed, food, shoe repairs.

'How was your blanket today?'

It was fine, thank you. I got what I wanted.

As the gap closed between the satisfaction of desire (the pleasure of acquisition) and the lack or longing to which it was attached like a shadow, 'home' did just come to mean the place of bed, food and shoe repairs. So that, at a certain point, inferring sadness from my brother's attitude as he wrote his postcard 'home' – or from any similar tableau – became pointless. Or, worse, morbid.

But the image of my brother writing his postcard won't submit to this reasonable discipline. I still feel for him, and don't believe it's only self-pity I'm feeling. As if setting off on one of our bike rides, I need to take the map of this image – the YHA hostel guide, as it were – and follow our route through the years after we left the kind of home you have when you're a child in a family, in a family home, whatever that might consist of. Which, in our case, wasn't what we had.

But there's another image to consider. Next to mine of Dave crouched writing his postcard at the YHA table on Dartmoor, I need to locate one that my brother, with gentle, smiling mockery, came up with when we were talking about our 'homeless' time in England. This image may be the parallel or companion of mine – Dave's version of what I saw when I saw him writing, and imputed his gesture to homelessness. He remembers an occasion when Reg and Peggy Markwell collected us from the junior boarding school we'd recently been enrolled in, and took us for a picnic on a high, chalky, rabbit-warrened range of hills near Yeovil in Somerset. The hills overlooked the farmlands where our school, called Hazelgrove, was situated close to the little village of Sparkford. Sparkford had a thatched inn with low ceilings and creaky wooden floors; we'd stayed there with Linda and Chick when they were checking out the school. There were large stands of old oaks, fields, rustic brick farm buildings, and sunken lanes flanked by thickets of hazelnut. It was at once picturesque and homely.

Hazelgrove was the junior preparatory cousin of a public school called Kings School Bruton, where we went when we turned thirteen. The junior school was in a fine eighteenth-century manor house surrounded by formal gardens, parklands and sports fields, with various out-buildings. The combination of manor house, forelock-tugging rustic hamlet, thatched inns and stands of oak was clearly beguiling; in addition, the school made some big academic promises. It greatly impressed our father, in particular: his impossible dream of betterment, superior education, meritocratic social mobility and Masefieldian hearts-of-oakism, was about to come true. I have no doubt that both he and Linda were convinced they couldn't possibly do better for their boys – they were vindicating all the hopes they'd fled Blenheim with;

they were paying off four years hard up the Karnaphuli River; they were investing in a family future that could only improve; they were showing the family sceptics back home what could be done if you put your mind to it; they were repeating a multi-stranded family history of leaving one home in search of a better or more interesting one.

But what Dave remembers, with affectionate derision, is his twin brother standing on the windswept crest of the hill overlooking the plain, with Hazelgrove emitting homelessness signals in the far distance. With a plaintive quaver in my voice, I said, 'That's where mothers and fathers send the children they don't love.'

Perhaps it's just as well I don't remember this – I would have to add it to the lamentable catalogue of performances that began with the ankle-dragging tantrum at Chandraghona. What's interesting about it now, viewed through the amiable lens of Dave's grin, is that he doesn't for a moment see my gesture as in any way mirroring his own feelings. He doesn't now; and he's clear that he didn't then. He remembers Reg Markwell, who had a scoffing sense of humour, enjoying the tragi-comic moment. But he doesn't remember sharing my sense of abandonment. In fact, he's even doubtful I felt that way at all. I think my melodramatic credentials were already well established; I'd cried wolf too often; no one took these demonstrations seriously.

This complicates the YHA hostel guide. There's a stretch between me seeing a mutual sadness in Dave writing his postcard and Dave not entirely believing my sadness on the hill overlooking Sparkford. I think he probably was sad on Dartmoor; he doesn't think he was. I think I was sad on his behalf on Dartmoor, as well as on my own behalf on the hill above the place for unloved children; but he doesn't entirely believe me, because he wasn't.

It's that pulling-together by pulling-apart thing again. What this elastic conundrum describes is Dave's and my double act – left handed, right handed; sons, daughters. Apparently, he does happy and I do sad. In reality, we are something like a unity. It's my knowledge of my brother that makes me whole: it's as though I don't always have to be happy because I know he's more likely to be; as though I'm confident I have a happy counterpart, at once part of me and not part of me. It's our knowledge of each other that makes us individuals. I have my own happiness, plenty of it, and have had it for most of my adult life; but I also have a larger concept of happiness, which I owe to my brother – a happiness that extends beyond what I feel in myself.

There it is: the big fish on its manuka stick, the prize that makes us pull away from each other; the trophy that pulls us together. And here it is again, the YHA guide to our journey through childhood homelessness, the map and narrative that we diverge from, that draws us together.

The Christmas card

We left Chittagong on 28 February 1958. I don't remember very much about it, but Mr Qureshi wrote me a letter in January 2005, after I'd made contact through Lina Chowdhury, in which he recalled seeing the Wedde family off from Chittagong Port Jetty, where he'd been waging my father's war against ticket-clipping miscreants. We were going on board a small Bay of Bengal coaster, the RMS (Royal Mail Steamship) *Aronda*; her destination was Colombo in what was then called Ceylon.

What Mr Qureshi also told me in his letter, and what caused a readjustment in my understanding of how things had proceeded from that moment of departure, was that Chick was already committed to another contract in East Pakistan – something we weren't told about at the time, nor something Dave or I remember, not me in my melodramatic way, nor he in his factual one.

This contract was at the Khulna Newsprint Mills at Khalispur, Khulna. Khulna is to the west of Chittagong, at the head of the vast network of Gangetic waterways that descend to the Sundarban delta on the Bay of Bengal, the largest mangrove forest in the world – the place to which the plausible Hasan Mansur was dispatching tourists and film crews no more likely to see a royal Bengal tiger than I had been to get to the Hill Tracts on the strength of his permit alone.

When I went to the old Chandraghona mill in 2005, the one at Khulna had been closed for years as a result of corruption and mismanagement; this was said to be depressing the publishing industry and driving down writers' royalties. Apparently, in 1958, as Qureshi would find out later, Chick was already plotting to get his goateed young offsider transferred to the Khulna mill, which was still one of the drivers of East Pakistan's modernisation project. Like the mill at Chandraghona, the Khulna mill belonged to the Pakistan Development Corporation, but was managed in a joint venture by Sandwell & Co. of Vancouver. This relationship with Sandwells was to be the launching pad for Chick's next Big Leap Forward. That didn't include keeping his and Linda's kids with them.

But back then, as we steamed out through the broad, muddy mouth of the Karnaphuli, with humid, green-brown hills shimmering in the heat, and the jumble of brick dockside buildings merging into the rattan-patterns of bamboo *bushti* along the river bank, all I knew – all Dave and I knew – was that we were going to England. Probably, Dave and I would go to school there. I don't think the likelihood of us going to boarding school was ever mentioned; nor was the option of going back to New Zealand; nor was the fact that Chick would be returning to East Pakistan. Nor, for that matter, was the obvious corollary mentioned: that our mother would be going there with Chick – would be going there without us.

Arriving at this moment in both our childhood story and my adult investigation of the meaning of home, I realise the extent to which this account has become a palimpsest. Its layers, erasures and additions begin with the simplest one, in which memory laminates the present where it acts and the past that is memory's resource. This laminate is paradoxical, ambiguous and unreliable. It may even be contradictory, as is the case with Dave's and my versions of events. The palimpsest has layers that are at once temporal and spatial: memories can exist only in the present but will always refer to the past; and this paradoxical temporality moves forward along a spatial narrative track that goes from place to place, or resides in locations that themselves change, as homes and neighbourhoods do while children grow up in them.

In addition, this account has always been randomly cumulative. It didn't proceed from a comprehensive body of research, nor from uncontested memories. Layers have been added to the palimpsest as I've gone along, much as they were in our lives as they went along. Disclosures and interventions have been either inserted into or pasted over what I'd already drafted – as was the case after I visited my cousin Norma, having already built a story around the photograph of my mother in a deerskin costume as the castaway Lady Mary Lasenby.

This accumulation itself has become a digressive, involuntary storyline. The project began in various texts before 2004, without any conscious intention to write about home. The question of home began to become purposeful after that, when I drove around New Zealand, talking to myself in a tape-recorder and wondering how to answer the question, 'Where am I?' This was overlaid by my time in Bangladesh, and by my attempts to find a viewpoint outside the compound of childhood memory. It was diverted somewhat by writing *The Viewing Platform* in 2005; but that, too, was a layer between the meanderings of 2004 and my first committed attempt to get this inquiry under way in 2009, in the opening section called 'The Grass Catcher', in which I tried out a strategy for ambushing memory.

What I've written since has been overlaid retrospectively

by conversations with my patiently amiable brother, and his responses to what I was writing or had already written. It was overlaid by time spent with my cousin Norma in Blenheim; by letters that have arrived from relatives who got wind of what I was up to. In effect, this layering, this toing-and-froing, this backtracking and pushing forward, has been going on for ten years.

And now, about halfway through a final rewrite of what I've believed is a comprehensive first draft, I open for the first time a packet my brother found among our mother's papers sometime after we'd started stirring up our collective memories. He hadn't looked closely at the contents before and, if our conversations are anything to go by, hasn't since. The items may have been returned to us when Linda died, as a gesture of sympathy and respect; or to Linda when their owners died. Who the owners were is not clear.

In the packet are a yellowing black-and-white studio photograph of our mother aged about three; her hair, which later became very dark, is blond and wavy; she's wearing a pretty white dress with lace trimmings, holding a bunch of daffodils and sitting on what might be a prop bearskin. This would have been taken in Blenheim in about 1913. In chronological order, the next item is a homemade Christmas card with a black-and-white photograph of a sampan on the Karniphuli River glued to the front. It's dated 1957, which my startled mind registers as forty-four years later – a temporal and spatial leap from the small-town photographic studio; a leap whose drama seems contrived, except that it expresses the sense I have of the bold trajectory of my mother's life once she left Blenheim, which is at once bound to and distinct from the exigencies of my father's work. This card was sent from Karnaphuli Paper Mills Ltd., Chandraghona, P.O., Chittagong, East Pakistan.

The third item is a similar Christmas card, this one with a colour photograph of Mount Kenchenjunga, taken near Darjeeling. The card is undated, but in it Linda writes that 'we leave here on "Aronda" on Feb. 28th for Colombo', so the card, which like the other one is a squared A4 sheet of heavy, now yellowed paper folded in quarters and covered densely with her tiny, neat handwriting, must have been sent before Christmas 1957, when Dave and I had just turned eleven.

The fourth item is a commercially produced Christmas card with a picture of thorn trees and roosting vultures silhouetted against a blazing 'Sunset over Luangwa', presumably sent from Zambia when Linda and Chick were there. It's addressed to 'Phyl, Ivan and family – Fondest love, Lin & Chick', unlike the cards sent from Chandraghona, which are signed off 'Lin, Albert & the Boys'. My mind lurches again – of course what my mother's trajectory now implies is the fact that 'the Boys' are not there, and haven't been since shortly after the card in which an embarkation from Chittagong to Colombo was announced. But this is hardly surprising, since by the time our parents were in Zambia both Dave and I had long since gone our own ways.

The fifth and final item in the packet is another Christmas card with a picture of lions in Zambia – but this one was sent from 47 Rarangi Rd, St Heliers, Auckland. This was where Linda's trajectory set down. In the card, she reports that Dave and Sue's first daughter, Sarah Jane, is ten months old ('the apple of Grandad's eye'); that Rose and I have bought a house in Wellington, and that Carlos ('a dear wee chap') is five. So it's 1977.

Along the track of these temporal and spatial *grands jetés* in my mother's card narrative there's a pause, for me at least, in which the trajectory stalls at an informative moment. In the card from 1957 in which the embarkation from Chittagong is announced, so is our parents' plan for us. I have never seen this before and until now had no idea that their minds were made up. The most momentous decision in their lives together since leaving Blenheim in 1954 – and perhaps in Dave's and mine too – was the one to leave us in England while they kept moving. In the card, whose addressees ('Dear All') may be the 'Phyl, Ivan and Family' mentioned in the thorn-tree-with-vultures one, Linda matter-of-factly spells out what is going to happen.

> . . . we've decided to send the boys to school in Eng. and have booked them in as day boys at Kings School (Prep.) at Sparkford, Somerset, where they will then go as boarders in Sept. We feel that at their age it is too sudden to take them from a place like this and just dump them into boarding as they can't play cricket or football & after life out here will have some awful shocks coming to them. We hope to get a house (or something) nearby so that for one term they can get used to the changed life with a home still there. During the August hols. the idea is to tour the Continent or rather 'on' it. Then I will continue to live in Eng., even tho' Chick may come East again, until after their Xmas Hols. That should see them fairly well settled. We are sending them to Eng. because we can keep them there for a year on what it would cost to just get them back to N.Z. and also because special planes run out back with school children and we hope, wherever we are that they will fly out to us at least once in 2 years for 6 to 8 weeks. . . . The world is such a wide, wide place & we've all got awful itchy feet!

Halfway through a final rewrite, feeling my way through the layers of this erratic palimpsest, ten years after starting this search for home, or for viewpoints from which to see what home might be, I feel my impulse tipping across a kind of fulcrum. The fulcrum is the Christmas card with its pretty picture of grazing cattle, weathered sheds, a valley filled with roiling cloud, and distant mountains from which a long streamer of wind-blown snow has been stopped in time and place.

Kenchenjunga - Darjeeling.

The absent-minded professor

In the palimpsest to which this late layer of the 1957 Christmas card hasn't yet been added, there's a Box Brownie photograph, taken by one or the other of us, in which an elegant Linda, wearing the familiar print frock and with a cigarette between the fingers of her right hand, is leaning on the rail of the *Aronda.* In her left hand she holds two sun-visored caps – ours. A dashing chap in whites and with a pipe clenched between his teeth is leaning on the rail near our mother. I think he was the ship's captain. In the background, a load of suitcases swings aboard in a sling. In other snaps, the ship's funnel smoke drifts across a vista of sailboats becalmed on the broad flood. The scene is languid – as though we're making a leisurely departure on a Somerset Maughamish holiday.

Neither Dave nor I retained any clear sense of the place we'd come from before the Karnaphuli paper mill, and had no idea about where we were going. From the time the old *Aronda* pushed past the clutter of sampans and overloaded, nearly-sinking barges in the turgid roadstead, we'd begun to live in the time and place of the moment. This was a transitional zone of which nothing much could be expected except surprises. There was no routine, or none that fixed time and place for long. We steamed off into a pleasant vacuum, into which rushed the fantasies that thrive on rootlessness, interfactuality, random phenomena; on shifting, unstable contexts contaminated by chance and by the language of storytelling, and sometimes by the boredom of the always-new.

This was a perfect breeding ground for delusions masquerading as plausible conditions: for what, as a grown-up, I'd call 'scenario-writing'. It was another new kind of home, different again from the one from which we'd just unsettled ourselves. It was a home fixed in transit; the world drifted past its windows; its horizon receded like an endless mirage.

I say 'we' and believe it's fair to do so. There we are, Dave and I, with our Box Brownies, in all sorts of different places (but first of all on the deck of the *Aronda*, snapping the approaching sunset). But in respect of the other force that steamed into this vacuum, I will speak only of myself. That force was sex. From the time we sailed off into a fantastic future, sex engulfed my eleven-year-old body and imagination. Like a humid monsoon deluge, like the sticky air inside my mosquito net, this incomprehensible, delicious obsession became the atmosphere I inhabited; it transformed my introversion into a furtive frenzy.

There was something non-negotiable about our parents' trajectory which, many years later, I measured with admiration. They were in transition too. Having shaken the dust of Blenheim from their feet, hardened up in the tough circumstances of the remote Karnaphuli mill, they were now moving further out, not retreating. We steamed across the Bay of Bengal (I remember that Dave was seasick; he denies it) and arrived in Colombo in time for a massive general strike. That, at least, is how it was described to us. Dave and I didn't know what a 'strike' was – it just explained the stench of rotting, uncollected food garbage around the hotel we were staying in; the humid stink-mist from the deserted kitchens;

the uncleaned lavatories and rooms; the strange, minimal snacks of biscuits and tinned Kraft cheese. I remember feeling bewildered by the extent to which we were dependent on our own resources. Now, I can measure how far we'd come from our grandmother's no-nonsense kitchen at Francis Street; how privilege had begun to nurture our presumptions of entitlement. These would soon be thrown back in my face, in an incident I now think of as 'the absent-minded professor'.

The hotel had easy access to a beach; there were changing rooms with cold-water showers nearby. This was where we hung out, away from the smell of rotting food and blocked sewers. There were waves we body-surfed on. One tore my togs off and dragged my cock through the sand – this had consequences later, also not unconnected with 'the absent-minded professor'.

We caught a taxi into the tense city of Colombo. There were army or police posts, and more piles of rubbish. I remember Chick getting out of the taxi to go to a bank. While we waited in the car, he half-ran with his characteristic urgency towards the glass front of the bank, one arm extended to push the door open. But a security guard saw him coming and opened the door, so that his momentum shot him across the bank's foyer with his arm stuck out in front. Linda laughed so much she ended up weeping and blowing her nose – perhaps Chick's Chaplinesque performance marked the beginning of a new phase of optimism in their lives.

We went inland to Kandy to get away from the smelly strike in Colombo, but also because that was what Linda and Chick always did: they *went looking.* By now, Chick had his first 35mm Leica and had begun to take the thousands of colour slides I'd inherit in two large tin trunks when he died.

4.1 To the Tin Trunk of Images

To me the Fates have given scorn for the envious.
Time's no flood, it bears nothing
Away, and only light catches it, shuttered on memory.
Let the heart rejoice in whatever it has right now.
What is this we hold up between us, my brother

And I? It's our father's satisfaction, it's food
For the table, it's a monument he never dreamed he'd see
In the Uffizi, it's his wife in a camelhair coat
By a DC3, with a camel in the Wadi
Araba and among the weathered pyramids of Dashoon.

Now it's a dhow, it's a thousand sunsets on the Nile,
On the Bay of Bengal, on the waters of Lake Constance,
And he was never satisfied with them. Far horizons, blue
And made of rocks, are what he also saw.
Sometimes he was happy with the spired horizons of cities

But which cities? And what Gods are worshipped
Beneath these turquoise domes? What was sacrificed
On these basalt altars, tumbled in black ruins
Across what valleys foraged by goats, sheep
Or llamas? What tunes have faded away?

Where are we now? No longer in
The picture, which is now a picture of my father's loneliness.
He survives in roguish snapshots taken in restaurants.
A plate of quail in Damascus. But never in the tin
Trunk of photographs, because he took them all.

But a more immediate record of Kandy is the Box Brownie one. The little black-and-white snaps show elephants being given a bath by their minders; the Temple of the Tooth;

our family in various poses against monuments, coconut palms, sunsets, or the kinds of surroundings that time makes anonymous. What time also did was file the smell of smoke and spices that then re-entered the car window eleven years later as a hallucination of the pattern on my mother's dress.

Back in Colombo in 1958, we boarded the P&O liner *Arcadia 2* to go to England. This was a state-of-the-art vessel, built in 1954. Dave and I had a cabin in which I immediately locked myself to examine my sand-scraped dick – which, despite its condition, proved irresistible. The result was pain that made me howl and refuse to unlock the door when an anxious crowd gathered outside it. Finally a peeved Cockney steward used his master key to get in; he gave me a strident telling-off and then demanded to know what the matter was. I refused to tell him. Linda arrived – I think Dave had been sent to get her. She, too, demanded to know why I was making a fuss. I could feel her concern tipping into anger, so I told her about my raw dick.

'Oh dear,' she said. 'Want me to have a look at willy?'

I didn't. And then I saw my mother's careful sympathy break apart. Her laughter came out first in a loud snort; soon she was weeping, as she had when Chick ran with his outstretched arm across the bank's foyer in Colombo.

'Sorry, darling,' she managed to gasp. 'I know it's not funny.'

So why was she laughing?

As she laughed and cried, dabbing her eyes with the edge of the bunk's sheet, I saw across her merrily shaking shoulders, framed in the cabin's narrow doorway, my twin brother's broad grin.

Nothing drives ambition as hard as humiliation, except the combination of vengeful humiliation and a sense of entitlement. I was set up for the catastrophe of 'the absent-minded professor'.

It was about the time the *Arcadia* crossed the Equator that the kids on board were marshalled by the liner's recreation staff to stage a fancy-dress competition. I got myself up as an absent-minded professor. I had total confidence in my winning concept. I ignored warning signs, the sniggers of the other kids. I remember a Tarzan I was jealous of but not threatened by. There were nurses, doctors, a policeman, and a cannibal chief with a blackened face. I saw the cannibal as a possible but remote threat. There was a ballet dancer who I didn't think counted, since the girl who'd put on a tutu and pointes was in fact a real dancer, not a made-up one; I may even have lodged a complaint about her. I don't remember what Dave went as: probably a pilot.

I was confident that my absent-minded professor concept would be strikingly original, obvious, but also hilarious. This would be my point of difference, my advantage. The laughter I anticipated would be a kind of applause, the opposite of derision; it would regain me the ground I'd lost to my mother's mirth on the night I'd locked myself in Dave's and my cabin.

One by one the kids stepped forward and paraded before the audience of dutifully proud parents and other passengers who, drinks in hand, were looking for any respite from the voyage's implacable boredom. I listened to their applause with condescending resentment – soon they'd see! The cheating ballet dancer had won the most applause so far, spinning on the toes of one foot to admiring cheers; this had added resentment to my confidence. When my turn came, I stepped forward.

Wearing my own owlish glasses, a false goatee beard, a top hat, a white lab coat, shoes and socks with a pair of my father's sock-suspenders, no trousers and an expectant grin, I paraded before an audience stunned into bewildered silence. No one got 'absent-minded professor', let alone that the absent-minded professor had forgotten to put his pants on. I might as well have been a cross between a steward and a flasher (but with a top hat). Linda and Chick were sitting at a table with bleak smiles on their faces. My own confident smile turned to ice.

'Anyone getting it? No one?' urged the on-board entertainment supervisor.

No one did.

And then the laughter built. I could still hear it after I'd retreated to the dress-up room, where the other kids took their hilarity cue from the grown-ups.

I learned then that when someone laughs at you, the best thing is to join in. That way you'll at least become complicit in your own degradation. Do it convincingly enough, and you'll persuade those laughing at you that you always meant them to: you *made them do it*. You yourself will become the best joke you could tell.

Thus began my short career as a clown: the fat kid who, panting last across the cross-country finishing line at Hazelgrove, had everybody in stitches, including the terrifying Indian sports instructor who could hit hockey balls the length of the pitch at waist height; the author of ruefully funny letters to my mother and father, as in one headed 'Same old Place, 31st May, 1958 A.D.', which ended:

> I hope you keep well, and don't catch typhoid. Good bye, lots of love,
> Yours,
> Ian

And the melodramatist who, gazing down at the distant site of his unloved-child torments, caused Reg Markwell to crack up. Of course, since I only have my brother's word for it, I can't really claim to remember Reg's mirth. But I heard the laughter often enough over the next few years to be able to guess, now, that the occasion asked for it.

Reg's nickname for me was 'Fishface'. I see Fishface often in photos of us as a family during the last weeks when we were one in the conventional sense, which is to say when mother, father and kids were together. Wearing an English prep-school cap, blazer and pants, Fishface beams while Trafalgar Square pigeons perch on his shoulders and shit down the back of his brand-new uniform. Beside him his brother also grins amid the pigeons – but, even now, I can detect the difference. Dave is just grinning unselfconsciously and flinching back from the over-eager birds. But I am performing my comic happiness straight down the lens of Chick's new Leica. Here we are on a trip around Scotland. Dave and Linda are gazing sideways at the misty vista of a loch, probably Loch Ness, but Fishface is registering the axis of his attention at ninety degrees to theirs, to camera, to my father as the keeper of records. See how happy I am? If my sadness isn't credible enough to gain sympathy, then perhaps my performance of being really happy will redeem it.

Or my performance of some other significant emotion – anything but sadness. We were in a Gothic cathedral – Ely, I think – full of fresh, pale light, on what was probably the farewell trip around England and Scotland with Chick before he went to the mill at Khulna. I was awestruck by the architecture and brilliance of the place. But the tears I managed to pump from my ducts at the sight of so much beauty were every bit as much a lie as my blurted-out wish to die the time I crawled across the polished red plaster floor at Chandraghona and climbed into my mother's lap. I was playing to the gallery of my mother and father, and making sure they had a good record of what they'd be leaving behind – what they'd see they'd left behind every time they looked at Chick's photographs of our happy family, when it was one.

What they saw was the absent-minded professor, or Fishface the clown. I became the obscure metaphor of myself. Neither my sadness nor my happiness was credible. Why should they have believed either? It was in the secret poems I was writing that the truth was being told.

But the 'poems' – my feverish, trouserless cryptograms – were not what I was posting to my mother and father. What they received were letters whose cheerful, newsy fortitude had been scrutinised and sometimes censored by the staff at Hazelgrove. It didn't occur to me back then that being asked to rewrite my weekly letter was wrong; the teacher who made a reproving note in the margin of my letter simply became its core audience. I wrote for him, and hoped to be rewarded with a chuckle.

The rooks' nests

My plan for this book has involved returning in memory and person to places where I've been, in one way or another, at home. And so now another physical return is necessary.

Montacute Park

Affective, affective. Also
my reactions to the place
were pre-shrunk. The cottage
had grown smaller, the great elms
spaced out like spokes across
the park were stuffed with ugly
clots of dead twigs. The rooks
had done that. Their dark
trajectories drew the eye back
& back to the trees they had ruined,
where they still lived. Their caws
tore the chill fabric of the air.
My feelings were cramped into a child's
perspectives. I could have run
without effort the return distance
to the cottage: man's legs, man's lungs.
But I wanted to arrive breathless,
the dark at my back, & be warmed.
Down the park a dog turned, poised,
its owner hurled a stick, the rooks
crashed upward into dusk, I

walked off with the long strides
of a seasoned tourist. Behind me
the cantankerous birds settled back
among their families, the man
whistled his exuberant dog to heel.

I wrote this sometime in 1970. Rose and I had left Jordan in June, after the first phase of the civil war that would culminate in Black September, when King Hussein ordered his hard-liner Prime Minister Wasfi al-Tal to call up the Jordanian Army's tank brigade to crush the Palestinian militias. We drove from Beirut to London in the old Commer van I'd bought in Amman. It was against the confused background of what I'd seen of the Palestinian diaspora during 1969 and 1970 that I returned to the place in England where, as a child a decade earlier, I'd believed for a time in my own exile. Though I wouldn't have called it 'exile' back then, I might, had I known the word, have been drawn melodramatically to the Palestinian *al-Nakba*, the Catastrophe.

Nor, in 1970, could I use words like 'exile' or 'diaspora', let alone *al-Nakba*, to describe my uneasy memories of misery in England between 1958 and 1962. It was with chagrin that I measured the combination of suffering and dauntlessness I'd seen in the Palestinian refugee camps against the paltry memories stirred up by visiting the small lodge cottage near the Tudor mansion, Montacute House.

Our school-holiday guardians Reg and Peggy Markwell rented Odcombe Lodge, which was located at a secondary gate to Montacute Park, the mansion's extended estate, covered in old elms clotted with the ancient wreckage of shambolic rooks' nests and grazed by cattle. The lodge had two bedrooms upstairs, and a living room, kitchen and bathroom downstairs. At first, Dave and I shared a double bed in one of the upstairs rooms, but for most of our time with the Markwells we stayed in a small caravan beside the house. On one side of the lodge, a secondary road ran from Yeovil to the ham-stone Odcombe Village. This was the road Dave and I would have taken on our YHA bike tours, usually towards the south-west. On the other side of the lodge was the estate with its big old trees, a pond and some adjoining fields. This was where we spent most of our time if we weren't biking. In many ways, it was another of those extended territories we'd made our own since we were little, something we could do because there were two of us and because we could always egg each other on.

We climbed into the elms and made forts in the ruins of the rooks' nests; we detonated weedkiller and sugar bombs on floating craft in the middle of the pond; we stampeded the skittish yearling cattle; skirted the perimeter of the tantalising mansion (we'd been warned off the grounds by the Markwells). For a short time towards the end of our stay in England, we had girlfriends from a nearby hamlet which I seem to remember was called Higher Odcombe or perhaps Mudford Sock; with them, we walked solemnly through the parkland, wondering who should make the first move: no one ever did.

I went there in 1970 on the way back to London from Devon. The Markwells hadn't lived in the lodge for several years, and I was at once glad they weren't there requiring a visit and guilty for not wanting to see them. I wrote the poem soon after visiting Montacute Park on a dismal, chilly day. Of course, the scale of the place was diminished, but so was the scale of the emotion I'd expected to feel. The place had the effect of making banal and dull a whole succession of enervated images of home or the absence of home: the cottage we'd never quite been at home in, the ruined rookeries, the longing to be welcomed home and warmed up, and a closing image of compliance, which I still remember vividly – the happily running and barking dog coming to heel and walking in a crestfallen way back towards the house by the road.

The man with the dog could have stood for Reg Markwell, since they had a spaniel we used to play with, and which Reg used to throw sticks for. But of course it wasn't Reg I saw that day. I think the glum image of the man with his obedient dog had more to do with the compliance I remembered as the overriding childhood cost of 'staying with' minders, rather than living with family.

It wasn't that Dave and I were always on our best behaviour. Once, when we were still sharing the upstairs bed, Reg burst into our room where we'd been having a noisy early-morning play-fight, and threw himself on me, lashing out with wild punches and slaps, and yelling furiously, 'You want a fight? You want a fight?' Soon after that we were moved out to the caravan. Early on, I wrecked one of his drills in the workshop-garage down the back by the chicken run, and lied that I hadn't; I saw by his expression that he didn't believe me. Once, Peggy caught me Bunterishly scoffing left-over roast potatoes that I was meant to have taken as scraps for the hens, and she told me off for implying that she didn't feed us properly. We kept our homemade weedkiller bombs secret. But, in general, our behaviour around the cottage was circumspect. We obeyed injunctions against filling the bath above a certain point, and against the excessive use of toilet paper.

What I was experiencing wasn't so much an exile or a diaspora as an extended period of behaving myself – of staying-at-heel – in the house, and of running wild out there in the parkland with Dave. It was a duplicitous existence, though probably different only in degree from that of most kids. And in many ways it suited the mode I was in or the nature I'd cultivated, so to speak: a large, anarchic imaginative life fuelled by addictive injections of sadness and self-pity, which I concealed behind a happy, approval-winning performance of decorum.

Looking at that poem now, though, it's not the taint of self-pity in the man-with-dog image that strikes me, but my memory of the shambolic rooks' nests. This much further on from both the childhood experience of Montacute Park and my subsequent adult visit to it, I see in those catastrophic, ancient wrecks of twigs, rubbish and seasonal quotas of dead fledglings, an image of disgust and fear. I remember climbing up into the stinking rookery thickets with a kind of crazy determination – pushing myself up into them and making a place to sit, while at the same time feeling revolted and afraid. Perhaps, as a child, this was a stubborn way of assaulting my disappointment with what home had turned out to be like; or of overcoming my distaste for the nests by forcing myself into them.

But now I also remember that, in 1970, the apprehension and stubbornness I recalled from my childhood were like the complex of feelings I experienced when I first went to the Palestinian 'camps' around Amman in 1969 and to work in Russeifeh. This association, bizarre in 1970, was nonetheless what I've remembered feeling. I don't think I admitted my feelings at the time; but I admit them now, in the tangled, shambolic, compounded rooks'-nest archaeology of memory and emotion, which also reminded me of the layers of improvised building in the camps. Those black, fearsome birds, with huge beaks like the pointy fronts of the mediaeval knights' helmets we saw inside Montacute House, were always homing in on the trees and the ramshackle structures that clogged them, their hoarse yells at once jeering and stupid.

In 1958, it was as though the rooks were jeering at me for trudging dutifully back to a home I didn't feel at home in. In 1969, the politely repressed scorn I sometimes encountered in the refugee camps told me I couldn't expect to understand the first thing about what being homeless meant. In 1970, I began to trace a trajectory through these moments. In 2011, re-reading the poem I wrote then, I could own the end of that trajectory with a certain amount of equanimity, or irony. And now I can ask, why the repeated 'affective' at the beginning of my poem? Was I admonishing myself for feeling what I did? For being seduced into nostalgia?

Most of all, I think, I was warning myself not to want to recover emotions it had always been better to leave behind. But now I'm keen to recover them. The only danger I see is the rueful one of admitting that I may not understand what happened after Dave and I were *made homeless*; after our *catastrophe* – our forced displacement, when we were obliged to live somewhere we hadn't chosen, to behave according to the prescriptions of others, to repress anger or sadness, to show a smiling face or risk punishment, to be separated from my family, to call 'home' a place my heart told me wasn't that.

Now, the tangled rookeries that frightened and disgusted me in 1958 and shamed me in 1970 seem to be metonyms for home and memory – as if the emotional impenetrability of one and the archaeological chaos of the other have combined in a single object, a home-in-memory: an archive that is at once shambolic structure and disorganised contents.

I can go to this confused place on the limited terms of long-ago jettisoned emotions – and also to reoccupy a vantage point high up in the elms of Montacute Park, from which to see the man throwing a stick for his happy dog, the quaint lodge cottage by the road with a plume of smoke rising from its chimney, the road on which two boys on bikes are pedalling off towards a YHA hostel about 150 kilometres away on Dartmoor: a scene that resembles a board game or model set like the ones we played with back then, little utopian vistas with no emotion present or needed.

Back in 1958, our intact but cheerfully homeless family arrived without catastrophe at the Port of Tilbury on the outskirts of London. I have the passenger list for 23 March 1958; it's got Dave's and my birthdays wrong, and gives our address in London as the Tavistock Hotel, Tavistock Square, in Bloomsbury. I seem to remember we fled this hotel because it was too expensive. It was late winter, and the view from the train window of warehouses and the backs of buildings on the way in to the city was the bleakest I had ever seen. There was no colour whatsoever. It was dark. You could see only a short distance through grey mizzle. Everything looked grimy. The *Arcadia* had been battered by a huge storm in the Bay of Biscay, its railings and lifeboats swept away, and Dave's face retained the ghastly, greenish pallor of his seasickness. But we were all happy – or rather, Dave and I were infected with our parents' happiness. They'd done it; they'd cleared the next hurdle.

After the Tavistock, we were staying in a hotel on the Strand, and the bleakness didn't matter. It made the lights brighter and the warmth of the Underground cosier. There was a black-and-white television set in Linda and Chick's bedroom, where we scared ourselves watching *Quatermass and the Pit* on BBC Television. We ate hot buttered toast in the cafeteria downstairs, and had to learn that in London you couldn't just order more butter. We went to movies in continuous-screening newsreel cinemas where spivvy men in winkle pickers were snogging their girlfriends and smoking; we hung out at the Science Museum and twiddled the knobs on the mechanical interactives; we went back several times to Madame Tussaud's.

We rode up and down the long, clattering escalators in the Underground, where the advertising billboards were sensationally glamorous. There was one handbill-sized one that repeated a concept for Smirnoff vodka: 'I was a . . . until I discovered Smirnoff!' I remember Chick's head whipping around and a look of shock and displeasure on his face the day he clattered up past a Smirnoff ad that read: 'I was a chartered accountant until I discovered Smirnoff!'

We went to the orthopaedic clinic at Great Ormond Street Hospital for Children, where the doctor admired the accuracy of Dr Bottoms' diagnosis and treatment of my wonky heels; I was equipped with firm pink elastic bandages that smelled rubbery and made my shoes tight. I was disappointed to hear that a lot of children had osteochondrosis and they nearly always got better: I could sense my sympathy credit running out. We went to an optician who also admired Dr Bottoms' improvisation with my glasses, which he'd managed to get more or less right. I was re-equipped with even rounder National Health glasses which everyone called 'specs'. Then we went to an orthodontist who admired the wire-and-rubber contraptions and plate that the German dentist with visible nipples had organised around my teeth. It was all ripped out and replaced with a new contraption.

Then, suddenly, as if we'd all been waiting patiently for my various appointments to finish, we were staying in the little inn at Sparkford and visiting Hazelgrove School. It was freezing cold, but the headmaster, who was a fresh-air and exercise freak, had the diamond-paned windows of his pipe-smoky study open. Then, humiliatingly, I was being fitted for a tailored school uniform because the second-hands weren't big enough. I lip-read the woman who measured me miming

'Oh dear!' to my mother.

And then, with no transition that I can remember, we were in a clumsy brick house on a hill outside Yeovil in Somerset. The place had some sheds with vaguely menacing farm equipment in them, and a slope of cultivated ground from which fresh mole hills regularly appeared. We had what Dave is confident was a 1957 Vauxhall Wyvern that had to be driven up a steep driveway to the house, which had been rented from the owners who farmed the land around it, including the mole-infested slope.

Just along the road lived Reg and Peggy Markwell, in the quaint little lodge to Montacute House. I have no idea how our parents met them, or when it was decided that they'd look after us once Linda and Chick had gone. It was a financial arrangement, so perhaps the Markwells had answered an advertisement, though that seems unlikely. We went there for morning tea one day – that was when I wrecked one of Reg's drills, and I saw him get my number when I lied about what Dave and I had been up to in the shed.

We went on a trip around England, Wales and Scotland. Chick photographed us mercilessly. He, of course, was never in the picture because he was taking it. Dave and I took Box Brownie snaps, and he appears in some of them, with a triumphant, slightly leery grin and usually with his arm around Lindy. By him we were posed next to lochs, monuments and the Vauxhall parked in historic locations. As we drove past shaggy Highland cattle and crossed the border into Aggie Horne's ancestral Scotland, Chick burst into song: 'Hi ho ye Heeland bastards!' Actually, Agnes Tait was from the Borders, and we did drive over the Tay Bridge at some stage. It was pelting down with slatey rain.

Chick wept during a piano recital of Chopin at the Edinburgh Festival and we went to the Tattoo in the castle, so it must have been summer. I wept in Ely Cathedral and remember it was cold, so maybe it was winter. I remember a Welsh valley that was at once vividly green and full of black rock; lambs were bouncing there, so it must have been spring. I remember ripe mulberries dropping from a tree at Stratford-on-Avon, so it must have been nearly autumn – but why were we all the way back at Stratford? Did we go back to London to say goodbye to Chick at the end of our trip? There we are, our new uniforms being shat on by pigeons in Trafalgar Square.

I have no idea when it was, though we usually appear with warm clothes on. Now I have an inkling why we were dressed like public school boys, not like kids on holiday – we were trophies. The letter in which I hoped no one caught typhoid was addressed only to 'Daddy', and included the news that Linda had brought Peggy and Reg for a visit to Hazelgrove; it was dated 31 May 1958, in the spring. Perhaps this trip happened before we went down to Somerset from London. If I ask Dave, he will know (he says he doesn't). But for now my truth is as tangled as the rookeries.

Back at the house outside Yeovil (or maybe before we went off on our trip), Chick tried to tell us about sex, but gave up and left the room after advising us not to believe most of what we would soon be hearing at school. Linda took over and told us that sex was wonderful but best when you were married. We still had no idea what it involved, and attempts to open the subject up by asking about the Virgin Birth were unsuccessful. In their private lives, my mother and father were not prudish – both walked around the house with no clothes on and had no objection to us coming into the bathroom when they were in the bath – but they were useless at talking about anything intimate, including feelings.

And then, suddenly, Chick was gone. Of course, by then

we'd known this was going to happen. I have no memory of his leave-taking, only the sense of an emotional gear shift in the dreary brick house where we began to settle into a dull routine and where Linda was clearly bored and biding her time. The house seemed chilly and foreign; it had other people's stuff in it. It didn't smell right. Once, as if repeating the clod-chucking incident back at Chandraghona, we lobbed snowballs down at the passing cars from behind the hedge at the bottom of the mole-hill field. A fat policeman pushed his bike up the steep driveway and told Linda to keep an eye on us or there would be trouble. She gave us a furious telling-off, which was as much about being exposed and foreign and needing to behave as it was about our crime.

We began to catch a double-decker bus from Yeovil to Hazelgrove School. The bus tore along narrow sunken roads with hedges or hazelnut thickets as high as the tops of the lower-level windows. Dave and I were in different classes – separating siblings seemed to be a policy of the school. We had sports, at which Dave distinguished himself by being strong and fast, and I by being strapped-up and fat. The classrooms were freezing – or maybe that came later when it was winter again – and the health-freak headmaster's regimen included a ban on extra clothing or congregating on radiators.

We sat at deeply incised, ink-stained desks with lids that lifted and slammed and ink wells whose contents blackened our fingers. We wrote with nibs on wooden sticks which were good for flicking ink. A lot of what I began to be taught was completely new. Though I could speak and read French and German, had a smattering of Latin, and could write fast and fluently, I had never encountered the kind of maths we were expected to be proficient in, didn't understand the point of history or geography, and extended my hatred of our snooty young Bible studies teacher to the subject he droned on about.

Instead of poems and stories I began to write subversive sketches using as much foul language as I knew (not much); I did this partly in the hope of winning friends by circulating my samizdat texts around the class. The Bible studies teacher found, or was sneaked, a sketch that ended, 'Come here bloody bum and shit on the bed!' The point of this obscure punch line had to do with a convoluted story involving puns and someone with a speech impediment. I've forgotten the story, which no one could understand, but remember the scriptures teacher gave me some cuts with a cane across the backs of my thighs and made me copy out a long passage from the Bible.

Despite the weirdness and unfamiliarity of the situation, I think we were having a good time. There was a big, lugubrious kid everyone teased to make him throw tantrums; when he did, he'd run roaring in a strange deep voice across the sports field, tearing up handfuls of grass and charging at the jeering mob. I could see *he* wasn't happy; his situation was different.

It was about then that Dave and I began to be apart sometimes. At school, we began to have different friends; we did different stuff at hobbies. At night, back in the brick house, we had different homework. That astigmatic focal length in which my twin was almost invisible because he just was there most of the time – that changed. Now Dave became oddly visible sometimes, because he wasn't *just there* – and then suddenly he'd go past a bit further away, running with some other kids, his broad grin in the midst of them, all of them yelling.

When Linda met us at the bus stop in Yeovil, we'd occasionally go to a basement cafeteria near the town square and have spaghetti on toast; they did a double portion which we both liked. It was here, one day, she announced that in the summer holidays we were going to drive to Rome to meet up with Daddy from Khulna, and then we'd have a holiday together, after which we'd be coming back to Yeovil without him – and then she'd be going to East Pakistan. She'd be going by herself. We were going to stay here, in England. We were going to be boarders at Hazelgrove, which would be much more fun than catching the bus every day. Before long, we'd be able to come and visit them in East Pakistan, and that would be fun too. In the holidays, we were going to stay with Reg and Peggy in the lodge. That would be fun – they were really nice people and there was lots to do in the park.

God knows what kind of effort it cost Linda to break the news to us, or how often she rehearsed the various approaches she might take. The fact that she fell back on the implausibly accommodating concept of fun was probably a good indication of her apprehension and perhaps grief. I don't doubt that she longed to be with Chick – to be getting on with the life they'd gone past the point of no return with. But where did that leave us? Was she as convinced as her husband that this was the best they could hope to do by their children? I doubt it.

Many years later, after Chick had died, she told me she'd worried; but she made this admission hesitantly, not as if she'd largely forgotten the doubts, but as though she was unwilling to imply any fault on Chick's part. I thought, fair enough – it doesn't matter any more. It hadn't really mattered for thirty years.

Thinking back now, I remember a kind of beseeching anxiety in her manner – though whether then or later I can't be sure. At the time she broke the news, I was scoffing my double helping of spaghetti on toast, and the pleasure of that took over my first reaction to the announcement. It was later, when the news sank in, that I committed my reprise of the egregious life-isn't-worth-living lie I'd inaugurated that day back in Chandraghona, when she'd scooped me up and murmured 'There, there' into my sobs.

Linda came into our bedroom and found me sitting on the edge of my bed, contemplating a pair of open scissors with a meaningful look. It was true, I told her when she asked – I wanted to be dead. And was that because Mummy was going to Khulna? She removed the scissors from my hand. I don't think for a moment she believed my intention, or my answer, but that suited both of us. By giving me an admiring, sympathetic hug when I lied that I wanted to die because I couldn't stand the thought of all the unhappy children in the world, she handed me the Pyrrhic victory of an honourable discharge. Years later, I asked her about this incident. I did so as one adult to another, hoping to share a rueful joke. But she didn't remember it. Just as well.

The boy soprano

I don't remember the transition period – which must have been around May 1958, if my typhoid letter is anything to go by – when Dave and I were first boarding at Hazelgrove while Linda packed up the rented brick house on the mole-infested hill near Odcombe village and prepared to go to Khulna. Nor do I remember her leaving; or saying goodbye and then leaving – presumably in the Vauxhall in which she'd earlier driven us to Rome to see Chick, and back again to go to boarding school. Or perhaps she'd already sold the car, and went to London on the train, having packed up the house? Sold our stuff? All Dave and I had would fit in our regulation Hazelgrove suitcases.

On the morning I wrote the sentence, 'Nor do I remember her leaving,' I paused and went for a walk. My writing task for the day was to be a chapter in which I returned to the time Dave and I spent at Hazelgrove and, as a kind of lamination, the time I spent in London in 1970 and '71. But I encountered a blank and so went out for a walk.

As I climbed through the wet trees and birdsong on the hill above Donna's and my home on Mount Victoria, Wellington, a lone black man singing 'Once in Royal David's City' in a gorgeous, syrupy, bass strolled into the blank space where my thoughts had stalled. The footprints he left in the snow that had covered Brixton Road in London were evenly spaced and paced, with a turned-out duck-walk shape that somehow expressed the large, overcoat-draped belly and chest that rested above his saunter; his saunter kept time with the song.

There was no one else around in the street, so it must have been early in the morning, and Brixton Road must have been closed to traffic because of the snow. I watched him from the first-floor window of the flat we were living in. It was too cold to open the windows, whose draughty edges we'd stuffed with newspaper, but I could hear that he kept singing the carol after he'd passed out of sight. This was in the severe winter of 1970, but the beautiful singing is what I remembered, not the discomfort.

Remembering this, I understood that, before going for my walk on Mount Victoria, I'd been about to follow a default track; to start writing along lines I'd already taken for granted. I planned to write about the sad impact of Linda's unwitnessed departure, about what Dave and I did about it in our different ways, about a morbid consistency in my narrative of home and homelessness.

But the default would not play.

Even now, I can remember the *quality* of happiness I felt hearing the black singer's beautiful voice, and seeing him walk along the snow-covered street that only the day before would have been grimy and bleak. What was so special about it? The moment was special enough in itself – unique, memorable, strange, uplifting – but in a way it just confirmed what I already knew: that I was happy then, despite conditions. The flat was cold and infested with mice; Rose, Kevin Cunningham and I shared a pissy toilet with the sullen Italian barbers on the ground floor; we were scraping by – but we were happy. The singer's small margin of strange bliss told me so. If you are pretty happy, an extra measure of it doesn't feel like a reprieve: it feels like a blessing.

Linda had been right a decade earlier – boarding school

was fun and I was pretty happy. The conditions were bleak: the health-obsessed headmaster had us taking cold baths in the morning and doing physical jerks outside in the snow before breakfast; breakfast sometimes consisted of hot-water cocoa and slices of toast on which Marmite had been baked (some years after we left, the school was investigated for malnourishment of children); the Indian sports master was a martinet; slightly bullying sex cabals gathered in the dormitories and changing rooms; some of the schoolwork was hard. But I was mostly having fun. Some of the boys cried at night when the lights were turned off, but I never did.

And I think the reason I have no recollection at all of Linda's departure to join Chick in East Pakistan, a place two weeks away by airmail, was because it didn't matter in the end. In fact, it was probably a relief when she went. And now, it's a relief to be able to admit that. At school, we got on with our lives in an environment like the territories Dave and I had always occupied away from the family home. I no longer had to perform my doleful masquerade of separation anxiety for which there was, anyway, no longer an audience.

Instead, I became a boy soprano. My introversion was pulled inside out. Here is my connection with the black caroller in Brixton. As I walked through the trees on Mount Victoria that day, he signalled to me that I'd been happy back then when our mother left us; and then I remembered why. Singing in the chapel choir provided the margin of bliss that told me I was already happy. I became one of two soprano leads and, one Christmas, got to sing the solo 'Once in Royal David's City' as the choir processed down the nave of the chapel towards the choir-stalls. This performance was not a lie; its audience was appreciative, not complicit; it made me feel good, not guilty; it was a blessing, not a reprieve. It was also only good while it lasted.

As part of our father's contract at Khulna, we were flown out once to visit in the summer holidays. There was a compound-type arrangement of houses there, also a swimming pool. Some other expat kids were visiting as well and most days we all played at the pool. Word of my boy soprano performance reached Chick, and he asked me to sing 'Once in Royal David's City'. I knew in my bones that this was the wrong place and the wrong time. Perhaps I sensed that this would be too much like those other performances, the ones I no longer needed to do, the Fishface ones. Perhaps I was just shy.

I agreed to sing on condition that I could do so in an adjoining room. My voice was cracking and strained. When I came back into the one where my parents were sitting, they were holding hands, and Chick was weeping. 'That was lovely, darling,' said my mother. But I was sullen again. It would have been different if they'd heard me sing in the Christmas procession with the choir, and the huge candle, and all the parents of the other kids. But they hadn't been there; singing in a room next to them in Khulna was stupid, and my father's tears were embarrassing. Also, I sensed that he was moved by his own achievement, not mine; he was *proud*, but of the opportunity he'd been able to give me.

The next time I saw him cry was worse. We were getting on the plane in Khulna to go back to England, and Chick began to weep again. When I asked Linda if it was because he was sad to see us go, she replied, No, it was because we weren't as hairy as he'd thought we'd be. He'd expected us to be *older*. Again, the tears were not about what I was; they were about what Chick had hoped I'd be. I took that peculiar disappointment with me on to the plane, along with an ear infection from some bug in the pool. I got off at the other end dripping green pus, as if the 'family home' had become poisonous; it had, anyway, become foreign – as foreign as the murky Sundarban mangroves we went to on an overnight boat trip without seeing a tiger, only the rotting remnant of a skull with teeth, whose stink was like the one that came out of my throbbing ear. School was better.

Of course I know *now* that my father's emotion was genuine enough, even if it did include a measure of self-satisfaction, and that Linda was making a joke about the disappointing lack of hairiness. Like many jokes made by parents to defuse emotional situations, its aim was wrong. It lodged in my child's mind as a nasty infection, and remained there as evidence that the family home had been poisoned.

But this also freed me. And then my voice began to break – the sign of another liberation. I grew quickly, shed my fat and became good at sport. The wonky bones in my heels had mended. Fishface was no more. I was booted out of the choir, but trained with the school swimming squad and was captain of the senior rugby team. This was partly because I was the coach's favourite – he was the school's French teacher. Thanks to crazy Herzig and the scrupulous Robert Lübker, I was his star pupil.

As well as happy, I was fortunate. Linda and Chick were far away; I missed them dutifully when we stayed with the Markwells in the holidays; I missed the *idea* of home rather than the reality. The twinges of sadness I felt at the YHA hostel on Dartmoor, for example, began to be redundant, as if the homeless sadness I'd become accustomed to feeling, or the fear of it, hadn't yet been flushed completely out of my system.

As I walked along familiar tracks in the Town Belt on Mount Victoria, the black caroller in Brixton in 1970 made the connection between that liberation and my brief time as a boy soprano. All these unpredictable, unprogrammed things made happiness possible: made it possible to be *at home* within a kind of Epicurean zone of fortune.

The departure of my mother and father, and the absence of the kind of home we had when we all lived together, also opened up a space in which happiness could ambush the dire scenarios I'd become accustomed to taking for granted back then. Like my mother and father risking their happiness and the happiness of their children when they left Blenheim and embarked on a life where home had no fixed address but was rather the place where fortunate circumstances converged, I was given the opportunity to find happiness where contingency was its agent. The boy soprano moment, and its liberating sequel, marked a time not only when home left me but also when I let it go. Thus began a new chapter in the story of home.

The Italian water pitcher

The story of the Italian water pitcher focuses the last substantial memories I have of being with my mother and father, and is therefore my story of leaving them and the kind of home they represented. But before telling the story of the pitcher, I find I have to backtrack to the photographs of Linda as Lady Mary Lasenby in *The Admirable Crichton*, and especially the one in which she's wearing deerskins and bending a bow: an image that has fascinated and haunted me since I found it after her death in 1986.

Along with a black cast-iron Korean pug-dog which my mother got when she and Chick lived in Seoul, and which was definitely hers, the brass and copper Italian water pitcher which is definitely mine stood by the front door of our house in Mount Victoria. The iron pug-dog sometimes doubled as a doorstop, and the pitcher as an umbrella stand. I walked between and past these useful but talismanic objects whenever I left or entered what had been my family home for twenty years. This wasn't a repetition I thought about – it wasn't meaningful – though sometimes a pang of responsibility or chagrin made me pick up the dog and apologise when he'd fallen over, and sometimes I straightened the umbrellas (and the feather duster) in the pitcher because it seemed respectful to do so.

But after getting out the photograph of my mother bending her bow as a youthful, somewhat Artemis-like Lady Mary

Lasenby, and trying to figure out when the performance would have taken place and what it told me about the quality of my mother's life when she was as young as she appears in the photo, I walked out of our Wellington house between the dog and the pitcher – between her talisman and mine – and felt a charge pass between them.

The home we're accustomed to is the one we're least aware of; the pug-dog and the pitcher, like electrodes, shocked me with a sudden awareness of how little I knew about my mother's life at Francis Street, and how much I'd elaborated that meagre knowledge with my own assumptions. When I looked back at what I'd written, I saw I'd built a narrative of dissatisfaction and boredom in my mother's life, from which such episodes as her role in *The Admirable Crichton* – along with the social life that took place in the Sounds, with boat trips, beach parties and the occasional jazz dance on the Cook Strait ferry (*Tamahine*, adds my brother) at Picton – were an occasional relief. I'd assumed that my mother, at forty-four, had chivvied my father into getting her the hell out of there because she was suffocating in the narrow confines of a house and home that had defined her whole life.

And even if this was halfway true, it played too conveniently to my own agenda, the self-pitying contours of which I was beginning to doubt more and more. The story I'd found myself defaulting to was all about the necessity for an imaginative life that could compensate for a home life characterised by absences, shortcomings or failures, and therefore by dissatisfactions and desires. My default narrative had begun to construct a *likely* reality that was neither unhappy nor a fantasy, but something original: a metaphorical home in which I (or my mother) could be happy in a way that was never going to be possible in a world of inevitable limitations.

But now I began to mistrust this model, and the extent to

which I'd let it shape my understanding of why Linda had needed to leave her home in Blenheim. Now, I wanted her desire to be unshackled from dissatisfaction – I wanted it to be something like the free-flowing, transforming energy that Deleuze and Guatarri celebrated with such brilliant longing in *Anti-Oedipus*.

Hoping to find out more about Linda's life as hinted at tantalisingly in the Artemis photograph, I phoned my cousin Norma Robinson at her home near Spring Creek outside Blenheim. While hunting at the National Library for information about the amateur theatre scene in Blenheim, I'd already encountered Norma as a glamorous young star in several Blenheim Repertory Society productions, and I thought she might know when *The Admirable Crichton* had been staged. Maybe she'd be able to fill me in on that part of her aunt's, my mother's, life.

Norma was eighty-four when I phoned her, and could still easily pass for a woman in her alert early sixties. She laughs a lot, tells a good story, has a sharp memory, is the vigilant matriarch of extended family businesses and leads a resolutely independent social life. She could, she says, have had a life as an actor, and her husband Gordon as an All Black, but children and farming took over. She had a lot to tell me on the phone, but couldn't remember when *The Admirable Crichton* was staged. We agreed that I'd come over for a couple of days and she'd introduce me to Terence Burtenshaw, a local actor, theatre and film nut, veteran of amateur productions in the province, and one of the keepers of the Operatic Society archives.

So, four days later, I caught the Picton ferry with the Artemis/Lady Mary Lasenby photograph in my bag. From the sun deck of the ferry, I squinted at Dieffenbach Point through a significant end-of-year-parties hangover, and then drove a rental car across the Wairau Plains to Norma's place. Since her husband Gordon's death, she's lived in a fine modern house surrounded by a landscape that bears no relationship whatsoever to the one I grew up with. In all directions the Marlborough vineyards stretch out in orderly rows; wine tourists pose for photo opportunities next to famous brand signage such as Cloudy Bay. There's a luxury hand-made chocolate business just up the road. The vineyards compete for the best chefs, and as the Christmas holiday season approaches the lunch bookings begin to logjam into weeks.

The hills across the Wairau River towards Nelson were almost familiar, and so were the blond mounds of the Wither Hills on the other side of Blenheim, with little white clouds suspended above them in a hot blue sky. Missing was the kind of ad hoc orderly pastoral landscape with cows and sheep that I associated with the Hastilow farm we used to visit at Tua Marina; and, most of all, the plumes of dust from shingle roads like those that mostly seemed to end at the broad, shingly, braided river of my childhood, whose water was always warmer than expected, and smelled of leaves and stone.

Already I began to feel my default narrative of metaphorised unhappiness and imagination being subverted by these signs of transformation which, of course, had long been taken for granted by those who lived there, like my bright-eyed cousin pouring us a glass of wine at lunch. The landscape hadn't really been strange for decades – not even to me when I'd come back to it over the years.

And yet, all at once, it *was* strange, unexpected – and subversive. It was as if an alternative truth about my mother's life in it had been lying in wait for me and had finally been given the chance to ambush me at my most vulnerable – faintly headachy and blurred, halfway to admitting that I'd run with a default narrative for too long, and encountering my cousin Norma's lively memory of my mother whom she'd admired and perhaps in some ways even emulated more than sixty years ago, before there were vineyards as far as the eye could see, in an age that seemed to have been geographically erased just so I could re-imagine it as a place people *came to* rather than left (or got stuck in) – where enjoying life seemed to be what the place mostly expected. It was as though my gloomy default narrative, and the place in it that I'd reserved for my mother, had been reversed or turned inside out.

At Norma's sunny kitchen table I enjoyed some salad, a salmon vol-au-vent and a glass of pleasant pinot gris. She began to tell me about Linda. She remembered being a bridesmaid at Linda and Chick's wedding. She was sixteen years younger than my mother, who was twenty-eight or twenty-nine when she married. To the twelve-year-old Norma, Linda seems to have been a glamorous figure. She remembers Linda doing her hair during the war years when it was the salon that kept the Wedde-Horne family afloat and, later, my mother's passion for make-up and costumes associated with the Operatic and Repertory Societies.

She has an earlier memory from September 1928 of Linda driving her out to see the hero aviators Charles Kingsford Smith and Charles Ulm, who emergency-landed their *Southern Cross* trans-Tasman flight on farmland which Dave later identifies as Fairhall, where the Woodburn air force base would be established. Linda seems to have been part of a young, fun-loving social crowd who rushed to see the aviators. On the way back, the car punctured, and in no time a dashing man pulled over and changed the tyre. The fact that Linda was driving a car at eighteen also surprises me – or surprises my narrative of dissatisfaction. Norma remembers her grandmother Wedde commenting somewhat tartly that, after the twins were born, Linda would often still be ironing at eleven o'clock at night; she wasn't much good in the mornings, was a night owl by nature, didn't like housework, but was very particular with the ironing.

I can't quite square up Norma's account of Linda and Chick's wedding with the dates in the official record, but I'm sure she's correct in her memory that Chick wanted to marry Linda before he went off to the war; she remembers the wedding took place in January, and that Chick joined up a few months later. Something like that is possible – New Zealand declared war on 3 September 1939. She remembers that they honeymooned on a yacht in the Sounds and came in to Endeavour Inlet where Norma and her extended family were staying for the summer; a bedraggled, salt-caked Linda came ashore asking for a hot bath and somewhere to do her hair.

I have two little black-and-white photographs from the vast trove my father kept; in each of them, one or the other of my parents is taking turns at the tiller of a yacht – they look wind-blown and sun-baked, with big grins. Nearby in the photograph folder is a picture of an elegant little cutter moored out in a bay – they probably rowed the yacht's dinghy ashore from time to time. I think these are photographs of their honeymoon, but can't be sure.

Norma remembers a lot of music in the Francis Street house, and in her own mother's house – Chick and his sister Phyllis both played the piano and sang, and took turns swapping the two between them. Apparently there was a strong music tradition in the Wedde family, which came from the Reepen side via my great-grandmother Maria: all of her and great-grandfather Heinrich August's children, Dave's and my great-aunts and -uncles, played musical instruments and would get together to perform. Reinhold – Ren – in particular was a gifted flautist. There's said to be a statue of a Reepen relative, Klaus Groth, whose wife was related to Brahms, in a public square in Kiel – I hope to see it one day. Grandfather Wedde, Albert Augustus (A.A. on the published sheet music), also composed hymns, songs, and ditties for children; Norma remembers that he approached his favourite poet, Walter De La Mare, for permission to set 'Silver' to music, and a letter of consent from the poet was once among the family papers. I have a copy of the sheet music for his setting of the poet and novelist Will Lawson's 'The Song of the Saws', with 'words reprinted from the "Sydney Bulletin" by kind permission of the Author'. Will Lawson, an acolyte of his namesake the bush-balladeer Henry Lawson, came and went between New Zealand and Australia – it's possible my grandfather knew him.

Later in the day, at the Operatic Society archives, I'd find evidence of Chick's and Linda's involvement in the music and theatre of the small town. I began to realign my impression of all this as Linda's imaginative refuge, the sign of her discontent. Instead, I began to see in Norma's account a pattern of vivid social life in which glamour, adventure, music and theatre flowed around homes, workplaces, performance societies, and the wider environment of picnics and boating. Times may have been hard, but they were not as grim as my scenario had made them. The subversive life of the imagination was not quite the client of dissatisfactions I'd assumed and even wanted it to be in my young mother's life.

Norma drove me to the Blenheim Operatic Society's rooms. Kids were walking on the sunny footpaths in bare feet where the tar was probably about to melt. Lawnmowers were working the berms of suburban streets – Masports and Flymos, not the chattering mowers with wire and canvas grass catchers of my childhood, but the smell of hot mown grass that came in the car window was the same.

'I love New Zealand towns on Saturdays,' said Norma. 'Everybody is so busy!'

At the archive we met Terrence Burtenshaw. He and Norma at once began a reminiscing conversation around the photographs he brought out for me to look at. She remembered most of the people in them. We found the Lady Mary Lasenby/Artemis photograph of my mother in her huntress deerskins. The production was in 1939. Linda was twenty-nine but looks much younger – almost teen-like. This must have been just before she married my father – the archive caption records her maiden name among 'Vera Dix, Clarrie Jamieson, F.C. Carver, Linda Horne, D. Ovens, P. Grieg'.

The name 'Vera' had a strange effect on me. I seem to remember my mother saying it. I remember the nasty taste of a green olive I spat out after I'd been given it from a drink 'Vera' and my mother were having. This woman had red fingernails, wore beige slacks, and rested one side of her bottom on the kitchen table of a two-storey house in Francis Street. Linda seemed to be laughing a lot on the day I was given the nasty olive from the drink – her laughter had a loudness I remember.

In a photograph from 1938, my father and his brother Paul appear wearing what look like Cossack uniforms in the male chorus of *The Belle of New York*. Linda was in the same production, wearing the ivory bracelet over her long white glove, and looking (thought Norma) a bit like Wallis Simpson. With his sister Phyllis, Chick appears in the chorus of an October 1939 production of *Rio Rita*. He must have gone off to the war very soon afterwards, though the company records show he was the Society's treasurer in 1939 and 1940.

Norma remembered that he sent home a great many

very long letters from Egypt, Palestine and Italy, 'beautifully written', with bits blotted out by the army censor; she remembered that 'he'd always wanted to write a book', but never did. I don't know where the letters are. Probably they were disposed of when Aggie Horne died and the household at Francis Street was wound up. Instead of writing a book, he took thousands of photographs.

'Most of them didn't come back,' said Norma as we left the archive. She meant the men in the Operatic Society chorus line who went off to the war at the same time as my father. Yes, she agreed when I asked, it was during the war that he began to study for his accountancy qualifications. He finished his degree after he came back from Egypt and Italy – in fact, after Dave and I were born. Norma remembered him studying late at night in the Francis Street house.

'I don't know how he did it – with crying babies. Mostly you. David always sat up and ate his food like a good boy.'

And so an alternative theme began to find the foreground of my narrative about my mother's and father's decision to quit Blenheim, and the consequences of that decision for the kinds of home I would live in. My father, who'd never settled to anything before the war (he was on the Ford sales team travelling the South Island, briefly managed a cinema somewhere near Gore, shot wallabies on the Canterbury Plains), returned to a small town from which many of the men he'd known were now buried on Crete, in the Western Desert, in Italy. Ahead of him would be the responsibilities of a father. Behind him was the daunting example of his own successful father, whose influence may have been cut short by his early death at fifty-three; and aunts and uncles who had gained university qualifications. Linda had waited a long time for her husband to come back from the war; she'd wait until she was thirty-six before she and Chick had children;

and she'd been forced to leave the convent school she loved long before she was ready to.

The darkness and dissatisfaction I've sensed around my parents' lives in Blenheim now seem to me to have been produced mostly by the war, and the damage it did to the social fabric of the small town; and perhaps, above all, by the sense of thwarted opportunity felt by both my parents, which the war accentuated, and which came to be represented by what they saw as the enforced (in my mother's case) or guilty (in my father's) limitations of their education. These frustrations became ambitions – my parents dislodged the chips on their shoulders by taking their twins to England and sending them to school there. In doing so, they cleared the way for their own happiness. This was not won at our expense, but rather by transforming their disappointments into our opportunities.

The basic architecture of my narrative hasn't been entirely wrong so far. But that metaphorising diagram of dissatisfaction and imagination generating a third-term reality has to be realigned. It has to emphasise the impact of the war and the sense of almost-lost opportunity, the threat of time running out, that the war thrust into the foreground. Here, the threat of it being nearly too late warped the pleasure I'd always seen in the photograph of Linda in her *Admirable Crichton* deerskins – a pleasure I'd stubbornly scripted as her imaginative refuge from the doldrums of her life.

But her life probably wasn't like that, then, in 1939 – only later, after the war, after Dave and I were born. And that was when the dauntless Artemis of the photograph deployed her desire and challenged her husband to get her out before it really was too late.

In his last few years, my father continued to express a yearning to write a book about his life. The closest he got to doing it was probably the long letters he wrote during the war, and the thick, blue-bound economics manuals and reports he wrote in Geneva between contracts for the UNDP. I sometimes sensed that he was afraid of writing the book, though he began to tap at his blue Olivetti from time to time when he and Linda had settled back in Auckland. After he died and we sorted out the contents of his desk in the house at St Heliers, there was no sign of whatever it was he'd been writing. But I did find some account books in which he'd composed what appeared to be imaginary balance sheets for fortunes that had never existed or that had ceased to exist (he did lose all his money once in a West Indian banking crash, and there's the story of his Uncle Fritz's mirage of wealth).

Perhaps these imaginary fortunes were sad – but then, perhaps they were just entertainments; and he had after all made many such stories come true in his life, beginning when he was the energetic guru of Mr Qureshi and Mr Qurim at Chandraghona.

Perhaps these impeccably presented fictional reports and balance sheets *were* my father's book – the scripts for a last performance. And perhaps my mother's last trip, the one that effectively killed her, was her version of the same thing. She *went home* to the wandering life she'd lived with Chick, to her friends in different parts of the world; then she *came home* to its banal aftermath, and died. This too was a kind of performance, whose end she'd dreaded but not avoided. Dave told me she didn't even unpack; she certainly didn't make up the drapes for her flat.

Norma and I went to find the family graves at the Omaka cemetery on the Wither Hills outskirts of Blenheim. We drove through streets that were almost familiar to me, past the public hospital where I almost remembered visiting the foul-breathed Dave after his tonsils had been removed; along an almost recognised grid of tree-lined suburban streets. Norma parked up on the closely mown berm in the shade of a large tree next to the old Omaka cemetery. Across the road in the newer one we'd find the plot with my tragic uncle Hugh Lancelot, the suicide; my Wedde grandparents, Albert Augustus and Mabel, whose headstones were missing; and my aunt Kay. Kay's husband, my uncle Paul, is buried with the returned servicemen in the war section of the cemetery.

It was a blazing hot day, the Marlborough heat full of the scent of drying mown grass, the talismanic aroma of the grass catcher. The feel of the rough lichens I rubbed from the family's headstone inscriptions was almost familiar too. Across the road in the old Omaka cemetery there was no longer any trace of my great-grandfather Heinrich August's grave, though I found what I thought might be my early Tait relatives' headstone – James Tait who died on 10 April 1897 aged seventy-nine, and Martha Mein Tait, who died five years later at eighty-one. I knew nothing about them and could only guess that they came out to New Zealand somewhat earlier than their young relatives William and his wife Susan, my Tait great-grandparents.

I later searched the Births, Deaths and Marriages records, and found that Susan, whose maiden name Ogilvie was my mother's middle name, died in what her death certificate describes as a Mental Hospital in Nelson, of 'senile decay', on 2 March 1918. The names of her mother and father were not known.

Nor, in any embodied way, at the time of Norma's and my visit to the cemetery, did I know anything about the others whose graves I'd touched with fingers that remembered childhood's summer heat on the lichened river-stone balustrade at our home in Francis Street. Following Norma's lead, I blundered along among the rows of tumbled and illegible headstones, through a layering of anonymous or affectless facts scattered across a half-remembered emotional topography and the grid of my own predisposed narratives. Trying to get my bearings in this hot, grass-scented maze, I began to understand or get the measure of the ambiguity I'd sensed opening up around my default narratives of home as shaped by these people whose marble memorials were themselves almost gone.

The following day, in teeming rain, I sloshed uselessly around the hilltop graveyard at Tua Marina where my maternal grandmother Aggie's first husband is buried. I hadn't known she had a husband before Bertie Horne until Norma told me. I didn't know his name, and Norma didn't know it either – he seemed to have disappeared from all family records. So of course I didn't find anything, only confirmation of my quandary and a reprise of that bewildering almost-familiarity, that recognition fogged as if by misty drizzle, that sense of a more complex narrative than the one I'd driven up the muddy cemetery access road with.

Below the north-west slope of the cemetery hill, the paddocks and low hills where the Hastilow farm had been were halfway familiar. I had the feeling that if I closed my eyes and went over there with my fragmented memory map, I'd get closer to what I'd known as a kid than I would with any retrospective knowledge; I'd *smell* it, as I had the pattern of my mother's summer frock when that aroma of dust, heat and cow-shit smoke came in the car window in Ceylon in 1969, ten years after she'd left us to go and live in Khulna. I'd smell the whey that ran to the Hastilow pigsty from the farm dairy where the cream separator whizzed around and cheese was stirred in a vat; I'd smell the poopy chicken run where the chooks ran fiercely after the bootlace eels we threw them; I'd smell the dry hay-bales we climbed on, sneezing, with the Hastilow kids; I'd smell and taste the black paddock mushrooms Nana Aggie cooked in bacon fat.

There had to be a connection to the Taits somewhere in all this – and if I closed my eyes and sniffed my bearings through the rain to the paddocks over by the river, I'd find the story; I'd see it written in a landscape that matched the one in my head.

Later, back in Wellington, switching codes to the factual, retrospective record, I found Aggie's first husband in the Registry of Births, Deaths and Marriages, that other graveyard. His name was Frederick Charles Cox, described as a grain expert on his marriage certificate and as a clerk on his death certificate; his father was a farmer from Crofton in the Rangitikei. He and Aggie were married in the Methodist church, Blenheim, on 23 March 1904, when they were both twenty-five; Fred died of peritonitis of the appendix on 11 December 1904. Aggie, whose father William the marriage certificate describes as a blacksmith, remarried to my grandfather Herbert Stacey Horne, described as a clerk, in Wellington on 24 July 1906, at the residence in Thorndon of someone called Porter. One of the marriage witnesses was James Tait. The other witness was one John Aston, an advertising agent.

James Tait could not have been the man whose headstone I'd found at Omaka, because he died in 1897 and was a joiner. The James Tait who witnessed Aggie's second marriage must have been a brother or other close relative named after old James; and, once I'd deciphered the hastily confident handwriting of the officiating registrar or minister, Thas. Porter of Thorndon, I saw that *this* James Tait was a 'Cheese Maker' of Tua Marina.

Surely my memory of the cheesy smell of the dairy at the Hastilows' farm in Tua Marina was connected in some way with James Tait, 'Cheese Maker'? But I didn't know this. All the same, the presumption of the over-confident (and self-serving) narrative with which I'd got this far was complicated by that aroma, so strong in my memory. And I knew (because my accurate brother Dave had told me) that Aggie had gone to live at Tua Marina after we left for East Pakistan, and had died there.

These lives began to sheet back into landscapes where families lived and where skills were deployed – where children were raised, horses shod, cheese made and grain assessed. There were tragedies large and small; romances and redemptions. The narrative tracks I had cut through all this to get to my mother's and father's home, to the nest of circumstances in which they'd raised Dave and me, began to branch into complexities I hadn't anticipated. It wasn't that I'd 'made up' my mother's unhappiness or dissatisfaction and my father's restless ambition. Rather, I'd believed that what I was 'remembering' was as close as I could honestly get to the truth of my childhood experience. Yes, these memories were assisted by various prompts such as photographs, and by the family's stories. But I'd tried to keep these in perspective, and to declare them.

Recently I received an email from Robin Hastilow, whom I would have known as one of the Hastilow kids back in the 1950s. She passed on a story about a shooting accident on Christmas Day 1927.

> In Tua Marina on 25 December 1927 after the cows had been milked and a cooked breakfast enjoyed by the Hastilow family on a typical hot Marlborough morning Mary and daughter Agnes turned their attention to preparing

> Christmas dinner on the wood fueled range, the Horne family from Blenheim had been invited to the farm for their traditional annual gathering and there was much to do before nine people sat down to dine at midday.

Though this was the first I'd ever heard about the longevity of the Hastilow–Horne family relationship, let alone seventeen-year-old Bill and fourteen-year-old Dud's shooting accident, the story immediately found its way to a chamber of my childhood memory where I could visualise the adult Dud's feet in wool socks going into gumboots on the back porch of the homestead at Tua Marina; I even think I can remember him squirting milk from a cow's teat into a tin can for us to drink. But I also know how contingent these memories are; how their triggers may be unconnected to events I experienced; how broad the narrative is through which I've cut my narrow path.

After visiting Norma, I knew I needed to adjust or loosen this viewpoint and see what else changed. For example, the photograph of the Swiss teacher called Herzig climbing a coconut palm, which I described some pages ago, was pasted to a Christmas card sent to my parents by someone called Donald. It contains a handwritten message that I can now read as slightly jeering: 'P.S. Can you recognise who is climbing? Yep – it's Herzig!!' The twin exclamation marks suggest that poor Herzig was probably ridiculed. At once I want to side with him against the snotty expats in the compound at Changraghona. I now want to suspect that the rumours we heard of Herzig going crazy and wandering the streets of Calcutta with his cardboard suitcase may in fact have concealed a different reality – that of an adventurous and fun-loving man who climbed trees with us kids and pre-dated the influx of hippy wanderers around India by a decade. This inflection of the Herzig story runs a few degrees counter to the one I've already told. *That* one wanted to move swiftly and even impatiently past Herzig (who I wanted to have gone mad with loneliness), and get to what I thought was more important, the story of Robert Lübker and the 'hat penthouse-like o'er the shop of your eyes'.

Now I think I need to move more slowly and uncertainly.

Which story of the Italian water pitcher should I tell? The one I thought I was going to tell, with its redemptionist sub-theme of triumphant imagination and a home in contingency and fortune, whose template I believed I'd found in my mother's story of impatient dissatisfaction; or the revised one I now find myself with after visiting cousin Norma? In the latter, the story tilts away from a drama of extremes towards something at once simpler and more complex. It's simpler because I now believe my mother and father, and in particular my mother, weren't as 'unhappy' with their lot before the war as I'd scripted them to be; but it's more complex because I now think they passed the baton of redemption to their twin boys, and themselves went on to live lives unencumbered by much need to gamble a life-wished-for against a less satisfying reality.

If I choose the second, I have to leave behind the gloomy, blame-full kid on the hill above Hazelgrove School, gesturing wretchedly towards his absconded parents, and relive the happiness of his successor and the conditions he was *happy enough* to be at home in.

The Italian water pitcher was in a shop mostly filled with tourist souvenirs in the hilltop town of Assisi, where we went to see the Basilica of San Francesco d'Assisi, with its frescoes by Giotto and Cimabue. The frescoes didn't mean much to me in 1959 when I was eleven years old, but coming back down the hill I stood my ground and insisted that my parents buy the large metal water pitcher whose lid was attached to it by a chain. The pitcher looked old but probably wasn't; it was sturdy and quite heavy, with molded brass animal motifs on its lid and spout. Its outside was dull copper but not tarnished, and I liked it that way. The inside was lined with tin or perhaps pewter. It was expensive, heavy and awkward to add to our carload of travel gear.

My mother and father protested, refused, cajoled, walked off. I stayed by the shop until they came back. The shop's owner, seeing her ally in this small drama, allowed me to hold the pitcher; I was still holding it when the family returned to put a stop to this nonsense. Dave was grinning as usual, Chick was angry, but I saw Linda hesitating.

Behind my obstinate arguments that this was a beautiful thing and why couldn't I have it, especially as I'd promise to give up any other treats for the rest of the trip, lurked a simple truth. The water pitcher was my ransom. It bought my freedom. And it bought off my parents' guilt at abandoning their twin boys.

Can a child think this way? Of course the water pitcher, which would always be 'Ian's Italian jug', didn't come back to school with me. It went with my parents around the world, first of all to Khulna, where I admired it with satisfaction when we went to visit, and subsequently to wherever they stopped for a year or two. I asked to have it when Dave and I divvied up the things in Linda's flat after she died. And when I brought it home to our house in Wellington, I remembered the feeling of triumph as I walked down the hill in Umbria behind my fuming father, conspiratorial mother and grinning brother. Of course I'd known what I was doing. Wherever they went, my stand-in went with them. I didn't have to remind them that I existed; they didn't have to remind themselves.

The transaction of the water pitcher freed me to be happy elsewhere, however fortune threw the dice.

And now my mother and father could also do whatever they wanted, seeing in the water pitcher the liberating sign of everything they'd been able to give their children, which was everything they'd been denied themselves until the moment when they leveraged our advantages off their own freedom. Even our peculiar education to that point, during which we'd learned French and German but not a lot else, was transmuted into an advantage of sorts.

I don't remember much else about our last holiday with Chick, before he and Linda made the final break and left us in England. There are photographs of us carrying Box Brownies with Mont Blanc in the background; Chick and Linda had a map-reading argument somewhere near Lake Como, and Chick got out of the car and stormed off, so Linda drove along slowly behind him with a hint of a chevron-shaped smile on her face. We're somewhere like Austria where there's a clock from which mechanical figures emerge and bash bells with hammers; we're grinning in a gondola in Venice. I remember eating a delicious sole in France, and being allowed a sip of wine with it. Once, desperate to pee during the night, I tipped the flowers out of a vase in an upstairs room and pissed into it, then emptied it out the window; below in the courtyard, some people who'd been singing yelled at me in a funny, guttural language.

And then we were back at Hazelgrove, with the scant food, mass dormitory wank-ins, cold baths and tuck-box wars. The loony kid ran about bellowing and tearing up sods of grass. The Bible teacher popped in on us in the changing sheds. We crash-rode bikes around a kind of dirt track through thickets of nettles. In our last year at the school we wore long pants. In the holidays, we went on bike trips to YHA hostels. Once,

Reg and Peggy took us with them to visit friends in Ireland, where we were on permanent best-behaviour. Mostly we stayed in a little caravan outside their Odcombe Lodge. We slept in sleeping bags on narrow squabs; we mucked about in the parkland. We were allowed to watch *The Black and White Minstrel Show* and Bruce Forsythe compering *Sunday Night at the London Palladium* on the TV in Reg and Peggy Markwell's front room.

It was better fun at school. Then we took a Common Entrance exam to see if we could get into the senior branch of the school, a few miles away in Bruton. We did well enough, at least in languages, which was a vindication of some kind. On our birthday we'd get a letter from Chick's lawyer, with a five-pound note each enclosed. 'Your father has asked us to wish you a very happy birthday.' When we passed our exam to go to senior school, we got a lawyer's letter with a cash present, and a letter from Linda and Chick telling us how proud they were.

Seven Samurai

The headmaster of Kings School Bruton, the senior branch of Hazelgrove where we went when we were thirteen, was an unusual man, as excellent as his counterpart at Hazelgrove was an incompetent health-freak wacko. His name was R.C. Davy – I don't know what the 'R.C.' was short for. I remember him as a big, leathery-faced, kindly, quiet-spoken, but unexpectedly frightening man with bushy eyebrows. He wore baggy tweed suits and a faded black schoolmaster's gown. He had very large hands and ears, and a smoker's yellowed teeth. Dave remembers the mop of straight dark hair that hung aslant his forehead.

He taught Latin and German across the whole school and English literature to the senior classes. It was rumoured that he was a poet. I remember him mentioning in passing that John Steinbeck had once spent several months in Bruton, working on a book.

The school was an old one, with buildings that sometimes stood alone and sometimes mingled with those of Bruton village. Many of the buildings were grand, built of tawny local sandstone; others were more modest, especially those that abutted the village high street; they were all comfortably run-down. The school was organised along traditional all-boys public boarding school lines, with 'houses' (whose names I've had to ask Dave about) in which a traditional governance system prevailed, with a housemaster, prefects, fags and a matron. Dave remembers the names of the houses. The first one we went to was old, with an entrance from the village high street; it was called Old House.

There was a chapel, a brass band, sports teams, many clubs or 'societies' as they were called, and we wore uniforms that included shirts with stiff detachable collars fastened with studs at the back: you changed the collar more often than the shirt. We had to shine our shoes daily, Latin was compulsory, and every night we did two hours prep after dinner.

There was a music conservatory, and a large art department run by a long-haired, chain-smoking bohemian in corduroy trousers. During the holidays, he and I once bid against each other for second-hand picture frames at a junk auction in Yeovil – at the time I was flirting with the idea of becoming an artist. The art room was located by a river, which was where the art teacher's pet, who was the school's resident moody genius, threw the art gear I'd bought with my birthday money (he'd also chopped the bristles off my brushes with a razor blade): thus ended my brief aspiration to be a painter. The remains of my gear were rescued downstream by a big smiling boy with a strong Dorset accent – he spent all his spare time alone by the river, catching little trout.

I have a copy of the school magazine, *The Dolphin*, for the Winter Term 1961. For some reason it was among Linda's papers. It opens with an anonymous editorial complaining about VIth Form 'apathetic indifference to or unawareness of important world-scale issues', and closes with a stirring quote from John Osborne: 'Let's pretend we're human beings and that we're actually alive.' There are various society reports, including one by 'D.B.' for the Film Society. The 1949 *Christopher Columbus* directed by David MacDonald and starring Fredric March is unfavourably compared ('a flat, superficial version') to the 'rebel psychology' of John Osborne's play *Luther*, which probably outs D.B. as the anonymous rabble-rousing writer of the editorial. *Gunfight at the O.K. Corral* (1957) is praised for working its clichés well ('the saloon brawl, the sluttish woman, the good men fighting outnumbered') but is apparently compromised 'by the monotonous succession of second-rate television cowboys'. *Viva Zapata* (1952) with Marlon Brando is D.B.'s favourite: '. . . the film lets the ideal of complete democracy live on, symbolized by [Zapata's] white horse.' I'd like to know where D.B. ended up.

The Gallows Society, which would have staged the Osborne play, went to the Bristol Old Vic to see a production of Brecht's *Mother Courage*, and watched the film *Blackboard Jungle* (1955) with Sidney Poitier and the first installment of a series called *Maniac Theatre* ('which aims to examine the trend of lunatic violence in to-day's plays') – this was devoted to 'Edward Albee's electrifying *Zoo Story*'.

I'm surprised to find myself listed as the captain of the Junior Colts rugby team, for which Dave also played. I don't remember this, or have lost it in the red haze of my rugby at Hazelgrove. The team had an undistinguished season, with two wins and six losses.

The school had a reputation for academic excellence. It presented itself as a small but distinguished traditional private school that might appeal to the professional middle classes of the south-west – the prosperous citizens of Somerset, Devon and Dorset, a few clicks out from the Home Counties, with a rural base.

There were dandies in our house (Dave and I were in separate dormitories and classes) who skited about hunting; they meant fox hunting. Apparently the best part was getting blind drunk afterwards. They had girlfriends with whom they boasted they had frequent sex in the holidays; girls liked it when you stuck your tongue in their mouths and your fingers up their cunts, but what they liked best was sucking on your cock – even more than when you stuck your cock into them, which was risky as they might get pregnant. The logistics of exactly where you stuck your cock continued to baffle me. The rural dandies imparted a glassy shine to their shoes by using homemade concoctions smelling of turpentine nicked from the art room. They went to balls.

They had homes. Their parents came to get them for the holidays, arrived with picnic hampers on sports days and sent them stuff in parcels. They had pocket money. I was wistful about this rather than sad – I've no idea how Dave felt. But it was the headmaster Davy who appeared to take note of our situation, which was probably shared by other expat kids at the school, and he began to talk to me, a gruff sentence or two at a time.

One day he said, 'You write a bit of poetry, don't you? That's what I hear.' My silence must have been familiar to him. Of course I was going to say yes, but I didn't know how to. The whole point of having a secret whose hiddenness was apparent to those who chose to notice was that it couldn't be spoken about. Before the silence could go on long enough to be embarrassing, he just said, 'That's good,' put his pipe back in his mouth and walked on.

I seem to remember that my face was hot with a combination of shame and pleasure; but that was a sensation I was to feel often over the next few years, and I may be remembering what was typical rather than distinct. I still have my Kings School Bruton copy of Ovid's *Metamorphoses* in Latin, a small red book whose spine has faded, as have my little scribbles in the margins. I think it was around the use of that book in Latin classes that Davy discovered what I was up to – or our English teacher, whom I don't remember, may have noticed my covert activity.

The 1961 *Dolphin* has three of my poems in its Literary Supplement. They are mawkish, and have over-elaborated metrical and rhyme schemes. One has the rhyme scheme pencilled in its margin: abcdcae. Another stumbles from an erotics of summer heat to an image of an itchy dog, 'which must nibble all day,/ And scrabble and twitch.' I know where the erotics came from, but not the formal obsession. Perhaps I was sending secret signals to Davy, who spent patient hours trying to get our heads around Latin prosody.

Looking back, I can see that what Davy was doing with the school as a whole was highly unusual. Beneath its façade of public-school conventions, no doubt essential to its brand and its appeal to the largely well-off parents of its pupils, Davy was subverting most of the school's institutional traditions. There was a prohibition on corporal punishment of any kind. Writing 'lines' as punishment was not practised either (I'd spent hours of excruciating boredom at Hazelgrove copying and re-copying passages from the Bible). The 'prefects' moved into quotation marks, since their role involved more obligation than privilege. I was assigned as a fag to a prefect whose name I don't remember; although I shined his shoes for him, he had to look after me and make sure I was getting what I needed. He showed me how to use the library, the telephone I was terrified of, and the post office I didn't understand; he tried to help me with the maths I never did get the hang of; he warned me that the scrumpy sold illegally by the local off-licence would make me vomit. It did.

Davy himself seems to have been a pacifist, or was at least sceptical of the school's military obligations. He'd devised a way of dealing with the army cadet corps which, dressed in hobnailed boots, scratchy khakis, and puttees plastered with mud-coloured muck, was mustered on the parade ground or the tennis courts where it drilled using old .303 rifles.

There was also an RAF corps, to which Dave belonged. Map-reading, rifle-range practice, drilling, and shambolic orienteering expeditions into the surrounding countryside took place; but if you said you didn't want to do any of this, you could join the brass band. It was common knowledge that the band was the best option, though giving up on the chance to fire .303s at the rifle range was a tough trade-off. As a result, the school probably had one of the largest and least-trained brass bands ever assembled.

Having expressed a dislike of drilling and running around the surrounding countryside with a heavy pack and a compass, I was given a battered euphonium and taught to play a rhythmical pattern of three or four farting notes. Then we marched about in poorly coordinated, discordant formations, with a small percentage of able musicians playing real music. On occasions when the whole corps paraded, led by the ludicrous band, Headmaster Davy, dressed in perfunctory khakis, would stand on a raised plinth to take the eyes-right salute with an inscrutably deadpan expression on his face. Thus he fulfilled what was no doubt obligatory within the school's charter while at the same time encouraging us to work around it.

Classes were organised in two streams – what was known as the academic one, and the practical one. This too may have been inherent in the school's charter, or in its traditions. The academic stream was directed towards gaining entry to universities, the practical one towards getting work. But Davy mixed them up in interesting ways. He had academic maths classes conducted in the woodwork shop, where calculations were applied to drawing up plans, working out ratios and extrapolating to three dimensions using algebra. He introduced us to Ovid's *Metamorphoses* by encouraging butterfly-collecting expeditions (he was a keen lepidopterologist), which he then cross-referenced to natural history classes and systems of Latin taxonomy.

There was no compulsory attendance at classes in the academic stream, and students marked one another's work. When he caught our German class involved in mass test cheats, in the course of which we'd worked out a system for rationalising our collectively higher marks, he punished no one, withheld no privileges, made no comment, but spent an entire class gravely, even woodenly pointing out the computational flaws in our system and what had made its scam ridiculously easy to detect; we'd shamed ourselves not just by cheating but by making fools of ourselves doing it. When he left the room after that session, we all sat in silence for a while. The dread and fear I felt may have been exacerbated by the fragment of one-sided conversation about poetry which I was still carrying around like an instruction on how to evolve, but I think my classmates all felt something similar. Davy let our marks stand as we'd awarded them to each other, but we didn't cheat again.

He conducted sex education classes in which he explained in simple language what even the boastful rural dandies hadn't been able to get across to me (what went where); he pointed out that no one in the school seemed to be going blind, and so masturbation wasn't as dangerous as some people would have you believe. He himself had a large animal presence and a beautiful wife, and we didn't doubt that they had lots of sex in the headmaster's modest house, which had a vegetable garden at the back where Davy could be seen at weekends staking up his tomatoes and beans, and forking over a large compost heap.

He'd also established a film society at the school. To join, you had to pay a small levy and get a letter of permission from your parents. This was because Davy, who operated the projector himself, showed films classified above the age range of his pupils. Thus it was that I saw (in French) Roger Vadim's *Sait-on jamais*, Jacques Tati's *Mon Oncle*, Claude Chabrol's *Le beau Serge* and Alain Resnais' *Hiroshima mon Amour.* We saw John Huston's *Maltese Falcon* and Robert Aldrich's *Kiss Me Deadly.* We saw Kurosawa's *Rashomon.* Davy ran the movies and changed the reels; he quite often smoked during the screenings, and his pipe smoke used to drift across the projection light shaft. At the end, he would usually say a word or two about the film. He had a standard answer for anyone who protested they hadn't understood what it was about: 'See it again.'

Above all, he screened Kurosawa's *Seven Samurai.* I was completely swept away by this film. Though I've seen it several times since, I still remember that first viewing. The film seemed to have a large, rhythmical shape – to be composed of tremendous material blocks or masses that presented themselves front-on, surging into chaotic close-ups, or that gathered at the sides of the screen and then rushed laterally across it. The rain that swept across the screen both darkened it and gave it a kind of harsh diagonal grain. The light appeared to be organised in sheets or planes, rather than diffused through the film's depth of field. The story seemed to dodge and thread its way through these great, counterpoised compositions; it was delicate, even minimal, so simple that you could almost forget about it – it seemed to be telling itself in spite of or oblivious to the big visual structures of the film.

At one point early on, the simple story and the large, blocked masses of movement came together – this is what I remember most vividly – or seemed to be still, like a clearing in a mighty landscape, or a silence in the middle of an ongoing tumult. It was also a silence or clearing in the mind. This was the moment when Kikuchiyo, the young wannabe Samurai whose humble origins enabled him to empathise with the poor farmers of the embattled village, paused by a mountain stream and caught a fish for food.

The delight of this small event, which established Kikuchiyo as resourceful rather than a hapless clown, had a lot to do with my own sense of inferiority. Unlike the rural dandies who went home to holidays of drunkenness, finger-fucking and fox hunting, Dave and I amused ourselves in the rook-cluttered elms of Montacute Park or pedalled our way staunchly through the YHA hostel guide. We didn't go and stay at friends' houses. We seemed to have less cash than the others, who bought sausages, toast-making supplies, cocoa and vomit-inducing scrumpy in the village; I scrounged these things from them.

Also, Kikuchiyo somehow reached across to our visit to the Chittagong Hill Tracts a few years back, to the time I fell down the waterfall and disturbed the monster that was waiting to emerge as the Gill-man of the Black Lagoon. The villagers of *Seven Samurai* reminded me of the people we'd seen at Chimbuk, including a group of women catching minute fish in the river that became the waterfall.

That secret moment – the horribly swarming waterfall-pond and the creature of the black lagoon – which had in some way inaugurated the furtiveness of my writing activity as an antidote to fear and the portal to another reality, now seemed to have been laid open. The stillness or lightness of the fish-catching moment in the film was like a window opening in my mind. I remember walking out of the screening with a sense of physical and atmospheric lightness. The Kikuchiyo I identified with planted himself resourcefully in the film's tremendous structure, its masses of movement, sheets of light, cross-currents of rain. He made himself entirely visible. He declared what he wanted, and was eventually accepted on his own terms. His personal triumph was notable not just in itself, but because it was contained – housed, homed – in forms that were all about the drama of making emotion visible. My excitement was at once personal and abstract.

Of course such moments are seldom the epiphanies we subsequently remember them to have been. My emergence from writing as a secret activity almost certainly took place over time. But I do remember very clearly that, at the end of the *Seven Samurai* screening, Davy made some kind comment about the film being more like a poem than a story.

I emerged cautiously from my poetry closet. The school magazine published some of my poems, and I was given a book of poetry recently published by an old boy of the school. I no longer have the old boy's book, and can't remember the poems I was being encouraged to emulate. In the summer of 1961, I won the school's German prize – a copy of the 1960 Oxford edition of the collected poems of Gerard Manley Hopkins, chosen by Davy. That oblique good judgement was typical of him. As a bonus, though without the signed prize-label on the inside cover, he also gave me a copy of Baudelaire's *Les fleurs du mal* in French. Of both he said mildly that I'd find them difficult. He obviously thought that was a good thing.

He once delivered a sermon in the school chapel on some occasion when it was full of the kids' families. He based his talk on T.S. Eliot's *The Waste Land*, from which he quoted at length. The congregation began to rustle and there was an outbreak of coughing. Davy was unperturbed. Somewhere out there, in one of those clearings or moments of mental stillness, someone – a Kikuchiyo – would be catching the bony little fish of difficulty and feeding his hunger to be part of something larger than himself. I think of this Kurosawa episode as a kind of homecoming – when the where and the who of me lined up, or rhymed, I want to say 'for the first time'.

Peggy Markwell's back

As we came in to Odcombe Lodge that winter holiday when Linda appeared out of the blue to pick us up from Bruton, the first thing I noticed was Peggy Markwell's back. She had it turned to us while she was doing something at the kitchen sink. My memory of the layout of the house is that the kitchen was at one end of the ground floor, with a door opening to the outside facing the park, and another into the bathroom and lavatory. The small dining room and parlour were to your right as you came in from outside, the kitchen to your left.

Linda ushered us to the right, away from Peggy, who didn't turn to greet us. There was something about her back that disturbed me. Leaving aside what appeared to be the unfriendliness of her stance, she appeared stiff, her head bowed towards the kitchen sink, as if oblivious to anything but what she was doing there. But then I noticed that she wasn't doing anything. She was just standing there with her head a little bowed and her back straight, her hands hidden in front of her on the edge of the sink, quite motionless.

Having come this far along my story of home, on a narrative track at once chronological and diverted into digressions where I've returned to places where I had homes in the past, I now confront a memory that is banal where the others have been dramatic.

The grass catcher whose talismanic ambiguity presides over my entire effort here; the smell of darkness that I encountered in the artesian well at Francis Street when I was a child, and its reprise that I encountered as a sixty-four-year-old's dream of death by the Vaikuna chasm; the illicit stink of the little white-faced girl's shit, and the desolating aroma of my mother's ball-gown perfume; the wedge that Robert Lübker's pedantic explanation of 'penthouse-like' drove into my mind, and the creature from the Black Lagoon that entered through that opening; the plums from my mother's tree at Chandraghona, and my father's ghost scuttled upon by silverfish in the paper-mill archive there; my brother's thumb stroking back and forth across his lips in the dreary YHA hostel lounge; the Italian water pitcher that still gives off a dull, metallic ring, and reminds me of the time when Dave and I parted company with our mother and father – when our home ceased to be with them; the liberating stillness in Kikuchiyo's fish-catching moment in the poem that was *Seven Samurai* – this catalogue of significance isn't one I've chosen in advance so much as a kind of guidance system that has lit up in front of me as I've groped forward without ever knowing what would come next.

I've been moving ahead and looping back through a layered reality that has been at once internal, composed of memories or the talismanic objects that seem to produce memory as their affect, and external, composed of facts such as the pebbly beach across the bay at Waikawa. The truth values of such hard, material facts are their own, in their own present; but they also may endorse the intangible truths of memories.

In *On Dreams*, Freud reminded us that we dream in pictures – in fact, in moving pictures with sound – but not in language. Understanding dreams involves looking at a collage, in which different times and places will be mixed up, and in which (Freud suggested) something like allegory makes the dream's meaning accessible. The dream-narrative is a jostle of symbols pointing away from themselves. The world of dreams is often filled with the visual babble of signs clamouring to be spoken or written of otherwise.

The key moments in the memories that have been my dream-like guidance system often resemble what Freud called symbols. There's an inherent paradox in this analogy. What Freud characterised as visual is implicitly aligned with allegory, a mode of annotation, and therefore of *reveals*. This insistence that, in dreams and memories, something must always mean something *else* is inherently dramatic. It anticipates a revelation, even a catharsis. The analysis of dreams and memories is theatrical, and often sensational.

What, then, do we make of memories that are banal? That seem to point nowhere else? That are without suspense, mystery, drama? That are mute? That is how my memory of Peggy Markwell's back appears. Though her behaviour was soon glossed dramatically in Linda's hushed explanation, my memory of its appearance remains flat, as if the emotion had been ironed out of it, as if it had been drained of narrative. This remains so even when its tragic circumstances are explained.

The home we entered when we went to live with Reg and Peggy in the holidays was 'childless'. Thus, by default, we became the children in it when we were there. But we weren't *their* children. Reg was an aeronautical engineer who worked at the big Westland helicopter factory near Yeovil. He was a dashing, swarthy man, with a Greek mother who came to stay sometimes. He wore his black hair swept back with a shine of Brylcreem in it; there were a few streaks of grey at his temples. I'd guess he was in his early forties when we went to live with him and Peggy. Peggy was a bit younger, in her mid- to late thirties. I remember her as a compact, attractive woman. They sometimes took us to the seaside at Chesil Bank on the Dorset coast, where they'd sunbathe on the steep shingle beach – they were a good-looking couple.

I suspect that one of the reasons we were moved out of the bedroom next to theirs in the top of the lodge was that they were trying to have a baby. And eventually we noticed, and were told with great delight by both of them, that Peggy was pregnant. And then Linda appeared suddenly from Khulna and picked us up from school. I didn't understand much of what she told us, but gathered that Peggy's baby had been born with a deformity and had either died or been allowed to die.

I saw Linda with Peggy a lot – she seemed to be supporting and comforting her. My guess now is that she was asked to come back to England for the holidays because it would have been too hard for Reg and Peggy to handle these children who in a sense represented what they'd irrevocably lost. And so Linda was there for a few weeks before we went back to school and she to Khulna.

Peggy's manner towards us had always been brisk and friendly. Her kindness was practical rather than warm. Reg, I understood early, had found me irritating; he mostly kept this in check, with the exception of the occasional 'Fishface' taunt early on, and his one furious assault when Dave and I were play-fighting in the double bed next to their room. But from the moment of Peggy's stiff, still back turned towards us at the kitchen sink, her manner changed. I don't remember how many more holidays we spent at Odcombe Lodge and in the adjacent Montacute Park, but I do remember that she became withdrawn towards us: practical and organised as before, but of necessity. I don't think she disliked us. But I've no doubt she was glad when we left.

It was an especially bitter, black-frost winter when that

happened. Reg was driving us to London to catch the plane back to New Zealand. For some reason, I remember the drive taking place overnight, in the dark, through driving rain, sleet and snow, which the Austin A35's headlamps could barely penetrate. But that's unlikely. Probably the weather was grim and dark, with heavy snow clouds; we probably left before dawn to get to Heathrow on time. I remember the grimness of that drive, with Reg silent and concentrating on the black road ahead. I felt as though we were escaping. Later, in a long conversation with Dave about the time we left England and came back to New Zealand, he reminded me that we drove to London and spent the night with Reg's sister May (of course he remembers her name) and their mother, that Reg took us to the airport the following morning.

Almost certainly, we wouldn't be seeing Reg and Peggy again. We'd been the occasional children in their home for five years. Then their own child had died and we'd become the children they couldn't have. I remember Peggy's perfunctory hug when we left to get in the car; and the back she turned again to go inside out of the cold. She was a good, kind woman, and I can't blame her for the ways her grief made her turn her back on the kids she'd made a home for but couldn't have been expected to love. I've been back to England many times over the years, and to Montacute Park when I lived in London in 1970 and '71. But I never tried to get back in touch with the Markwells. I probably should have; I wish I had. My brother Dave did, as you'd expect – he went to see them a couple of times after they moved north. It's he who is able to fill in the details – that they went first to Preston for Reg to work 'on the BAE Tornado Multi Role Aircraft', then into retirement in Falmouth, Cornwall. That would have been where Linda visited them on her last trip.

They're both dead now. The clearest memory I have of

them is also the least sensational, an image that seems entirely factual and, because of that, almost emptied of meaning, a kind of abstraction: it's Peggy's back turned not against us, but against the childless home we haplessly rebuked with our presence.

The punnet of strawberries

And then we were returning to be in a home again with our own mother and father. I remembered this when Donna and I drove north to Auckland from the big old house in Wellington where we'd lived and worked for twenty years, where our kids had lived, and come and gone, and come back again; where we'd all sat down together at meals to celebrate yet another return, another embarkation. (. . . *It's great to be home/ Again, say our wandering sons, as they wave goodbye.*)

We were driving up in separate cars with our office gear and minimal possessions. It was high summer, and on the southern motorway approaches to the city I saw the shimmer of heat rising from mirages of water on the asphalt, the approaching high-rise horizon, the gassy, hot blue of the sky with its motionless heaps of grey-white cloud, the trashy signage and brightly coloured bunting of the service areas and used-car lots – and market-garden signage advertising strawberries. All this rushed into the space in my mind and the adjacent breathless chest-space where memory resides, and I let out a yell of exhilaration; my eyes filled with tears. I felt as if I was coming home, or coming home again.

Three of our boys, Mischa, Conrad and Penn, were back living in the house on Mount Victoria, together with Mischa's girlfriend Laura and her baby girl Bella. We expected some of them to follow us north once the house sold. Jack had settled in Melbourne but most of his stuff was still at the house in Wellington. Carlos, Sarah and their son Sebo were back there too, but in their own cosy house on Ohiro Road that leads down to the stormy, rocky Cook Strait coast I'd loved for thirty-odd years – the one that connects, through the tides I sailed in my cousin John's yacht, with Dieffenbach Point and my mother's ivory bracelet, my father's Seamaster watch.

My exhilaration on the southern motorway approaches to Auckland City wasn't at the expense of the kids or a sense of home grounded in the sight of our children and their girlfriends and cousins sitting down together to eat at the big table Carlos and I built in our house on Mount Victoria. Rather, whatever sadness I'd been transporting north was swept aside by a memory of arriving in Auckland as a fifteen-year-old, in 1961, after crossing the space between the dark, bitterly cold drive to London from Odcombe Lodge, and the hot, mown-grass-scented sunshine we drove through from Whenuapai airport to our new home in Rarangi Road, St Heliers, Auckland, on the wide Hauraki Gulf.

Linda and Chick met us at the airport; they were both tanned and wearing sunglasses. Chick had shorts on, Linda a light cotton sunfrock. We hadn't seen them for over two years. The immigration officials' uniforms had short sleeves, and I remember a kind of incredulous excitement building from the moment I watched one of those bronzed, freckled arms reaching over to stamp my passport. Where was this? Where was I?

The guy gave Dave and me a droll look – we were still dressed in versions of our best-behaviour English clothes. A Masport mower was revving around the grassy area by the car park; as well as the scent of hot grass-clippings and aviation fuel the place seemed to smell of space and light.

We drove past market gardens and roadside fruit and vegetable stalls with honesty boxes. At one of them Chick pulled over, and Linda came back to the car with punnets of fresh strawberries. The fruit was warm from being out in the sun; we ate our way through a couple of punnets while driving into the city. We flicked the stems out the car window into warm, humid wind.

Soon, we were driving past second-hand car lots festooned with strings of brightly coloured plastic bunting. The footpaths outside some of them were shining with hose-water where the cars had been washed. This is what I remember most vividly after the strawberries – a bright glamour I associated with California, as different from the dark drive to London as you could get. Soon, we'd be hastily sinking our pale bodies out of sight in the tepid water of Ladies Bay below the headland at St Heliers; Rangitoto floated its exotic volcano shape on the turquoise horizon; there were immense piles of sodden cloud motionless in the glaring sky, and when rain fell out of them the asphalt steamed and dried in minutes.

Before long, we were tanned like the others at the beach, and we lay about on towels or walked to the dairy on the corner to get ice creams. We hopped back to 47 Rarangi Road in bare feet along red scoria footpaths that were so hot we had to jump sideways on to the springy Buffalo grass of berms that people mowed with Masports at the weekend. It was a paradise that couldn't be home because it was so fresh and unfamiliar, but that was *going to be home* because our mother and father were there; because they'd asked us to be there, to be *here*, with them.

When I talk to Dave about this, he remembers a similar feeling of exhilaration. In his case it's not the punnets of warm strawberries or the bright second-hand car-yard bunting he remembers as representing this paradise that was going to be home, but the awnings and canopies that were supported on posts along the shopping strips we drove through towards

St Heliers. My paradise of strawberries and coloured plastic bunting was Californian; Dave's reminded him of the Wild West. Both of us had come home to a place that was more like a movie than . . . what?

I don't remember when the letter came to England from our parents telling us they'd decided to return to New Zealand, and I can't, now, find it. Sometime around my first year at university in Auckland in 1965 I burned a whole lot of stuff associated with the years between leaving England and moving on with my own life after finishing school in Auckland. I remember that their letter said they were going to live in Auckland, and they wanted to know if we'd like to leave school in Bruton and come back to New Zealand to join them.

What I remember as the choice we were being offered was also their admission that they couldn't take our compliance or wish to be with them for granted; they'd forfeited both. The possibility that they may secretly have hoped we'd prefer to stay put in England did occur to me during the sour years that ensued. Now I know that wasn't the case; I recognise a kind of honesty in their invitation. We'd earned the right to say no to them. But of course we didn't.

I was happy at the school in Bruton, perhaps happier than I'd ever been except as a small child, and certainly happier than I would be for some years subsequently. I was at home there in ways I couldn't be during the holidays at Reg and Peggy's. I felt safe at Bruton: in the homeliness of its knockabout rooms and in its tolerant, congenial culture. I mostly liked the schoolwork and felt valued for what I was good at, especially writing and languages. My furtive imaginative life was coaxed from its secret places. What I brought out was rewarded. Both Dave and I had fun with our friends at school. I even lost my virginity with a girl from a neighbouring all-girls school, behind a white-flowering hedge full of bees. She had a slightly French-sounding name and no breasts that I could find; she made me sniff the fingers she'd pressed against her cunt. The deflowering had nothing to do with my initiative, but it gave me boasting capital with which to approach the rural dandies and their rich social lives – though not enough to make me a desirable house-guest during the holidays when, wearing glassy leather shoes, I might have learned to dance, ride horses, crack jokes and fuck. In the holidays, for a short time, Dave and I paraded in solemn silence around Montacute Park and the surrounding lanes with a couple of girls we'd met from a village near Odcombe Lodge. We had nothing to say, and for the girls the appeal of our tongue-tied, hand-holding strolls quickly wore off; they were soon seen with locals who wore their hair swept back Elvis-style, and whose cultivated sneers froze us in our tracks.

Why did we say yes to our parents' invitation to join them in Auckland? Now, my answer has to be, why wouldn't we? Yet I do remember hesitating. Linda and Chick had also written to the headmaster, Davy. They must have put the possibility of us leaving in contingent terms, because he asked if we wanted to go. I remember him suggesting there would be opportunities for us if we stayed. For example, we might be able to go to a good university in England.

I don't remember the discussion Dave and I had, if any. Perhaps the decision made itself; perhaps the childless unhappiness in Reg and Peggy's house made it; perhaps we both, deep down, hoped for the kind of home we saw our school friends had.

I remember Davy's air of resignation when we, or I, said we wanted to go to New Zealand. He made arrangements for us to sit three O-level exams early, in French, German and

English. Perhaps, a little patronisingly, he saw these as the least he could do to help us make our way in backwater New Zealand. More likely, given what I remember of him and his oblique strategies for generosity, he just wanted to do the most he could for us. I have a copy of Dylan Thomas's collected poems which I'm sure he gave me as a goodbye present, but the book was published by J.M. Dent & Sons in 1962, so he can't have, unless he had an advance review copy. In any case, I want the book to have been his farewell present. Even if I bought it myself after getting to Auckland, I'd have done so because of him. And so I left what had become a home, and the father-figure in it, and went home to what, at first, looked like an exciting film set, and a father I no longer felt much connection to.

While working through these memories I had a bizarre dream. I was dressed in clothes that were inappropriately natty – a pale linen jacket, a pair of stylish Italian loafers – as if I was anxiously expecting someone I needed to make a good impression on. The jacket and shoes were splattered with blobs of plaster and paint that came from work I was doing to fix up what resembled a kind of boarding house, old and somewhat decrepit – it could have been our house on Mount Victoria, with a full complement of family in it and the usual list of things to fix at the weekend. In my dream there was only one of my children in the house, a little blond boy who looked like Jack, or like my grandson Sebo, but a large crowd of other people was moving about in the dim rooms.

Then my mother and father came in. It was an anxious moment. My father at once began to remonstrate with me about the state of the place – he got peeved about an old sofa (in real life there was one, with stuffing coming out of it here and there, on the back veranda of the Mount Victoria house). He began to lecture me about the proper way to finish off gib-plastering and how to do a decent job of stripping and painting doors. I was annoyed – couldn't he see that I'd been ruining my special clothes in the course of doing the renovations? And why was he interfering? This wasn't his home, it was ours. I told him to mind his own business and then, as if to make a point, picked up the small child and began to make a fuss of him. '*See?*' I seemed to be saying. 'This is how it's done.'

It feels disloyal to admit that I may have preferred Headmaster Davy to my own father; may have wished that my father was more like him; may have wanted Davy to be my father, not Chick. It's even harder to admit that I may not have, or may no longer have, loved my father. For a time I didn't really know who he was, and he didn't really have a clue about me. He had ambitions for me that were irrelevant, given what interested me – and about which he knew very little. He thought I should be a lawyer because I was argumentative; he thought I should be a diplomat because I'd been lucky enough to get a good start in languages; he considered the English accents Dave and I had come back with to be career assets when in fact they were social stigma.

He didn't consider writing to be anything more than a hobby, and when I began to look for ways to say it was central to my life, he'd respond with advice about making writing pay – I could send stories to *Argosy*, for example, a magazine he subscribed to, which published short fiction. It was clear that he believed the investment he'd made in our education deserved to pay out a substantial career dividend. Now, I can see how his ambitions for us grew from his own early disappointments; but, back then, as the film-set bliss of our first weeks at home in St Heliers began to generate its own routines, I wanted him to be more like Davy and help me to feel good about what had become central to my happiness.

I'd begun to build a belief system around the idea that happiness was the result of being at home in the world, which could happen only when the imagination acted as an open channel between inner and outer realities. But I couldn't get Chick to buy into the idea that it was more important to make happiness than money through writing, that having an imaginative life was more important than having a career.

Many years later, this changed; his pride in what I did was unconditional if slightly baffled, and I even discovered his own desire to 'write a book' about his life. Later still, after he died, I sat up night after night clicking my way through the thousands of 35mm colour slides that had been his own rich and complex imaginative channel between the places he and 'Lindy' passed through or lived in and his own inner life. In the months before he died I even saw a kind of bewilderment come over him, as though the limited circumstances of his life had begun to close those imaginative channels down; he became introspective and moody in ways that were at odds with the energetic, resourceful man I'd re-encountered at intervals throughout my life.

What I did like about him after we came back to live in the house at 47 Rarangi Road, and what began to restore the channels through which love could circulate again, was the Chick who began to emerge during the brief time we were all back together. I think that in some ways this was the father who'd been left behind in Blenheim when we went to Chandraghona. Now, he had a job as the chief accountant at Fisher & Paykel in Panmure. He'd come home and have a beer down on the back lawn he mowed with zeal and enjoyment at the weekends. He established a vegetable garden with a compost bin, and under the house he built a workshop with a heavy-duty bench-vise, with saws and other tools hanging on nails against the wall, and screw-cap jars of recycled nails, nuts and bolts fixed to the undersides of shelving above the bench. The old, crusted gluepot from my childhood was there, and so were various timber oils and varnishes whose aromas I remembered. They must have been stored somewhere while my parents were away all those years. I took over much of this stock when Chick died twenty years later. Some of the tools had been his father's, including a set of sash cramps used to tighten tongue-and-groove timbers or pull together widely spaced joinery. His grandson Carlos and I made the tongue-and-groove matai table with the cramps – as the boards drew together and the smell of linseed oil rose from them, I felt my father's workshop at 32 Francis Street, Blenheim, being gripped into a present forty years later.

Chick began to accumulate a stash of timber among the cobwebby foundations of the house, in dim spaces that extended beyond the workshop, where the piled-up evidence of his and Linda's travelling years were stacked: suitcases, tin trunks and tea-chests in which they'd shipped home their accumulated household stuff and a trove of exotic furnishings, rugs and ornaments. The house above was filled with these trophies.

My father seemed to be relaxed and at ease in these surroundings. Number 47 was on a knoll at the corner of Rarangi Road and Glover Road. It was a modest, single-storey, two-bedroom weatherboard villa with a drive-in garage and a laundry underneath. Out the back was a grassy section with citrus trees. The large front picture-window faced north-west from a lounge and dining area; off this room was a small kitchen that looked out over the back garden. On summer afternoons the front room had to be shaded by venetian blinds. Linda and Chick had a front bedroom that looked out across the neighbouring houses below ours, but not as far as the sea.

The room Dave and I carried our suitcases into that summer day in 1962 was at the back, along a short corridor with the bathroom and a lavatory opening off it. There was a door to the outside at the end of the corridor. After dropping my suitcase on one of the beds in our room, I stuck my head out this door and encountered an inquisitive neighbour looking at me through a hedge.

'Gidday,' he said. 'Welcome home.'

Lunch with Dave

But the most dramatic aspect of this fabulous homecoming was that we almost immediately left again. We went to boarding school at King's College out at Otahuhu, a place I loathed. In the end, my hostility paid off – I got booted out after three years on grounds of 'incompatibility'. We went 'home' for the holidays at first, as we'd sometimes wished we could have during our time in England. But then the mother and father who'd suggested we might like to come back to New Zealand and live with them packed up the home at St Heliers, rented it out to a young family called Brown, and returned to their wandering life, first of all with Chick's posting to a UNDP job in Seoul, South Korea, and thence, with spells in Geneva between times, to Egypt, Jordan and Zambia.

Dave and I saw them for a few weeks in Seoul over Christmas and New Year 1963–64, after we'd been at boarding school in Auckland for two years; again when they returned to New Zealand on a brief sabbatical during my first year at university in 1965; and (for me) again when I went to Jordan in 1969–70.

An unsettling dissonance plays around these stretched-out dates, and around the sequence of events that led up to our coming back to New Zealand.

Soon after moving up to Auckland with Donna, and remembering the bliss of Dave's and my arrival fifty years earlier, I walked the short distance from our home in

Ponsonby to a small Herne Bay beach. I was feeling very happy. I swam out through the tepid water far enough to be able to look around at the shoreline, the harbour bridge, the Chelsea Sugar Refinery, the diminishing, hazy view down the Gulf. I began to remember a lot about those first months when we came back to New Zealand from England at the beginning of 1962. And then, in the midst of this happiness, I experienced a sense of dismay.

It's one thing to write about *memories* which are, after all, only objects of a kind. Sometimes, as in the case of the grass catcher or my mother's ivory bracelet, memories are barely separable from the things that embody them, or that we hold while speaking or writing these memories, as if the talismanic object we're turning over from hand to hand is itself speaking – as if we are the tranced mediums through which the magic object speaks from a past we have, ourselves, forgotten. But it's a more difficult thing to write about *memory* itself, that untrustworthy engine of consciousness.

The vivid memories I do have fill me with confidence in *memory*. They persuade me that my consciousness is doing a good enough job, even if it's getting some facts wrong, rewriting the narratives, relocating or layering events. The memories I don't have, for example the ones that my brother Dave does, give me another kind of confidence, since what I don't remember belongs with what Keats, in his grandly offhand letter, called Negative Capability – the licence to see an imaginative opportunity in whatever you can't be sure of. *Fled is that music:—Do I wake or sleep?*

But where memory is neither confident enough to be undeterred when challenged about factual accuracy (I trip therefore I run), nor capable of taking an interest in what might be imagined out of some kind of devoid condition (I lie therefore I think) – when memory fails to generate *anything* in the space between knowing and imagining, then I'm scared. I'm unable to compose an account of events that I haven't so much 'forgotten' or re-imagined as lost the sense of.

I felt scared all at once in the midst of bliss that was lapping around me like the murky water of the Waitemata Harbour at the bottom of Hamilton Road, where I was swimming and looking across at the Chelsea Sugar Refinery on Auckland's North Shore. I wasn't scared of the memories I was having while floating out there, nor was I scared of what I couldn't remember (I was confident Dave would). I was scared of a senseless incoherence.

Never afraid of deep water, I nonetheless swam for shore, as if my old childhood fears of the Gill-man were rising up again from the harbour muck. Back at our new apartment, I phoned my brother and arranged to go over to his place for lunch and a talk.

Some days later, Dave and I sat outside at the large, hospitable, alfresco table on the patio by his back garden. Through the open French doors to the living room I could see an array of objects and furnishings that had come from our parents' house, from their travels and various homes. There was a large, inlaid, beaten-copper and brass table-top from Syria hung on the wall; a cumbersome, brass-handled wooden chest-of-drawers and escritoire from Korea; some elaborate silver faux-Empire candlesticks that probably came from Cairo's French antique quarter; some wooden African curios; the long-stemmed silver opium pipe from Burma that my son Carlos had loved to play with when we visited Linda and Chick's house at St Heliers after they returned to New Zealand for the last time.

I'd not wanted to have many of their objects after Linda died, and was happy that most of them were in my brother's house, along with our mother's jewellery and other stuff – I'd found the objects oppressive; the memories they embodied crowded a present I wanted to fill up with my own life. But there they were, these prompts to memory, these props and properties, and I was aware of them as Dave and I sat in strong sunlight and drank tea, with the little digital recorder we'd got used to having on the table between us. I didn't ask him if the objects we could both see out of the corners of our eyes spooked him in any way – if he ever felt crowded in on by memories smuggled into his life by these things that spoke so emphatically of our mother and father and the life they'd chosen to live without their children. Had I done so, I can guess that his humouring gaze would have rested on his over-complicating twin for a tolerant few seconds before he said 'No' – with that hint of questioning perplexity I know well. After all, the things had been there in the house for more than twenty years and no one had run screaming from the place or covered the beaten-brass table with a concealing veil.

I was also looking at my brother's strong, brown arm and noticing how like our father's his hands were – capable, broad, the finger-ends slightly spatulate – and that, like mine, they were now the mottled hands of a sixty-five-year-old. He was wearing a baseball cap to keep the sun off his head which, like mine, is barbered very short, with a receded hairline and not much left on top. I felt like saying something like, 'Shit, we're getting old!', but I didn't. The Linda-and-Chick objects in the adjacent room, and our alligator-skin arms were in any case beginning to play into the line of questions I wanted to engage Dave with. They were about memory, rather than memories, and the panic that had disturbed my bliss out in the harbour a few days previously – the bliss that had come from remembering Dave's and my arrival in another Auckland summer fifty years earlier, when I was seduced by the warm punnets of strawberries and the colourful plastic bunting of the used-car yards, Dave by the Wild West awnings over shop-fronts, and both of us by the prospect of a home that had our mother and father in it, and the glittering Waitemata Harbour within hopping distance along the baking red scoria footpath.

Dave and Sue's two Siamese cats were half-heartedly annoying each other on the lawn – one ran to a gap by the fence and the other pulled up short and then sat licking her shoulder, as if the reality of her sister had been extinguished with the flick of her tail-tip as she bolted. A ticking sound came from the furled awning over the patio, and a similar sound from the corrugated-iron roof of the house – the day was heating up. I could see where Dave, with the kind of attention our father had devoted to his lawns, had re-seeded a bald patch of turf and covered it with some green plastic mesh. The shiny leaves of citrus trees fluttered a little; there was a faintly overripe smell on the breeze, as if loquats were rotting in a neighbour's garden. It was as though memory was folding the past of our return fifty years ago into this present where Dave poured tea; he waited with a familiar look of amiable patience. We'd been enjoying these talks, even though what they'd occasionally turned up had been troubling – but mostly we hadn't been all that troubled. Mostly we'd laughed; at worst felt wry.

Then I asked my brother if he could piece together the sequence of events from the time we'd first arrived in London with Linda and Chick to the time we'd come back to New Zealand five years later; if he could remember our parents' comings and goings after that. We'd arrived in London off the *Arcadia* – when did we go down to Somerset? When did we buy the car? When did we go on that holiday around Wales and Scotland – was it before Chick went to Khulna?

Or after we'd driven down to meet him in Rome, and before he and Linda both went away? But when did he go? Did Dave remember him going? When did Linda go – did he remember that? Did he remember her coming back when Peggy lost her baby – or did that happen some other time, even before Linda had left? Did he remember how we got the news that our mother and father were back in New Zealand, and wanted us to come there? What did he remember about the school at Bruton? How long were our parents in New Zealand after we joined them, and when did they leave again? When did they come back for a short stay? How long after they came back for good did Chick die?

I saw him begin to put his excellent memory to work – and then an uncharacteristic expression of perplexity or even bewilderment came over the face that I, with unwavering confidence, have always associated with lucid recall and with an easy, untroubled charm; with the peacefulness of someone content with their situation and how they got there; at ease with *memory* as the designing agent of that equanimity.

Like me, he'd encountered a place that consciousness seemed incapable of getting a purchase on; as it had me, this seemed to shock him. Neither of us had been surprised when we couldn't remember the exact sequences of events that took us from Blenheim to East Pakistan when we were seven – that was a long time ago. But, sitting in the hot Auckland Indian-summer garden and thinking back to our arrival there in that first New Year summer of 1963, we both felt close to that time but couldn't make it cohere.

We went back and forth across this territory that our collective memory seemed to have subverted, churned up, sabotaged. We couldn't make any sense of it. For once, my *ficcione* weren't reproved and improved by Dave's reliability; his facts weren't incubated in my Keatsian 'negative capability'.

We'd ended up together in a no-man's-land where neither of us could help the other to get his bearings.

And it was while we sat there drinking tea and sharing a certain anguish that Dave reminded me he'd been bullied at school in Bruton; that he'd hated the fag system and resented having to make milky instant coffee for 'his' prefect in a pot whose bottom was crusted with slimy, burnt milk; that he'd resented having to shine the prick's shoes; that the bullying had got worse when he reported it to the housemaster, and that he and I had both volunteered to go to a newly built boarding house partly to get away from the prefect and the bullying. There was no more fagging for us at the new house because there was a large quota of new boys; for Dave that was a relief as well. The thought of my sanguine, strong brother being bullied shocked me when he mentioned it with his usual lightness and equanimity – it suggested that there may have been a darker side to his experience, one that linked somehow with my image of him writing a postcard in the YHA hostel on Dartmoor.

Why didn't I remember any of that? I did, after he'd talked about it. But how shameful to have gone to my brother's place expecting him to soothe the unease I'd felt – how selfish to have sat waiting for reprieve at his hospitable table, without considering what might have been happening for him during the time that my memory seemed to have become infected.

No, all had not always been as well as my brother's sunny disposition had suggested over the years. But on we went. By now we both wanted to. We talked for a couple of hours without straightening out the narrative, but along the way we agreed that neither of us could remember the sequence of events that led up to our parents leaving England, we couldn't remember when we'd gone on that holiday around Wales and Scotland, and neither of us could remember either our mother's or our father's departure. It was as though our entirely separate consciousnesses had failed or shut down at that time; and although Dave could remember the makes of the Vauxhalls Chick bought (first a Wyvern, then a Cresta), and that he'd gone with him to Wincanton on the A303 to London to buy the first of them, neither of us could remember how or why there came to be a second (the Cresta), which had been shipped to Auckland and had met us at Whenuapai when we came home. Nor could either of us plot the moment when our parents did their U-turn and left New Zealand again.

It was by imagining ourselves getting back into the cars that we attempted to recreate what had happened. Dave was sure the car we travelled around Scotland and Wales in was the Vauxhall Cresta that had replaced the Wyvern that must have been sold when Linda first left for Khulna after we'd had the holiday with Chick in Europe. That's to say, Chick left England for Khulna, later Linda drove us to Rome in the Wyvern to meet him, then we all drove around Europe. We can't remember how we got back to England, but presumably in the Wyvern on the Channel ferry. Then Linda left for Khulna – after selling the Wyvern? At some time in the future they must both have come back to England, bought the Cresta, gone with us on the Wales and Scotland tour, and then shipped the car to New Zealand – expecting to return there? But that didn't happen for several more years. Dave remembered an incident during the Wales leg of the trip when Linda stopped what he was sure was the Cresta at a T-junction to let an articulated truck make a turn 'from our left across the front of the car – its trailer crabbed and despite Linda's desperate attempt to get into reverse and back away, the trailer snagged the right wing of the car and dragged it about 45 degrees before releasing it.' At least Dave remembered this. Neither of us remembered how the bigger story fits together.

The inanity of this forensic car-brand narrative shut us both up. What was the point? We opened a bottle of wine.

By checking obvious milestones, we thought we'd worked out that we must have gone to Khulna immediately after sitting the 13+ 'Common Entrance' exam that admitted us to the school at Bruton, to which we returned as new boys in the new year of 1960 (I remembered getting my infected ear drained in the infirmary). That may square with my boy-soprano memory, since it's plausible that my voice began to break around that time. But neither of us can get it to square with any memory whatsoever of either of our parents leaving Somerset.

We worked out from the visa dates in Dave's expired passports that we'd gone to Seoul in the New Zealand summer (the Korean winter) of 1963, having arrived back in New Zealand at the beginning of 1962. We worked out that we'd gone for a bike tour up the North Island to Kerikeri with a friend from school, Paul Martin, in the week's holiday after sitting School Certificate in 1962. It was blisteringly hot, our tyres stuck to the melting tar in the asphalt on the way up the Brynderwyn incline, and Linda was still in the house at St Heliers – she took the black-and-white snap of us lined up with our bikes prior to departure. Chick must have been there too, though neither of us had any memory of him leaving then or subsequently; but he must have done so during our second year back in New Zealand. Dave remembered us going on a farewell trip in the Vauxhall for Linda to say goodbye to her brother Keele in Palmerston North, and he remembered that the car got dinged and had to be panel-beaten before we could drive back to Auckland. We had our driver's licences by then, and took turns driving the car. But neither of us remembered Linda leaving after that trip.

I remembered us both spending a winter holiday at our Uncle Keele and Aunty Margaret's place in Palmerston North: that must have been in mid-1963, after Linda had followed Chick to Korea. We went for early-morning runs in bare feet, having been told it was part of the 'toughening-up' training regime for rugby, which I gave up soon after.

Later, Dave used to go to Palmerston for the holidays, and I began to stay with a friend's family in Otahuhu. 'Wan' Temple taught maths at King's College and his son Bill was my best friend there, though he was a day-pupil and went home after school. He went on to become a distinguished professor of psychology. The Temples were my surrogate family; after I was told to leave the school, I lived at their house and Bill's parents were my kindly advocates – Wan negotiated my re-admission to the school for long enough to sit the final Scholarship exam that paid for me to go on to university, which I did the following year after working over the summer with Dave on an orchard near Kurow. Dave went to Canterbury University as an Air Force officer cadet, and we seldom saw each other for a time after that.

It doesn't surprise me now to realise that 'Wan' probably reminded me of Headmaster Davy at Bruton; he had a regional English accent which explained his nickname 'Wan' (that was how he pronounced 'one'), a gentle, laconic manner, and a disdain for the school's faux traditions and discipline which he deployed with expressionless passive resistance. He and Bill used to play memory-chess during their standard breakfasts of boiled eggs and toast – they would sit staring at each other across the table, and then whichever one of them had to make a move would speak its code and put another spoonful of breakfast in his mouth.

Dave and I were remembering all this, telling each

other stories we already knew, skirting around the voids of our parents' departures and the weirdness of our combined memory failures. Dave went on a memory extravaganza as if to compensate for the spooky voids – he remembered that the dormitories at Hazelgrove were named after British battleships such as *Hood*; he remembered Reg Markwell installing a thumping diesel generator so the lodge could have electricity, and the smell of paraffin lamps before that; he remembered the .303 firing-range at Bisley, and how as cadets we used to stick pennies on the target silhouettes in the hope they'd get hit; he remembered being in the Air Force cadets at Bruton and flying in a Britannia and in a university squadron Chipmunk; he remembered being on the verge of applying for a cadetship with the RAF just before we left England; he remembered that at Guy Fawkes anarchy reigned at Bruton and salvos of rockets were fired at passing trains. It was during this session in his sunlit garden that he remembered the girl who'd called us 'poor little buggers' after we first came back to New Zealand was the daughter of an old friend of Chick's, Lewis Fitch; that she became a psychiatrist with the New Zealand Navy.

Was he right about all this? He remembered *The Seven Samurai* when I reminded him. We went back and forth. Throughout the recording of Dave remembering these things, there's the sound of a bird chattering aggressively in the background, and a gusty wind keeps battering the microphone. Dave's voice emerges calmly through this intermittent tumult. He remembers that we went for a holiday with Linda and Chick, and with Uncle Keele, Aunty Margaret and our little cousin Jocelyn at Oakura Bay in Northland; this would have been at the end of 1962, during the second summer after arriving from England, and after our bike trip up north with Paul Martin. I remember going to a dance at the beachside hall, and leaving early, crippled with shyness, and being gently mocked by Uncle Keele. Dave remembers learning to water-ski. I remember sailing back and forth across the bay in a Moth. Though the Moth was a one-person boat, Chick came for a sail and badgered me to sheet in and let her rip. I knew we'd can out, and we did; my father emerged gasping from under the sail once I'd jumped on the centreboard to haul the yacht back up. Later at the bach, Uncle Keele cracked jokes about how I'd almost succeeded in drowning my own father, and how I should try harder next time.

Then, for the first time since I'd started writing this account, and for the first time since Dave and I had begun to talk about our lives together, I heard my brother say that yes, he'd probably been pretty hacked off around that time after we came back to New Zealand, when Linda and Chick took off again, and that things hadn't always been so sweet during our time in England for that matter. Nor for that matter had things gone too well after he left school in Auckland; even worse when he didn't make the grade at officer training.

His wife Sue walked cheerily into the silence that had fallen over the table where my sanguine brother was looking at the backs of his hands. His happiness has had a lot to do with her, and her amused scepticism of me has had a lot to do with her suspicion that I might be out to taint that happiness – or even, perhaps, poison that well much as I'd once defiled the artesian spring at Francis Street, first with a frog and next with old sump oil, though of course she doesn't know about that. Dave greeted her affectionately before she could notice anything odd – for a split second I saw image-splinters in which our father was grinning adoringly at his Lindy one moment and in the next gasping for air from under the Moth's sail – and then he went to get lunch ready.

We had a delicious grilled squid salad and another bottle

of nice pinot gris. The cats came back, attracted by the fish. Dave remembered some other stuff from those strange years we'd been talking about, but by now his memory had recast these *memories* as jokes – like the time I went to the toilet on the train from London to Yeovil and ended up in a carriage that had been uncoupled and re-routed to Exeter. I'd forgotten that. We had a good laugh about it. Watching my brother tip wine into his smiling mouth, I remembered the incident as funny, whether it had been at the time or not. That's how memory works.

Somewhere just to the side of our laughter, though, was the silence that had slid out of our conversation into Dave's hot garden that resembled the one at 47 Rarangi Road, St Heliers, back in 1962, where a neighbour had peered at me through a peppery-smelling hedge and said, 'Welcome home.'

I hear that silence on the recording which I turned off just as Dave is saying 'Welcome home sweetie,' when Sue comes around the corner of their house with salad for lunch and some seedlings for the garden. We're all about ten years older than Linda and Chick were when they collected their tongue-tied, Pommified twins from mown-grass-scented Whenuapai in the purple and grey Vauxhall Cresta. We're about the same age they were when they finally came home and didn't leave again, a date neither Dave nor I can remember exactly, but around 1973. This time they came back with a white Mercedes. Sometimes Dave looks a lot like our father, especially when he's having a glass of wine with his lunch and glancing adoringly at his wife. At such moments he *reminds* me of Chick.

Of course such *reminders* are not memories; I'm not even sure what functional relationship they have to memory itself. They seem to slide like filters – or like my father's 35mm colour slides in which Lindy so often features – across those blank, uneasy spaces where memory has failed or been infected.

It's paradoxical to suppose the past exists; I know that. I know that memory, whose job it is to make sense of that paradox, to make the palimpsest transparent, or to present slide shows from a parallel time, may sometimes seem to fail. Sometimes it fails as if to protect us, sometimes to give us a fright. Perhaps *reminders* like my brother's affectionate glance at his wife are there to tell us to let the past go; if any of it matters, it's in the present, anyway.

'So,' said Sue with a hint of mockery in her tone, 'have you boys been having a nice chat?'

'Pretty fucked up, really,' said my brother cheerfully, filling our glasses.

The transit lounge

Following that conversation with Dave, I'm left with a question for which an answer appears so smartly it's like the flipside of the aphasia that made us both lose the plot the day we had lunch at his place. The question is: So where were we when we went to be with our mother and father in those places they'd made their temporary homes after leaving us?

The answer that appears quickly isn't the obvious, factual one – the house at the paper mill in Khulna, the house on the corner of Glover Road and Rarangi Road in Auckland, the house on a hill above Seoul. Yes, those are the places we stayed in for a short while: where I sang 'Once in Royal David's City' in a cracking soprano voice and got an ear infection from the mill's swimming pool; where Dave and I helped to scrape and paint the weatherboard back wall at number 47 Rarangi Road and daringly mowed the steep bank with a Masport; where we prowled the PX Store strip mall in Seoul, went to the bowling alley in the vast USFK Army base at Yongsan-gu, and threw a necking party on a night when our parents were out of town.

But the real answer to my question, *Where were we when we went to Linda and Chick's homes?* is: Going there, and then coming back. That's what first comes to mind – the transits, not the homes. I remember how my infected ear hurt on the way back to England from Khulna, especially during the plane's take-off and landing. A stewardess gave me aspirins;

next to me, Dave was throwing up expertly into successive sick-bags. Typically, Dave's memory is taxonomically exact: he remembers 'being utterly entranced by the sight of the methane-blue exhaust flames from the Wright R3350 Turbo Compound engine nearest to me on a night-time leg'.

For me, this memory of transit has a strong, connecting, satisfying narrative feel to it. It's a *type* of memory – it connects up with little black-and-white snapshots of Dave and me asleep with teddy bears in our seats on the DC6 when we first left Blenheim in 1954; with Dave's resigned, wan grin as he reached yet again for his sick-bag on the flight to Khulna at the end of 1959; with our blasé stocktake of the in-flight facilities, colognes, hand creams, snacks and drinks on the flight to Vancouver when we were coming to be with Linda and Chick in Auckland at the end of 1961; with us lighting up duty-free cigarettes immediately after take-off on the flight to Sydney en route to Seoul at the end of 1963; with our memorable excursions to the Tokyo Onsen bath-house and a bar in the Ginza during a stopover on our way back from Seoul to Auckland.

I notice how the word 'memory' seems once again capable of eliding the object of memory with the function of consciousness – how the uneasy gap between them has closed up.

We were together on the planes, coming and going. We became seasoned travellers together, or thought we were – we were twinned in our adjacent seats and in our joint progress through check-in and passport control; we were *with* each other in ways that no longer applied once we'd arrived. Once there, either side of the transit, more and more we got on with our own lives, had our own friends, did our own thing. But the coming and going was different. The transits were our joint home. We were *at home* in those interstices – suspended between ambiguities, liberated from uncertain loyalties, sealed off; secure; in adjacent seats.

On the way back to New Zealand from England in the northern winter of 1961, we stopped over in Vancouver and spent New Year with a Canadian family called Locke. Mr Locke had been the director of the paper mill at Khulna, which was run by the giant Canadian firm Sandwell. The Lockes' blond daughters had suave high-school boyfriends who smoked filter-tip cigarettes and drove their own cars; they had hip-flasks of strong liquor. There was a rumpus room under the house, with a bar, a record player and a table-tennis table. The atmosphere was friendly, casual and utterly foreign. We had no idea what to do. We didn't even know why we were there and not spending New Year with our parents.

We had burgers and shakes in a diner with booths, and were told by Mr Locke that this was the quintessential Canadian and American meal. It, too, was completely foreign. I don't think either of us had said a word up to this point other than 'Please' or 'Thank you'. We munched on our burgers. Dave was bent over the straw of his shake – his silence was as thick as the beverage he was politely sucking up. I remember the deference of his pale profile beside me as I drew on the sensational, malty flavour of my drink. We were both struck dumb by shyness, by the family's hospitality and friendliness, and most of all by their questions. What had it been like back in England? Were we glad to be going home to our mother and father? How long had it been? Did we remember New Zealand? Did we like the burgers?

We spent New Year in a resort hotel with them. They danced and kissed; we sat. We went skiing on Mount Seymour outside Vancouver, where I tore a cartilage in my knee – we'd never skied before and I didn't know how to turn once I'd launched myself down a slope. Our hosts' generous patience wore out. The last days of my stay passed in a haze of pain and embarrassment.

Then we were back on the plane, back in the familiar zone of transit – together again, having neither left home nor got there.

Sometimes I think that transit is where I'd like to be; to be there with Dave again. It's not going to happen, because we're both glad to be at home where we've landed. But still. And sometimes, in this odd longing for the transit, I recognise the narrative flicker, like a succession of Chick's 35mm colour slides, of our mother's and father's happiness, which we seldom saw but which I know about because of the expression on Linda's face when she decided, after Chick had died, that there were better things to do with the last years of her life than run up a set of new drapes.

Acknowledgements

Although this book isn't a family history it contains information (and probably misinformation) about my family. Of those who helped with this (not the misinformation), my first debt is to my patient and sweet-natured brother Dave who even seemed to enjoy the time we spent together trying to get our family's perplexing story straight.

A number of relatives I don't know personally have compiled narratives and records I've used, and I thank them all, in particular Alan Stephens and Bill Whitmore. Some of these resources arrived speedily when word got out that I was writing this book; they include an amazing 66-page 'Ahnentafel Report for Ian Wedde' and a giant Reepen family tree dating back to 1775. I don't pretend to have done justice to these gifts – perhaps next time. This book is more about what I haven't known than what I've learned late in the game. For now, my thanks to the generous and friendly members of a family whose extent suddenly seemed to expand.

I've had to learn to count family relationship interstices on my fingers. My second cousin Sam Robinson has been a committed researcher and writer for many years, and I'm indebted to the materials he's made available. His mother, my cousin Norma Robinson, whose bridal train Dave and I appeared to be holding up when we were little pageboys, was a charming and informative host. She also introduced me to Terence Burtenshaw, who opened the Blenheim archives of the town's amateur theatre productions and released the ghosts of my mother and father in various get-ups.

Another second cousin, the redoubtable pacifist Reverend Peter Wedde, has been generous with information, photographs and memories – for example, of our great-uncle Reinhold (Ren) Wedde, a bankrupted backblocks lawyer who lived out his last years with Peter's family in Mangere, arriving with complete sets of the German philosophers Kant and Fichte in his luggage, as well as a Cremona violin and a first edition of *Oliver Twist*. Such anecdotes, even if they don't appear in this book, greatly enriched my sense of what Clifford Geertz might have called a 'thick description' of home.

In the context of this book's main preoccupation with home, I'm especially grateful to Mr R.D. Qureshi and his niece Lina Chowdhury for their help with my slightly dodgy 2005 return to Dave's and my childhood home at Chandraghona in Bangladesh. In many ways, this event gave my intention the narrative shape it needed to go somewhere.

My wife Donna read an early draft of the book and said she thought it was pretty good. At the time I wasn't so sure, and her opinion meant I finished the job.

I'm grateful to many people, like Reg and Peggy Markwell in England, who provided the provisional homes that sustained me as a child. They died many years ago, which leaves me as an adult thanking their ghosts for the kindness I didn't always perceive back then.

In the same spirit I want to thank my mother and father, Linda and Chick Wedde, whose extraordinary lives deprived me of a conventional home – whatever that is – for much of my young life, but gave me a rich if sometimes delusional expectation of unpredictable possibility as a good way to be at home in the world.

I'm grateful to my publisher Fergus Barrowman at Victoria University Press for his continuing support, to Jane Parkin for her scrupulous and sympathetic editing, Philip Kelly for the cover design, and Adrian Young at Auckland's Museum of Art and Technology for the cover photograph of the lawnmower with its wire and canvas grass catcher which, not surprisingly, has become an historical artefact. I saw it in a social history exhibition about home while visiting MOTAT with my grandson Sebo. He had no idea why his grandfather was trying to take his glasses off and blow his nose at the same time.

Much of the groundwork for this book was made possible by a Creative New Zealand Investment Grant in 2010, for which I am grateful.

Photographs

Cover image courtesy of Adrian Young © Museum of Transport and Technology (MOTAT), Auckland.
p. 5: Ian and Dave, Menton, 2005. Photograph: Donna Malane.
p. 51: Linda as Lady Mary Lasenby in *The Admirable Crighton*, Blenheim Operatic Society, 1939. Gordon McCusker Studios, Blenheim.
p. 78: Chick and Linda, Karnaphuli River, East Pakistan, c.1954. Unknown photographer.
p. 103: The house at Chandraghona, February 2005. Photograph: Ian Wedde.
p. 112: Karnaphuli Paper Mill, Chandraghona, Rangamati, February 2005. Photograph: Ian Wedde.
p. 129: Heinrich August Wedde and Maria Josephine Caterina Wedde, with six of their eight children. Left to right from the front: Reinhold Henry (Ren), William Frederick, Elisabeth Frederika (Freda), Albert Augustus, Bertha Mary, Frederick Alexander (Fritz). Herman Conrad and Herbert Edward still to come. Wrigglesworth & Binns, Wellington, 1880s.
p. 160: Chittagong, February 2005. Photograph: Ian Wedde.
p. 175: Bandarban, February 2005. Photograph: Ian Wedde.
p. 189: Photograph of Mount Kenchenjunga glued to folded A4 sheet, 1957. Unknown photographer.
p. 199: Image-capture from company archives, Karnaphuli Paper Mill, Chandraghona, February 2005. Photograph: Ian Wedde.
p. 284: Dave and Ian with fish, Waikawa Bay, c.1950. Unknown photographer.

Quotations

p. 31: '4.5 To My Sons', from Ian Wedde, *The Commonplace Odes*, Auckland: Auckland University Press, 2001, p. 37.
p. 34: '1.4 To My Twin Brother', from *The Commonplace Odes*, p. 10.
p. 35: from '1.5 To Donna's Young Dogs', from *The Commonplace Odes*, p. 11.
p. 41: from John Masefield, 'Cargoes'.
p. 46: from Ian Wedde, 'Inside Job', in *Figuring the Pacific: Aotearoa and Pacific Cultural Studies*, eds. Howard McNaughton and John Newton. Christchurch: Canterbury University Press, 2005, pp. 107ff.
p. 61: from Arthur Rimbaud, 'Les Poètes de septs ans', in *Arthur Rimbaud – Selected Poems and Letters*, trans. Jeremy Harding and John Sturrock, Penguin Classics, 2004, p. 58.
p. 98: William Shakespeare, Moth's soliloquy from *Love's Labour's Lost*, Act III, Sc 1.
p. 110: from Alfred Lord Tennyson, 'Maud'.
p. 134: Frederick Alexander Wedde, 'A New Hypothesis or Theory of the Universe', typed pages, June 1957.
p. 193: '4.1 To the Tin Trunk of Images', from *The Commonplace Odes*, p. 33.
p. 200: 'Montacute Park', from Ian Wedde, *Made Over,* Auckland: Stephen Chan, 1974, p. 72.